Peter Herrle, Uwe-Jens Walther (eds.)

Socially Inclusive Cities

Emerging Concepts and Practice

With contributions from
Peter Herrle, Uwe-Jens Walther, Horst Matthäus,
Reinhard Goethert, Alicia Ziccardi and Arturo Mier y Terán,
Christoph Stump, Debra Roberts, Monika El Shorbagi,
Neelima Risbud, Anne Power, Mary Corcoran White,
Heidede Becker and Hans-Peter Löhr

LIT

Cover design: www.fumagi.de
Layout: Christian Dubrau

Bibliographic information published by Die Deutsche Bibliothek
Die Deutsche Bibliothek lists this publication in the Deutsche Nationalbibliografie; detailed bibliographic data are available in the Internet at http://dnb.ddb.de.

ISBN 3-8258-6971-7

A catalogue record for this book is available from the British library

Grevener Str./Fresnostr. 2 48159 Münster
Tel. 0251-62 03 20 Fax 0251-23 19 72
e-Mail: lit@lit-verlag.de http://www.lit-verlag.de

Distributed in North America by:

Transaction Publishers
Rutgers University
35 Berrue Circle
Piscataway, NJ 08854

Tel.: (732) 445 - 2280
Fax: (732) 445 - 3138
for orders (U. S. only):
toll free (888) 999 - 6778

Contents

Introduction: Socially Inclusive Cities - New Solutions for Old Problems - or Old Wine in New Bottles?

Peter Herrle, Uwe-Jens Walther

This book is based on a series of papers that were originally presented to a forum on *'Socially Inclusive Cities'* at the XXI World Congress of Architecture organized by the International Union of Architects UIA in July 2002 in Berlin. The response to this theme was overwhelming and continued well beyond the original event. This led us to the decision to widen the scope of the publication by including contributions from authors other than those who had attended the conference in 2002, rather than just publish conference proceedings. The widening of the scope has both further enriched and differentiated the topics and has eventually resulted in this book.

When we first developed the idea for the forum at the UIA conference, we wanted to bring together different groups of people - different in terms of the problems they are dealing with, different in terms of their professional backgrounds, analytical judgments as well as strategies proposed - and of course different in terms of the geographic regions they come from.

Despite the obvious economic and cultural globalization trends and the fact that in a few cases cities in the developed countries of the North have slum-like pockets of poverty with conditions close to what can be observed in the developing world, there is no sign of convergence. Still, cities in the South continue to have political, social and spatial characteristics of their own, shaped by local and colonial history, by local and international factors, producing social and economic and spatial patterns different from cities in the North. Global economic disparities and political power imbalances are certainly among the factors perpetuating these differences. They become apparent in discussions on all major issues of the urban agenda such as poverty, governance or environment.

With the increasing variety of the issues involved a variety of circles of 'experts', government advisors and academics emerged who specialized in their own professional geography. There have been few links between the camps, partly because of the implications of 'development' which was difficult for researchers and practitioners from the North to permeate. Only with growing international networking of city governments and NGOs has a process of mutual exchange of perceptions and ideas begun. Our forum at the UIA conference was an attempt to promote cross-thinking between professional groups and geographic regions.

However, notwithstanding the differences one overriding theme seems to have emerged in the past decade. It is a formula that has been able to interlink practical efforts from different parts of the globe and gather various streams of academic discourses. The unifying strand of the debate is provided by the twin term 'social inclusion/exclusion'. It seems that this twin term captures previously disjointed debates and integrates various strategies and concepts. What used to be discussed in other terms such as 'marginality' and 'participation' has now come under the broader umbrella of 'social exclusion' vs. 'social inclusion'. Such a short-circuited use of the terms, however, seems to devaluate both their analytical and practical potential .

To us, the important question is: does the new umbrella term suggest that there is more than just old wine in new bottles? Are the same old concepts being perpetuated under new labels following the global trend for permanent renewal of brands? Where is the value added to urban development theory and practice, if the terms inclusion/exclusion are adopted? What is it that helps us to better understand and conceptualize urban developments in a global arena when strategies of inclusion are advocated?

A few arguments in favor of the novelty of the approach come to mind instantly. They are more of a principal order and suggest that the twin terms exclusion/inclusion are more than yet another fashion:

- Firstly, the concepts of exclusion/inclusion marry the concerns of both thorough analysis and differential practice; they invite and call for a combination of diagnosis and therapy.
- Secondly, exclusion/inclusion has many faces and facets. Whilst there is strong evidence of the economic bases of exclusion, it is also a cultural, hence multidimensional phenomenon. As such, it cannot be reduced to being an epiphenomenon that just mirrors the unequal distribution of wealth even if closely connected with it.
- Thirdly, because the terms are a systematic pointer towards the cultural variety of exclusion, they also help us to understand the cultural diversity behind – as well as reminding us of the universality of the basic problem behind.

Hence the umbrella terms make it possible to capture multiple dimensions of inclusion and exclusion. This perspective, then, could also be used as a possible corrective – to capture the variety of both exclusion as well as that of combating it; to correct the promising globalized rhetorics of developmental planning. For, currently used policy concepts such as *decentralisation, devolution, local authority, partnerships, civil society, citizen participation* and *network building* claim universal validity. In doing so, they seem to ignore such variety of inequality and particularity. Given the central importance of these concepts for future planning in, and for, developing countries, the potential and limitations of urban planning and politics can be looked at in more detail.

There are also good arguments in favor of the new perspective on a less conceptual but more historical plane. These arguments relate to the very nature of cities and what they stand for: cities have long been places of social integration. Ancient urban cultures adopted and merged people of different economic classes, different ethnic origins and different social status; their integrative power is well known. Cities have been able to deal with unequal distribution of wealth without fundamentally threatening the legitimacy of their ruling elites or creating mass exclusion. They did so through providing mechanisms for socio-cultural inclusion and the building of social cohesion. Is it possible that in our modern globalized world the civilizing consensus of cities is no longer valid and that their inclusive mechanisms are functioning less and less well? This would indeed justify a concept beyond the level of regional or local particularities such as the twin concept of exclusion/inclusion. If a general lack of cohesion is the major problem, it can be conceptualized in terms of inclusiveness and can be translated into a strategy by using different sets of tools adapted to local standards and requirements. The level of social and spatial fragmentation, poverty, violence and physical decay that many cities around the world are experiencing - no matter where they are located - supports this assumption. Against such background, then, it does make sense to re-evaluate the old participatory strategies and their contribution towards social inclusion - and hence in terms of the social and economic coherence of the city.

Today, strategies of social inclusion are under way in almost every continent. They are put in the contexts of urban and regional development for good reasons. Here, the issue of social exclusion and related strategies can be discussed on several levels:

- In many cities in the South we see a huge informal sector, which in some cases amounts to 80 per cent of the city's GDP. This indicates exclusion of a major part of the urban population from formal working relations, credit facilities and social security.

- Informal and illegal settlements accommodate up to 60 per cent of the urban populations in some cities of Latin America, Asia and Africa. While the proliferation of these settlements is the real engine of urban growth, the settlers are often deprived of even the most basic infrastructure such as water, drainage or sewerage systems and legal security. Access to land is one of the key issues for 'including' the urban poor in the South.
- On the other hand, despite the existence of formalized social networks in wealthy countries of the North, there is an increasing number of people falling out of these networks. This has given rise to counterbalancing policies and strategies in almost every country within Europe and North America and the discovery that there are also commonalities with the situation in the South.

What this brief sketch of inclusion strategies intended to demonstrate is the common denominator of attempts that deal with the complex issues raised. They all look at people *and* the places where they live and work. Strategies of inclusion do not separate them. In other words: they try to solve or mitigate the problems caused by exclusion by working *with* the concerned people *in* their own environments and neighborhoods. It seems that such a combination of *people and places* constitutes the conceptual paradigm underlying the inclusive policies and strategies discussed in this book. In fact, the evidence from numerous case studies shows that structural policies at national levels need to be complemented through localized measures combining the notion of place as a social and economic realm with structural policy. In one way or another all the case studies presented in this book elaborate on the precarious relation between 'programs' and localities, or in other words: between systems and people.

Reinhard Goethert's contribution to this volume is on the key role of people in their places and how they can participate. He unravels the interrelations of 'inclusiveness' with other development concepts and raises some critical questions about the concept's meaning and usefulness. From his background in participatory planning techniques and methodology he argues that formal procedures would have to adapt 'informal' mechanisms and thereby gradually be 'included' into informality, which is the prevalent mode of urban growth in a major part of the world. He argues for a reverse type of 'inclusion', rather than including the poor in mainstream top-down planning and implementation procedures.

Horst Matthäus reports on experience from Recife, Brazil, a city well known for its innovative approaches. With 60 per cent of the population below the poverty line and living in unserviced slums, there has been a strong popular movement of the urban poor. This has led to internationally recognized programs such as the ZEIS (1983) and a participatory urban upgrading program called PREZEIS starting from 1987. Recife was among the first state capitals in Brazil to experiment with participatory budgeting, thereby introducing an earlier form of the 'orcamente participativo' for which Port Alegre became famous. Based in Recife as coordinator for a capacity building GTZ project, he draws the conclusion that the effectiveness of the new instruments is still largely hampered by inadequate funding and bureaucratic structures.

Alicia Ziccardi with *Arturo Mier y Terán* tell the context and history of a remarkable house upgrading projects which assisted about 53,000 families between 1998 and 2003. The program offers loans to social groups with very low incomes to improve their housing conditions without any collateral. It transforms the beneficiaries into borrowers based on confidence and a simple procedure and without requiring them to mortgage their property. The scheme is considered largely a success, not only because of its output but also because of its benefits to the local economy and positive effects on the building of a network wherein government institutions, academics, NGOs and CBOs cooperate. However, through its focus on house improvement and extension, the program has so far not been able to address the infrastructure problems typical of very poor areas.

Christoph Stump provides an insight into the planning and development of the Bronx in New York since the 1970s. He argues that urban decline, poverty and social exclusion are a consequence of non-participatory planning and development strategies and explores the implications and partial successes of participatory concepts in Melrose, a small neighborhood community in the South Bronx. He concludes with what he feels is the most important effect: the restoration of "a sense of community and civic responsibility" and physical upgrading, while typical social problems, particularly of youth, prevail.

Debra Roberts reflects on inclusiveness from the experience with implementing the Agenda 21 in Durban, South Africa. Durban has been in the forefront of a movement that started with the advent of democracy in 1994. It has successfully developed a Local Agenda 21 Program which recognizes the importance of sustainability and stakeholder involvement. The contribution shows that inclusion policies should and can be embedded in a broader social movement.

Monika El Shorbagi reports on a GTZ-supported project in Cairo, Egypt. Using the project as a reference base she explores the typical mechanisms of exclusion and possible solutions for the improvement of informal settlements in Cairo, which accommodate some 60 per cent of the Greater Cairo population. The article presents experience from the Participatory Urban Development Project for Manshiet Nasser, which is one of the most densely populated inner city districts of Cairo. The project addresses problems related to service delivery, tenure security, and empowerment. While there are positive results in promoting collective action and community processes and thereby linking local initiatives with local and national government institutions, the author remains doubtful about the long-term impact.

Neelima Risbud provides a comprehensive account and analysis of 'inclusive' urban policies in India. She reports on changes in national and state policies starting from slum clearance and welfare approaches in the 1970s up to the 1990s, when under the influence of the World Bank the emphasis was shifted to poverty alleviation. The most widespread policy has been the provision of basic infrastructure while the provision of land for the poor has been limited to a few states. While there is an increasing realization that top-down planning is inadequate, NGOs have played only a limited role in the process. With little or even shrinking opportunities to get legalized access to land, squatting remains one of the primary options for poor settlers even today. The lack of managerial capacities, coordination and institutional capacity are among the factors which aversely affect inclusion policies.

Anne Power focuses on the English experience of Neighborhood Management - how to improve the conditions of everyday life in low-income neighborhoods by organizing and managing them differently. She puts her contribution in the context of long run attempts in England to tackle deprivation at the local level and of the central role of local government and housing organizations in changing conditions on the ground. The author argues that Neighborhood Management "addresses environmental and social problems within neighborhoods as part of a wider understanding of social exclusion, sustainable development and the need for greater care of our urban communities. Although its perspective is shaped by British examples, many of the issues are relevant to other countries".

Mary Corcoran White investigates a deprived housing estate in one of Europe's booming capitals, Dublin, Ireland. She depicts the case of a single social housing complex—Fatima Mansions—which is now the target of a major urban regeneration project. What she calls "the re-imagining of the Fatima Mansions" turned out to be "an ongoing process in terms of its physical structure and layout, social structure and composition, economic potential and cultural creativity". The project is also "the outcome of a hard won partnership between local champions, community groups and activists, municipal authorities and central government representatives".

Heidede Becker and *Hans-Peter Löhr* report on the state of policy formation towards social inclusion in German cities. They give an account and appraisal of a joint program of the German federal government and the German Länder. The program is called "Districts With Special Development Needs – the Socially Integrative City" ("Soziale Stadt" - *The Socially Integrative City*). Like similar policies in other European countries, the program responds to overall changes to the urban fabric. It was launched in 1999 as an addition to conventional urban development aid. Its main objectives are to make urban regeneration a more socially responsive, co-operating, integrative area based policy.

The contributions in this book present a breathtaking variety of responses to combat the different forms of social exclusion in particular urban contexts respectively world wide. They come from national governments such as England, Germany or India, they may be deeply entrenched in regional and local politics and planning such as Recife, Mexico or Cairo. Or they may even come down to the level and scope of individual housing projects such as Fatima Mansions in Dublin, Ireland or Melrose Commons, Bronx/New York. This collection of international examples, we feel, presents both an intriguing and encouraging diversity of approaches. We have made no attempt to streamline this diversity because it is exactly the broad and colorful patchwork that makes up the new urban landscape of Inclusive Cities in the making.

The reader will hardly be surprised that such an internationally mixed bag of articles invariably entails problems of language as well. It posed problems of an editorial order, to say the least: to what extent should one tamper with the manifold backgrounds of nationalities, personalities and cultures involved that manifest themselves in different uses of language? Should it be edited in British English or American English for better coherence and readability? Or should one respect the local and national idiom? Again, we decided in favor of diversity in the end: we maintained the original color (or should it be *colour*?) of each contribution at the expense of coherence of presentation of the book as a whole. So this is a word of warning to the benevolent reader. Readers will not only be able to enjoy the indigenous lingo, but will also have to put up with *programmes* and *programs*; *Multi-Storey* and *Multi-story buildings* and will *talk to* someone as well as *talk with* someone to name but a few examples. At one point in time we just gave up the idea that there should be a universal set of rules about these questions. Why indeed should there be one in the first place, one might well ask.

Last not least, we are grateful to all of those who have made this publication possible. We are deeply indebted to Rachel Marks for proofreading and harmonizing all references at various stages, Franziska Berger and Tosca Piotrowski for their sustained technical support. In particular, we would like to thank the authors for their patience and their never ending belief in what to us became a wonderful, but never ending project. Now that we see the result in full shape, we are becoming more aware of its shortcomings, too. So the last words are directed to the editors' pride: Nobody but us should be blamed for any such flaws or blunders that remained uncorrected.

Planning with People – Challenges to the Paradigm

Reinhard Goethert

Ideas are powerful. They underpin programs and projects by giving legitimacy and direction. But as ideas take hold, new ideas evolve, and previous strongly held truths are often discarded. Ideas may be discredited from failure, or they may slowly be compromised by the desire for change, which is often driven by the notion of progress. It becomes a cycle: an initial unchallenged euphoria is increasingly tested, leading to tinkering with the basic concepts, and subsequently modified as remedy. Eventually the original idea is replaced, followed by a shift in projects and programs to reflect new thinking. To quote a common saying: "nothing seems to endure but change."

The replacement is not always complete, for it may only relinquish its place as the primary focus and shift to a supporting role. But in some cases it is unceremoniously forgotten and leaves little impact.

Powerful and sustainable ideas must meet four criteria to avoid being marginalized:

- Clear, identifiable and understanding of what it is, and what it isn't;
- Recognized value with tangible results;
- Support of a broad coalition of interests from different sectors; not captured by a few interest groups to the detriment of others;
- Institutionalization into the mainstream decision structure.

Social inclusion policies and methods have been promoted for many years in the development field. It is rare to find any development program or project that does not explicitly require participation in the development and implementation of a project or program. It has become accepted to be a basic precondition to success, and the involvement of beneficiaries in all aspects is a given. The momentum of inclusionary practice has gained in the last years and the concept is spreading into many fields.

Social inclusion is perceived as being mainstream, although there has always been disagreement as to what exactly it is. Techniques and methodologies that purport to be participatory exist and have been proven in practice. 'Action-Planning,' 'Micro-planning,' 'Planning for Real' are other accepted and well-established techniques.[1] The well-known PRA (participatory rural assessment) family of techniques is widespread among practitioners. Social inclusion will not fade away because of inadequate methodology.

One wonders if social inclusion – community participation as it is commonly known – will follow an evolutionary cycle of euphoria, testing, modification, and replacement. Will it fall away completely to be replaced by a new paradigm, or will it be continuously modified, and perhaps evolve into a different form?

But it is not so simple: an additional consideration in the development field is the overbearing role of large agencies. They have increasingly become the main funders of programs, and hence the drivers of development ideas by default. The disillusionment and abandonment by the large agencies is not necessarily followed by disillusionment at the implementation level, but the redirected funding often severely affects the programs. But more troublesome is the 'tone' that the agency sets – the example which it sets – and consequently a 'cloud' becomes associated with a previously strongly held idea.

Including the large development agencies, there are four key sectors to be considered and particularly noted for their inherent bias and inclination toward participation:

- The large development agencies: participation considered suitable if fits within agency time and organizational constraints and delivers in project implementation;
- NGOs: inherently supportive of participation as a basic right and not necessarily from a project implementation perspective;
- Municipalities, government: often reluctantly accepts participation if it fits within structure and delivers on implementation with minimum disruption and added administrative and cost burdens;
- Communities: inherently participatory, but must deliver.

---

1 For a summary of the most common families of community participation method, see Hamdi/Goethert (1997). See especially Section Two: Tools for Practice.

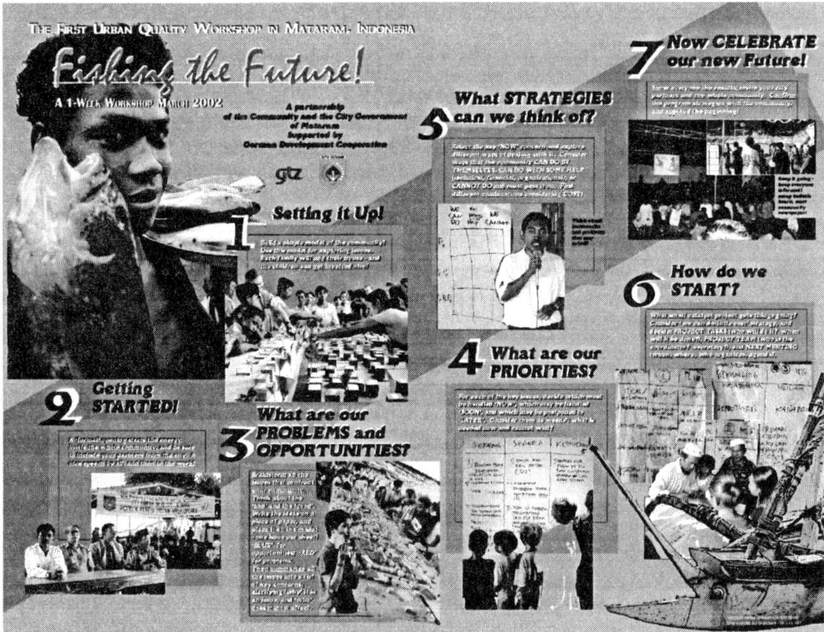

Figure 1: Participatory techniques and methodologies exist and have been proven in practice.

One seldom remembers the 'site and services' programs of the 1970's. Site and services represents an idea that was replaced by the large development agencies, and even the term has fallen into disrepute. Essentially these were mimics of squatter settlements but with official support and legalization. Land was subdivided and a plot was given to families with legal title, and sometimes with a rudimentary 'starter' core house, along with basic water and sanitation provisions. Families were expected to mobilize their own resources in constructing their houses, similar as to what is found in squatter settlements. These programs had been strongly promoted as the 'perfect' alternative to previous direct-construction housing programs. The merits of the approach had been real, but it has, nevertheless, all but disappeared in contemporary practice and planning literature.

Although as a concept it was rejected, in practice the essentials continue, though under different names: resettlement areas, overspill developments, expansion areas, etc. Clearly the need for land allocation to poor families remains.

Will social inclusion follow the same fate as site and services? Hypothesizing a cycle of ideas, three futures may be speculated:

- Inclusion is a fundamental imperative; it has been tested and found to be a vital driving force in development. It continues to remain a focus of programs, although some modification would occur in response to experience.
- Inclusion is desirable and very useful in specific situations; it has been tested and proved to be a useful supporting tool. It no longer enjoys being a key element and is not automatically included in programs, but it is still considered relevant.
- Inclusion is not essential in development, and there are other approaches available to achieve development goals. It has been tested, modified, and is slowly being replaced by new thinking. Perhaps it was all a passing fad?

How comfortable we are with our ideas on inclusionary practice? How convinced are we that this is a prime fundamental? An examination of practices and contradictions may offer some insight as to what may lie ahead.

What is in a name

Social inclusion is already known by a wide variety of labels, and 'community participation' and variations thereof are the most common. 'Community empowerment' is widespread. 'Micro-planning' has also been used to differentiate from 'macro-planning' representing 'top-down' practices.

Several terms extend to what inclusion does and refers to the concept indirectly. For example, 'action-planning' has been appropriated as implying community participation but linked to output. And more recently, 'demand-driven development' is linked to communities as the determiners of actions.

Does the variety of terms reflect the strength and breath of the concept, or does it reflect the lack of clarity and confusion?

What actually is inclusion?

In all cases, the overriding consideration seems to be the sharing of power as the fundamental parameter. No longer are decisions reached through a top-down, non-consultative approach, but rather active, effective involvement of impacted communities is required. The notion of community is important – it is not an individual but rather a shared group activity.

There are a variety of ways to characterize inclusion which reflect the variety of ways it is practiced and perceived. One way to map the scope of inclusion is to frame the alternatives through a matrix of stages of a program or project on one axis, from initiating an idea to planning, design, implementation, and through to maintenance, and on the other axis, the levels of participation ranging from no participation to full control by the community. This offers a positioning of relationships and the degree of involvement and power/control and highlights the range of ways to perceive inclusion.

All of the different combinations represent a possible form of participation, and have been characterized as such in various projects and programs. For example, early programs with participation tended to view it as a form of providing cheap labor in implementation. Or often participation is seen as where the key role of the community is to ratify suggestions. These 'easy' forms of participation require the least power to be given away, and the crucial decisions are still held by the traditional formal structures. Perhaps more 'true' participatory practice allows more meaningful inputs and empowerment by communities. The legacy of these early perceptions is the feeling of 'being used' by the communities, leading to mistrust and discrediting the approach.

Does the large number of ways that participation may be seen suggest the flexibility of the concept and its ability to adjust according to circumstance, or does the multiplicity imply a 'free for all,' under which many things could be considered legitimate participation, dependent on the beholder? It is a worry that if practically everything could be categorized as participation, then in effect it loses clarity and with it credibility and purpose, and simultaneously presents a 'false' front of participation.

My personal bias toward a 'best' form of participation is the intersection of 'plan' and 'shared control': here the communities and the 'outsiders' see themselves as equal and exchange knowledge. It is the decision stage of what to do and how to do that offers equal representation and shared ownership.

'Real' participation slow in being adopted

Most agree that there are many experiences in participation from which to draw that offer a coherent body of practice. Lessons from many countries are readily available and generally widespread. Despite this, inclusion does not seem to be as widely practiced as would be expected from its recognized value, the general availability of information, and the many experiences that are seen in the literature. I was startled to learn of a very recent project funded by an international development agency that totally ignored inclusion, and only after an outcry did inclusion become a prime consideration. Why is this so?

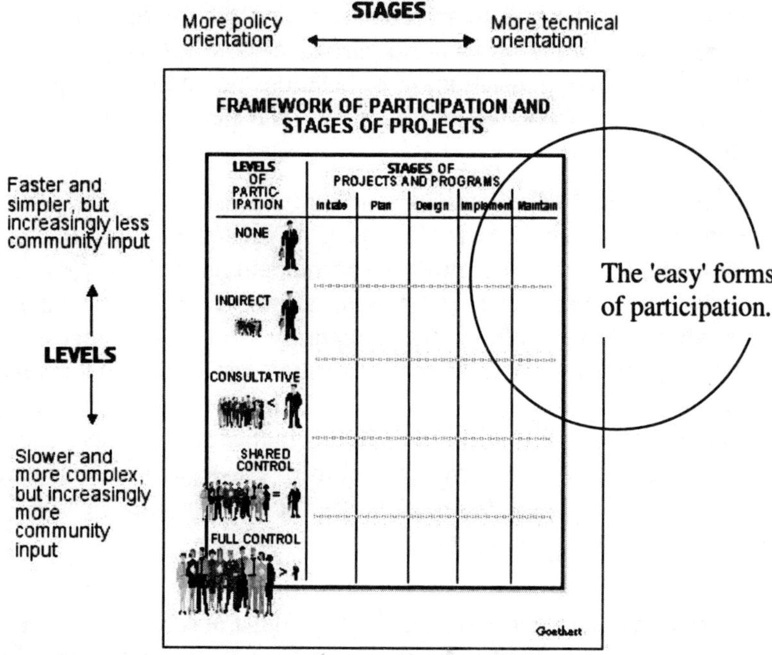

Figure 2: A matrix of alternative levels of participation.

Perhaps this may be characterized as ‘ability to do’ vs. ‘willingness to do’: it can be done, but the willingness for all parties to embrace inclusion is not as enthusiastically taken up as would be expected. For governments and development agencies, the clear loss of power by sharing control with communities inherently makes it difficult to incorporate. For professionals there seems clear hesitation for them to stake their careers on the outcome of a participatory process.

Inclusionary practice may also be slowed by the lack of knowledge and experience in actual hands-on practice: the rationale may be clear and accepted, but implementation skills are less known. And if they are known, few have the experience or the training necessary to carry it out.

Perhaps participatory practice is a push from the ‘outside’ and less of an ‘insider’ desire – ironically a form of ‘top-down’ pressure. Communities may have more immediate priorities than engaging in an activity perceived as a 'planning exercise.'

And lastly, perhaps the slow pace of participation is out of touch with the 'hurry-up, rush-rush' planning pace of professional practice, unaccustomed to a more deliberate process of change.

Perception as an activity of the poor

Inclusion, if perceived as only involving the poor, limits the power and potentially marginalizes the concept. Some argue that the higher-income groups already practice participation, although perhaps not as transparently as practiced in development projects, and clearly not labeled as such. In effect, the too strong association of participation with low income places a stigma on the concept and makes more difficult its acceptance by communities.

A 'one-shot' process

Experience suggests that once a specific goal is reached through participation, participation tends to cease. This implies a one-off, short- term process that is eventually discarded and reinforces its use as a limited tool. Long-term, continued participatory dynamics are difficult to achieve. Often a group disbands when a goal is achieved and reforms when new issues are confronted. Is the ideal the formalized acceptance of participation as a normal, standard mode of action?

This points to participation as an effective tool particularly useful when needed to achieve specific goals: limited, but effective.

Too inexpensive

The direct cost of setting up participatory social programs is relatively low. This is a problem for large development agencies, in that overhead costs are high and large sums of funds need to be allocated. Even more detrimental, participatory involvement is generally coupled with more high-cost components which tend to command more emphasis in the course of a project or program. But for NGOs, the relatively low cost is a benefit.

Money taints

When agencies begin to fund communities in their participatory endeavors, two issues emerge. One, the communities – like others – can readily become dependent on the funding and lose their ability to freely act. Secondly, they can become more beholden to funder's wishes and probably will lose their community perspective and self-reliance.

A dilemma: how to support communities without destroying their sense of community?

Disconnect with government organization

Still lacking is an effective interface between communities and government. In practice, organizational structures often fail to consider a clear flow between participatory decisions arrived with government staff and their incorporation into government policy. The hierarchical structure of government and development agencies is not designed to accommodate the different rhythm of participatory practice. Government models may not be available to incorporate community inclusion, but perhaps it is more an indication of the reluctance of government to relinquish control and power. As a result, the approach remains marginalized and is barred from mainstream shared decision-making.

At the individual level, professionals are reluctant to accede power to 'unskilled' communities and to seriously accept their inputs. It is rare to find ambitious professionals willing to base their careers on the 'give and take' and unpredictable outcomes of participatory planning.

Ends or means?

It is generally accepted that inclusionary practice is more time consuming and requires intensive administrative support. If the 'ends' is the goal, inclusionary practice is not the fastest and most direct, and other methods are suggested as more efficacious. Related is the debate of a rights-based, social-equity perspective as the end goal of sustainable development. From this perspective, it is not *what* it does, but *how* it is done that is important. However, if the 'means' is seen as the important element, the risk of frustration and disillusionment may set in by both agency and community if the process becomes too drawn out with no noticeable result.

Development projects tend to be bound by fixed schedules with direct impact on costs, and it is difficult to fit participatory planning into the rigid bureaucratic demands. Clearly recognizing the possible dilemma, there are examples early on where projects experimented with participation, but with the caveat that direct methods would be used if the process proved to be too slow.

But perhaps customary practices do not adequately consider the need for tangible and timely results as demonstration and reinforcement. In other words, the practice of participation needs further development to address emerging problematic areas. The goal ideally, would be to satisfy both 'ends' and 'means.'

'Competitive city' vs. inclusion

In the increased focus on poverty alleviation, the recognition that cities are the drivers of economies, has intensified the competition among cities in attracting industry and commerce. The increased time consumption and added administration from inclusionary practices may work against presenting a city as a desirable place to do business.

Cities with strong participatory practices may be viewed as potentially troublesome and shunned. The shift of industries traditionally found in the northern US to the southern states was in large part due to the non-unionized work force that was considered more compliant and accepting lower wages.

Children as new participators

Participation may be well served if it is broadened to include the young. It is being recognized that children provide a fresh input into planning through more unbiased insights, and increasingly children are used as informants in the planning process. They are also involved in generating ideas and getting a 'sense of the community.'

Children as 'change agents' in informal area upgrading are starting to be noted. Developing awareness in children through traditional techniques of participation has become a potentially potent mechanism. Not only does this sensitize future citizens to issues, but it also infiltrates and impacts the adult realm. In some sense, this may be characterized as developing a long-term sustainability element in planning.

Children are also cultural transmitters. They are not just effective as change agents, but, on the contrary, also function as cultural transmitters.

The participatory process becomes a true two-way flow: *from* children a fresh input is offered, *to* children the values of the society are passed on.

But bringing children into the process may further the perception that inclusion is a specialized approach and detract from it broader applications, and therefore may not be taken seriously in the mainstream of practice.

Participation is also exclusion

Well-intended inclusion and a deliberate bias in addressing gender concerns result in unintended exclusion. There is always the difficulty in redressing past imbalances while still maintaining the existing structure, and generally the existing structure becomes deliberately shunned in the process. In effect, it may be characterized as the transfer of power from one group to another, creating exclusion, but in the group previously dominant. Using participation to redress previous imbalances may just shift exclusion from one group to another. It may promote an image as a confrontational tool and discredit the process as not neutral to the mutual benefit of all parties.

All these issues raised suggest a rethinking of inclusionary practice. In summary, is this a stabilizing, emerging fundamental element, or will it become a passing ‘good idea’ that is slowly being replaced?

But who is excluding whom?

But perhaps all this is irrelevant: the majority in cities in the developing world are very poor – representing up to 70-80% of the population in many cases – and the bulk of new housing is informally constructed and expected to continue to be so. Moreover, recent studies worry about the rapid expansion of cities – expected to double in population in the next 20-30 years – that are disproportionately poor. The informal mechanisms seem to be the dominant method for land development and housing supply, for we have few of any concepts that contemplate dealing with this rapid expansion. The informal are developing, expanding, and defining their own world, despite our best efforts at bringing them into our formal world.

Figure 3: The informal sector is the dominant actor in land development and housing supply for many cities in developing countries

The customary perspective has been from the formal sector. But in the context of our helplessness and the dominant role of the informal, who then is excluding whom? Perhaps it is us, the minority formal sector of development planners that are the excluded and irrelevant? To paraphrase Gandhi, "There go my people, I must run and catch up, since I am their leader." And in the future, will there be a new development model yet to be invented and a form of inclusion that is unlike what we know today?

At the least, participation may still be practiced but undergo change – and perhaps the reverse of what we are now considering.

Instead of striving toward a model from a formal perspective, the trend appears to lean more toward an informal derivation. This 'hypothesis of convergence' is a shift toward the informal by the previously dominant formal reference model.

Evidence suggests that we are already shifting toward recognition and acceptance, although not recognized as such. Even in naming, the shift has been from 'illegal squatters' to 'informal settlements.' But there are also other more profound shifts:

- Formal land tenure is no longer a prerequisite in many upgrading projects by development agencies. A formal title is no longer considered as an absolute, and an internal local system of land 'ownership' appears satisfactory. Despite this, a recently acclaimed book and a key development agency argue that legal title is a vital component, particularly necessary as collateral in mobilizing funds, and thus a fundamental way out of poverty. From the formal perspective this is undoubtedly true, but from the new reality this may not be the key.
- Informal 'realtors' are increasingly recognized as providing an orderly development framework. Although perceived by some as exploiters, they do provide a mechanism for orderly development, which facilitates installation of basic infrastructure, future regularization and incorporation into the formal world.
- The informal service providers of water and in some cases sanitation disposal services are increasingly being recognized and embraced. They are seen as positive approaches in extending service to the unserviced lower income communities. Throughout Africa informal small-scale water suppliers are being accepted at the norm in many cities, and in Latin America, for example, the 'Aquaterros' as they are known in supplying water, are well established.
- Small-scale micro-loans improving on traditional loan mechanisms are now in the mainstream throughout the world. The traditional money-lenders – often characterized as loan sharks – are being overwhelmed by the worldwide availability of micro-loan programs.

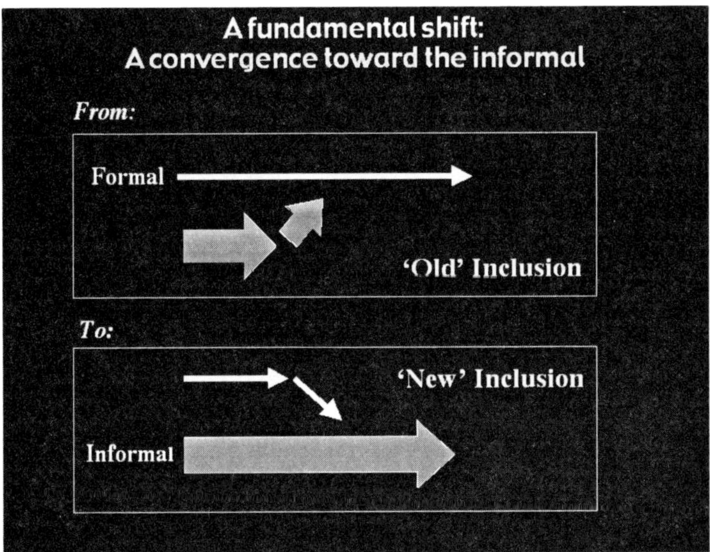

Figure 4: We are moving toward a world defined by informal mechanisms

But more important, perhaps the process of inclusion is essentially a traditional, customary form of local self-governance. Examples of small-scale participatory governance are found probably in all societies that provide a forum for identifying problems, considering alternatives and seeking agreement on actions. Have we professionals – after much struggle – 'reinvented the wheel,' in this case, a traditional form of governance?

The inclusionary paradigm lives, nor is it disappearing, but perhaps the reverse of what was expected. Inclusion models the customary form of small-scale governance in traditional society. The danger is that participatory practice will become ritualistic in development agencies, who co-opt the process but are unwilling to cede power and control. And it also may become discredited by communities because it fails to deliver when more formally structured.

Epilogue

And if inclusion fades, what would be next? Increasingly a market-centric orientation is emerging in development strategies. 'Privatization' is the increasing watchword. Public-private partnerships and direct private sector responsibility is becoming more widely used as the development tool of choice. At the smaller scale, 'community-contracting' has been shown to be an effective approach. A recent Harvard Business School paper even proposes that multi-national companies should enter and invest in the world's poorest markets – the bottom of the economic pyramid – as a way "to radically improve the lives of billions of people and help bring about a more stable, less dangerous world."[2] Among other arguments, they argue that "the high-cost economy of the poor could benefit from the scope, scale, and supply-chain efficiencies of large enterprises, the same as their middle-class counterparts do." Essentially this is a shift away from the strong social-welfare beneficiary basis to a client-market orientation.

Would market-derived concepts be readily compatible with social inclusion?

References

Hamdi, Nabeel / Goethert, Reinhard (1997), Action Planning for Cities: A Guide to Community Practice, West Sussux, England.

Prahalad, C.K. / Hammond, Allen (2002), Serving the World's Poor, Profitably, Harvard Business Report, September, p. 48-57.

---

2 Prahalad/Hammond (2002).

Towards Inclusion?
Lessons from Recife, Brazil

Horst Matthaeus

Introduction

The Inclusive Cities Initiative of UN-HABITAT defines its objectives as "promoting inclusiveness." This is not only an inherently socially just objective, but it is favorable for growth and central to sustainable urban development. Inclusive urban governance thus:

- reduces inequality and social tension;
- incorporates the knowledge, productivity, social and physical capital of the poor and disadvantaged in city development;
- "increases local ownership of development processes and programs."[1]

The inclusive city is described as follows:

An inclusive city promotes growth with equity. It is a city that practices inclusive urban governance: everyone, regardless of their economic means, gender, race, ethnicity, religion is enabled and empowered to fully participate in the social, economic and political opportunities that cities have to offer. Participatory planning and decision making, therefore, are at the heart of the Inclusive City.[2]

This paper intends to describe and analyse the situation and efforts of the city of Recife, Brazil, in its struggle towards "inclusiveness." It will give a brief overview about the situation of Recife, the central of city of its metropolitan area with about 3.5 million inhabitants, where today more than 50% of the population lives below the poverty line. Historically Recife was in the nineteenth century a very wealthy city based on the exploration of sugar. This wealth is still present in its great cultural heritage but in steady decline since the economic basis disappeared and the political and economic elites were unable to modernize, explore and promote new

---

1 UN-HABITAT website.

2 ibid.

economic development. The stagnating region in the Northeast of Brazil, of which Recife is one of the most important urban centers, contributes to the continuing flows of migration from rural to urban areas or from secondary cities to capital cities.

Seen in the national context of Brazil, Recife has always been a politically (and at certain times also economically) important city. Recife was one of the last to surrender to the military coup in the sixties of the last century; it was a center of opposition during the military regime and created innovative and "inclusive" urban regulations shortly after the beginning of the eighties – regulations that are still applied today. These progressive municipal laws were the basis for a political movement of slum and squatter organizations. It still is an important factor in city policies and has survived city governments of different political ideologies and programs.

However, even this long tradition has done little to overcome the social, cultural and economic divide of the city. In my contribution, I will try to explore the background of Recife's present social structure, the social movements concentrated in the struggle for urban upgrading, and some newer tendencies of the city government in widening political participation through the extension of the participation in the definition of the city budget in a process known principally from Porto Alegre as *orcamento participativo*.[3]

The structure of the paper is divided in the following sections: Recife and the metropolitan area, pressure from below: neighborhood associations and movements, innovations by municipal governments: Policy responses, technical cooperation and the search for financing inclusion. To this, I will add conclusions that put the efforts of participatory planning and decision making, stressed by the Inclusive City Initiative, in a wider context. My point here is that even the best planning and participatory decision making processes do have only a limited influence on the move towards social inclusion if investment levels in deprived neighborhoods do not increase substantially.

Especially in Brazil, participatory procedures on their own cannot produce socially inclusive cities. Brazil's so-called deep social divide (*divida social*) can only be reduced if the participatory approach is complemented by massive public and private investments. Initiatives in this direction are under way in nearly all metropolitan cities of Brazil. However, it may be too early to evaluate its impacts beyond the physical improvements.

---

[3] Souza (2001). Laranjeira (1996). Matthaeus (1995).

Recife and the metropolitan area

In order to understand the situation of social exclusion within the city and metropolitan region of Recife, a brief look at the history of the formation of the city seems necessary, as the rich/poor, formal/informal dichotomies started practically with its foundation.

From its foundation in the seventeenth century up to approximately 1820, Recife experienced a period of steady but slow growth based on commerce and the beginning of plantation and export of sugar. The following century, approximately up to 1920, was described by Singer as "the century of accentuated growth."[4] The wealth accumulated during this period made Recife a city comparable with European cities in terms of infrastructure (extensive railroad system, university), cultural establishments (theaters, churches) and cultural events. The city grew in the delta and swamp areas of the Capibaribe and Beberibe Rivers with an inherent shortage of adequate land for construction. This shortage led already in the beginning of the 20th century to the development of two towns: the formal, rich and wealthy city on the one hand and the settlements within the Mangrove-swamp-forests on the other. Slaves (or former slaves) and migrants started to settle within the Magrove forests in shacks constructed above unsecure landfills on *palafitas*, which were subject to frequent flooding and lacked any kind of infrastructure. In 1913, these so-called *mocambos* (hideaways) housed already approximately 40% of the population and numbered aproximately 20,000 mocambas according to municipal census of 1913.[5] In the 1923 census, this number had already reached approximately 40,000 or 51% of all houses registered. The "accentuated growth" in an economically favorable environment did not have any effect on improving the housing situation of the socially and economically weak sections of Recife's population.

The economic growth and expansion of the "formal" city could not be sustained towards the end of the 1920's. The world economic crisis and the resulting competition on World Markets that led to falling sugar prices, besides increasing production, eventually led to stagnation and the loss of importance of Recife. Compared to the more dynamic south and southeast of Brazil, where a modern industry followed the "coffee cycle" and consolidated Sao Paulo, Belo Horizonte and Rio de Janeiro as growth centers, Recife lost out. As a result, Recife transformed to a "metropolis of an underdeveloped region" in which the following decades where characterized by "explosive growth, attributed largely to the decomposition of the rural

---

[4] Singer (1968).

[5] SEDHUR-PE (1990).

complex" with massive lay-off of former rural workers who migrated to the city and the metropolitan region.[6]

The first relocation programs of the *mocambos* began in the 1940's with the shift of its population to the hilly hinterland where social housing was built by private and public investment. The shift from the plains and the mangrove swamps to the hills did not solve any problem: the hills around Recife are geologically unstable and are subject to frequent land slides and erosions during the rain season. The cleansing of the city center and the continuing migration led to the development of the informal city of Casa Amarela with approximately 350,000 inhabitants.[7] Already in the 1950's, various movements against the eviction programs started. The organization of the *favela* population negotiated with landowners and public housing programs. The continuing "explosive growth" through natural reproduction and continuing migration was impossible to stop or reduce: *favelas*, slums and squatters grew at an exponential rate. In the beginning of the 1980's atthe end of the military regime, the situation became more and more dramatic: in the years from 1978 to 1981 approximately 250,000 migrants participated in illegal land occupation. New public housing and the first attempts of upgrading the existing *favelas* started in 1979 but had little impact on the overall situation.[8]

In 2002, the housing situation of Recife shows the highest deficits of dwellings in Brazil. Not only in percentage of the total but also in actual numbers, Recife has a higher deficit as São Paulo and Rio de Janeiro.

---

[6] Singer (1968) quoted in Assies (1991), p. 43

[7] SEHAB/URB (1988).

[8] One of the successful programs was the upgrading of the *favela* "Brasilia Teimosa", with more than 20.000 inhabitants. This *favela* became in the following years the symbol of resistance and inspired legislation to guaranteed land tenure (municipal law ZEIS).

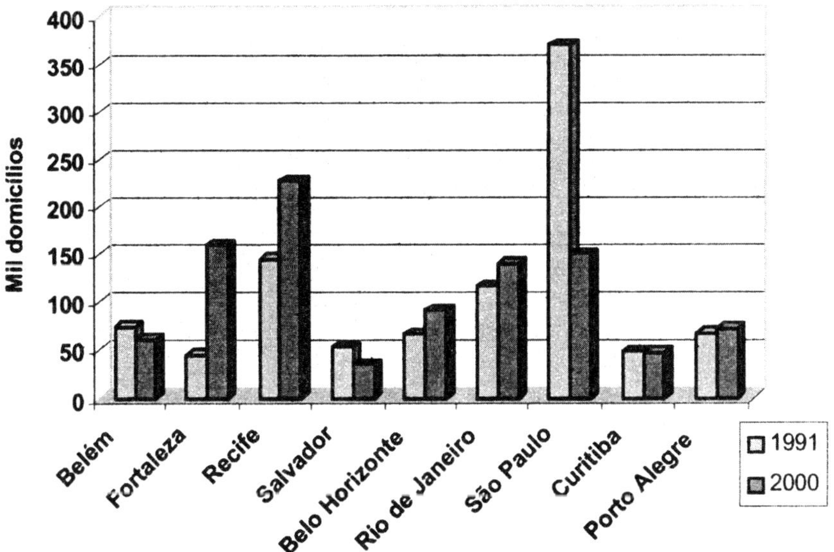

Figure 1: Numbers of Housing Units (in millions) with inadequate Infrastructure and Sanitaion in the Metro Areas of Brazil (1991-2000). Source: FJP/CEI 2001

Responding to the relocation and slum clearing program, a real explosion of the neighborhood organizations took place from 1955 onwards. These organizations were stimulated and supported by parties on the left and municipal governments. This resulted in a struggle for power and influence over the community organizations. The fight over political dominance became a new dimension when leftist mayors promoted *audiences populares* and improvement programs, such as street paving, lighting, water supply, etc.

Various movements and neighborhood organizations started in 1962 to form the first state wide *Federação das associações dos Bairros do Estado de Pernambuco* (FEBAP), and a similar organization on the city level. However, the initiatives supported by the then Governor Arraes were cut short by the military coup in 1964, which prohibited all activities of the FEBAP and the related neighborhood organizations.

The following years up until 1979 (when the first signs of political liberalization started) were marked by political suppression through the technocratic-authoritarian development model. Political rights were suspended and participation made impossible. The military regime produced a profound restructuring of Brazilian economy and society. At its end, the urban population had risen from 45% to 68% of the population, paralleled by a polarization of income levels that still today is one of the highest worldwide. In respect to urban development, the period was marked by the creation of the metropolitan regions, technocratic planning processes and the execution of large scale projects in infrastructure. The National Housing Bank was supposed to produce low-cost housing for the urban masses but subsidezed instead middle and upper middle class residences.

In Recife, as in all other major cities of the country, the "cleaning" and "development" of the city centers continued. Thousands of slum and squatter dwellers were transported to places far away from their original homes, hardly equipped with basic infrastructure. During this time, the church, under the leadership of Dom Helder Cámara, supported neighborhood organizations in areas under threat of eviction and helped organize land invasions. Under the influence of the "base community cristianism," the new movements developed in two different directions: one tended towards human promotion through communitarian-self-help and the other was inspired from urban social movement theories which tended towards confrontation with the state.[9] The growing pressure of these movements – together with the union movements and strikes in the more industrial regions of Sao Paulo – forced the bureaucratic-authoritarian regime to soften its grip and initiate the process of *abertura* in the late seventies.

The growing unrest and pressure from social movements caused in Recife – what Assies called a "metamorphosis of the political discourse"– was expressed by the last appointed mayor Gustavo Krause in the following terms:

> *... The government will be from the city to the Prefeitura and not from the Prefeitura to the city. The people are the source of power and the government is the instrument of their will ... stimulate ... strengthening neighborhood associations, because without participation society is anemic and without mobilization the people will not make themselves the masters of their destiny.*[10]

The *Plano de Desenvolvimento of Recife*, elaborated in 1980 and approved in 1983, stressed the necessity of "social integration" and "ordering of urban space." Community participation received a dominant space and was seen as "identifying social needs....to be realized with priority;...executing works, aiming at broadening employment opportunities by incorporating individuals in labor-intensive programs and in managing community equipments."[11] Besides this shift, the plan also called for "a maximum of realism in the face of consolidated situations." This new pol-

---

9 Assies (1991), p. 135-6.

10 Krause (1979), quoted in Assies (1991), p. 143.

11 Prefeitura (1980), p. 31.

icy marked the end of the large scale resettlement policy and gave way for developing new instruments of urban policy directed towards inclusion and reduction of inequality.

Towards inclusion 1: Pressure from below

The pressure of the neighborhood associations, supported by the *Comissão de Justiça e Paz* and other NGOs, made it possible that in the development Plan of 1983, twenty-seven neighborhoods of subnormal settlements (out of 300 registered areas) were spatially and legally defined and designated ZEIS (*Zonas Especiais de Interesse Social*). For these areas, differentiated parameters of land use and occupation applied. They were to be established in a specific planning process. The regulation was intended as a protection against forced eviction and was seen as a means to reduce land speculation. The declaration of ZEIS was the first official recognition of the subnormal settlements in a municipal planning document. It provided the inhabitants with a sense of security of tenure as well as with the hope for improvements of infrastructure and services.

In 1987 the number of ZEIS was increased to sixty-six, covering some 1,100 hectares. In 1990, approximately 600,000 people – 45 % of the total population of the city of Recife – lived in ZEIS areas.[12] The creation of the ZEIS in 1983 was a victory for the popular movement; however, in the following years, no systematic action was taken by the city government to improve the living conditions, including the regularization of the land occupied. Once more, the popular movement, assisted by progressive sectors of the church and NGOs, elaborated the draft for a municipal lawwith the objective to establish both a governance and funding structure for a continuing upgrading and land regularization process called PREZEIS. This law became a historic land-mark in Brazil, as it was the first popular initiative for a legislation passed by a legislative assembly. Only in the 1988 Constitution was this procedure (popular initiatives) incorporated as a constitutional right.

The organizational structure of PREZEIS consists of the following bodies:

- **Forum PREZEIS:** Deliberating council of representatives from all ZEIS, public sector, NGOs, university and municipal council. The Forum meets monthly and is attended by 60-100 representatives from the ZEIS areas.

---

[12] URB-Recife (2002).

- **Coordination Committee:** Implements the decisions of the Forum, elaborates proposals and monitors the execution of PREZEIS activities. The Coordination Committee meets weekly and consists of three representatives of the population, one representative from each NGO and municipal government.
- **Technical Committees:** Discusses specific issues of their competence and report to the Coordination Committee. Presently, four committees or working groups are operating: i) planning and infrastructure works, ii) regularization of land use, iii) environment; iv) income generation activities.
- **Local Commission for Upgrading and Land Regularization (COMUL) formed in thirty-five ZEIS:** COMULs form the basis of the PREZEIS structure. They consist of two elected members from the community of the ZEIS, two representatives from the municipality and one NGO representative with advisory functions inspired by the concept of advocacy planning.
- **Fundo PREZEIS:** Finances the upgrading activities a special fund. It received resources from the municipal budget and a minimum was negotiated between the popular movement and the municipal administration, fixing the municipal annual contributions to 1.2% of the municipal investment budget and later turned into a simple budget item, which amounted in the last years to approximately 4 Mi. R$. Upon the recommendation of the Coordination Committee, the Forum decided on the application of the resources, thus establishing priorities on what type of works should be executed in which area.
- **Executing Agency:** Within the municipal administration the Municipal Construction Corporation (URB-Recife) was made responsible for the management of the program. A special unit (DGZ- Departamento de Gerenciamento das ZEIS) was established and made responsible for the coordination of the relations with the forum, Coordination and Technical Committees and the COMUL. The elaboration of the upgrading plans and projects, as well as the tendering and supervision of works remained in the regular divisions of the URB. This division of responsibility was to become a major bottleneck in the functioning of the PREZEIS. I will come back to this point in discussing the PRORENDA urbano project.
- **NGO involvement**: The PREZEIS reserves specific functions for the NGO sector as assistants or advisors to the popular movement in its articulation with the technically better equipped and organized municipal government. In the planning and implementation processes,

the NGO worked within the COMULs and assumed functions known from advocacy planning. However the growing number of COMULs and diminishing external financing made it difficult to implement the legal provisions for having one NGO assistant for each COMUL. In the technical committees, they became a constant critic of the municipality on procedures, timing, contracting and assigning financial resources and in the Coordination committee the NGO voice was often the most articulate.

Political importance and management of PREZEIS

Elaborating, discussing and passing the law PREZEIS showed the political strength that the popular movement and its supporters had gained in the post military regime. In the following years, PREZEIS survived different municipal governments and grew into an important actor in municipal (and to some extend state) politics. This strength became visible once more in the beginning of 2001 when the new PT municipal government introduced the reformed Participatory Budget process and tried to abolish the Fundo PREZEIS. The mobilization of the PREZEIS structure and population forced the government to withdraw these proposals and the PREZEIS (as program or institution) become an "institutional member" of the Participatory Budging Committee (see below).

The management structure of PREZEIS within the URB Recife can be characterized by a continuous lack of personnel and lengthy and a bureaucratic process of coordination between the PREZEIS division and the sector directorates (planning and execution). The URB was not able to structure itself in a way conducive to the program in its management structure. The movement and the NGOs often interpreted the continuous internal frictions caused by bureaucratic procedures and management deficiencies as political obstruction and a situation of continuous confrontation.

One of the reasons to request external technical assistance was the existence and persistence of these problems. I will deal with this point in the analysis of PRORENDA *Urbano*.

In its fifteen years of existence, the PREZEIS produced approximately twenty-five upgrading plans and infrastructure projects in eighteen ZEIS. The total investment of PREZEIS in these years comes to approximately 16.5 Mi. US$.[13] The distribution of the very limited resources to many different areas produced as a consequence limited results in terms of in-

[13] The annual expenditures varied between 1 million and 3 million US$. URB-Recife (2002).

stallation of complete infrastructure systems in some of the areas. The strategy used could be described as an attempt to strike a balance among emergency measures, long term improvements and political pressure of the representatives of the COMULs in the Forum.

In relation to the social inclusive cities discussion, the PREZEIS can be seen as an example of active citizen involvement in the agenda-setting and decision-making processes related to the situation of their neighborhoods. PREZEIS grew over the years to be a city-wide institution and a major political actor as the voice of the poor; however in terms of practical achievements, the limited funds provided to the *Fundo* PREZEIS produced few improvements in the infrastructure and the physical integration of the city. Schroeder concludes that PREZEIS is an appropriate instrument for the upgrading of *favelas* but its application shows series of deficiencies and that consequently basic restructuring was required.[14]

Additionally, the PREZEIS with its concentration of political issues and articulating demands did little to promote self-help activities and creativity to contribute to solving local problems. The lengthy discussions and decision-making process as well as the deficits in the management structure of the PREZEIS within the URB-Recife contributed to the inefficiency of the system even more. It is interesting to note that besides the low physical outputs, the system PREZEIS enjoys very high prestige among the poor and any attempt to modify it fundamentally was confronted with great opposition.

Towards inclusion 2: Innovation of the municipal government - Prefeitura nos Bairros and Participatory Budgeting (PB)

Parallel to the installation of ZEIS/PREZEIS, the first directly elected mayor Jarbas Vasconcelos (1985-1988 and 1993-1996) introduced in 1986 decentralization to the city in creating the Political Administrative Regions and the program *Prefeitura nos Bairros*.[15] The objective of this program was "to guarantee that the institutionalization of mechanisms of popular participation is consolidated through a democratic practise of direct articulation between the city government and the social movements."[16] The pro-

---

14 Schroeder (2000).

15 Initially there were twelve PAR, but they were later rearranged in six PAR with a subdivision of so called micro-regions, which number eighteen until today.

16 Prefeitura Recife (1987), p. 16.

gram, together with the PREZEIS, was part of a "model of participatory governance as envisaged by the new democratic administration."[17]

The Political Administrative Regions (PAR) and its subdivisions (micro-regions) were to become stable substructures of the municipal administration with decentralized regional offices, responsible for a number of municipal services like maintenance of roads, building permits and control, etc. The PT administration is using this subdivision for the elaboration of Microregional Development Plans.

The program *Prefeitura nos Bairros* consisted of a series of public meetings on the PAR level. Its objective was to discuss the problems, needs and priorities of the regions, which were incorporated in a "plan of action," a document accompanying the more generic municipal budget. These meetings were open to the public, but only representatives of registered community organizations could vote. This gave the formal organizations an important new status, but produced as a counter-effect a bureaucratization and a rapid increase of organization, which had as its main objective the participation in the voting of priorities of the Program.

The political nature of the program, i.e. the dialogue of the municipal executive with the population, seems to have been the major objective. This political dynamic created a dilemma for the program. It found itself in an uncomfortable position between various fronts: the demands raised in the regional public meetings were far beyond the financial capacity of the municipality, the bureaucratic apparatus of the municipal administration was not adapted to clear and transparent, technical and bureaucratic procedures and adapted to a continuous monitoring by the population.[18]

During the initial years of the *Prefeitura nos Bairros*, the mayor Jarbas Vasconcelos introduced a great dynamic and received popular response to the program. The dependency on the mayor's leadership became a fatal drawback, however, when the following mayor (Joaquim Fransisco/Gilberto Marques, 1989-1992) abandoned the program. This was considered by the national and local presses as "the end of the most promising efforts of municipal democratization during the 1985-1988 period."[19] It should be noted that the mayor Joaquim Fransisco was not able to discontinue the PREZEIS; however, the resulting relation between PREZEIS and the municipal, administration was characterized by continuous conflicts and disagreements.

---

17 Melo (2001).

18 Lehmann (1990, p. 205), quoted in Assies (1991), p. 250.

19 See Assies (1991), p. 260.

The return of Jarbas to mayorship in 1993 brought back to the agenda the topic of participation and integration of the poor into city development and policy. The Jarbas administration remodeled the program *Prefeitura nos Bairros* alongside with the experience of the *Porto Alegre Participatory Budget* (PB) process.[20] The objective of the PB is clear: to discuss the budget and priorities of municipal actions with a maximum of representatives of all segments of the city. The PB structured by the Jarbas administration was essentially continued also by its successor Roberto Magalhães (1996-2000); however, the PB did not afford Magalhães the same leeway as his predecessor.[21]

The very basis of the PB are the "delegates." These delegates are selected through nomination by ten participants during plenary sessions in the micro-regions. The delegates of all the micro-regions form the General Forum of the PB, which then elects a General Coordination Committee. The General Coordination Committee is assisted by a variety of Technical Chambers. On the Micro-Regional level a Local Coordination Committee and local Monitoring Groups are installed. Melo summarized the organizational structure as presented in the following table.

20 Melo (2001) reports on the interrelation of the two cities in shaping their programs. According to Melo the first ideas for the participatory budget in Proto Alegre were similar to the ones of the *Prefeitura nos Bairros*. After the return of Jarbas to mayorchip he incorporated important elements of the than already consolidated Porto Alegre experience.

21 Magalhães is a conservative politician, who came to power with the help of Jarbas and the assurance that he would continue the PB and PREZEIS.

Level	Actions/functions	Actors
General Forum	- Assesses the program and sets general guidelines - Establishes the program's methodologies based on proposals from other organizational levels - Evaluate the implementation of the program's general and sectoral budget plan	Mayor, municipal secretaries, municipal officers, Chamber of Councilors, NGOs, associations and federations of CBOs, delegates, rep. from sectoral councils, and from the local universities
General Coordination	- Implements decisions taken by General Forum and monitors the activities of plenaries, micro-regions, commissions etc. - Monitors the program's budget execution publicizes the program in the media and among the population - Prepares proposals for publication and for training schemes within the program	1 rep. from the following secretaries: social policy, planning and finance 2 rep. from NGOs 1 rep. from Chamber of Councilors 1 rep. from the local Universities 1 rep. from the association of the CBO's 6 delegates, 1 from each of the 6 PAR's
Plenaries at PARs and microregions	- Deliberates on the budget - Consolidates information provided from the various monitoring commissions - Discusses and evaluates the various executive's programs	All Delegates, Secretaries and sectoral departments Residents of the PARs and micro-regions
Local coordination	- Provides training schemes for delegates - Coordinates the program in the PARs (supervises Plenary, inspections and election of delegates)	1 rep. from Secretary of Social Policy 1 rep. from associations, and 3 delegates, 1 from each micro-region
Chambers for Technical advice (health, education, culture, economic development and infrastructure	- Provides advice to plenaries and commissions	1 delegate from each PAR in each Chamber 1 specialist from sectoral departments 1 specialist from Secretary of Social Policy 1 rep from NGOs 1 rep from the universities
Local Monitoring Groups	- Monitors the planning and execution of the activities approved on the plenaries	6 delegates from the micro-regions in each commission (health, education, culture, economic development and infrastructure) 1 specialist staff from sectoral department 1 staff from Secretary of Social Policy

Table 1: Participatory Budgeting, Organizational structure and formal roles.
Source: Melo (2001).

The use of the PAR (and its micro regions) by the PB consolidated these sub-divisions of the city created by the *Programa Prefeitura nos Bairros*.

Melo calculated that the budget discussed in the PB does not exceed 10 to 15% of the municipal investment budget or approximately 3.5% of the total municipal budget.

The coordination of the program became the main responsibility of the Secretary of Social Policy. The secretary and its staff were able to re-establish cooperative relations with the popular movements and NGOs and contributed much to the fast recognition of the (new) PB as a legitimate and important channel for discussion and decision making on municipal budgeting and municipal policies.

As in the earlier program of the PB and the *Prefeitura nos Bairros*, the expectations were very high; however, a marked discrepancy developed between the high expectations, the financial resources and the executing capacity of the municipal administration. All municipalities (and state governments which introduced PB) went through this experience. The program also encountered certain resistance in the technical secretariats, which were reluctant to accept the proposals from below. The program also had to deal with resistance from councillors who saw it as an intervention into their sphere of influence.[22] This conflict led to a clash between the executive and the legislative branches during the Magalhães administration (1997-2000) when the councillors tried to abolish the PB, and the mayor played a dubious role in supporting/opposing this motion.[23]

The figures of the municipal budget affected by the PB show the only the relative importance of the process in the overall political decision making process of the municipality. However, in terms of political participation and the creation of a new political culture, the PB seems to be one of the most important innovations in municipal governance since the 1990.[24] I support Souza's argument, when she concludes her comparative analysis of the PB in different Brazilian cities with the remark that "the Participatory Budgeting in highly unequal societies like Brazil should be valued more for providing citizenry to formerly excluded groups in society rather than for the material gains it may bring."[25] Melo concluded his analysis of the program *Prefeitura nos Bairros* and the PB up to 2000 by stating that

---

22 A similar situation developed during the introduction of the PB in Porto Alegre. Matthaeus; see also Souza (2001).

23 See Melo (2001) for details.

24 Matthaeus (1995).

25 Souza (2001).

the Recife PB has resulted in a shift in expenditure towards social programs and local infrastructure benefiting the poor.[26] The lessons from Recife's *Prefeitura nos Bairros* and PB were summarized as:

> *Whatever the limitations, the PB process has made budgetary choices more transparent, especially since the executive is required to publish information both about budgetary options and about implementation. Above all, community level participants have gained new, more institutionalized opportunities to participate in rule-based rather than clientelistic decision-making.*[27]

The mayor João Paulo (Labor Party), who defeated Magalhães in the 1999 election, reformed the PB and re-established the status it enjoyed under the Jarbas administration. As in all PT governed municipalities (more than 100), the PB is the principal modernization program of the Labour Party. The Recife PT government has already introduced new elements in the PB discussion similar to the *Porto Alegre* experience. These include the creation of thematic chambers, discussion (although not deliberation) of the entire budget, and transparency of the municipal action (and expenditure) in form of publications, public audiences, etc.

To summarize this section, it can be stated that the *Programa Prefeitura nos Bairros* as well as the various forms of the Participatory Budgeting were government initiated programs, aimed at introducing "good governance" principals. In this respect, these programs are different from PREZEIS, which started on the basis of popular demands.

The success of all these programs, however, depend to a large extend on the politics of the governing mayor. The remarkable survival of PREZEIS, even under mayors who opposed it, shows that PREZEIS has stronger roots in its constituency than the *Program Prefeitura nos Bairros* had.

Besides their difficulties and limitations, the programs show the emergence of new political relations between the governed and the government, changing from the clientelistic policy of personal favors to institutionalized political negations. All of the programs, however, tend to underestimate the influence of the bureaucratic apparatus of the municipal administration. As the procedures and culture of the municipal administration remained largely unchanged, the effectiveness of participatory government seems to remain limited. Additionally, the difficult relationship between the legislative council and the delegates of the PB points to a

---

[26] Melo (2001).

[27] Devas (2001), p. 45.

structural problem of relations between the prevailing representative democracy and the introduction of elements of participatory democracy.[28]

In respect to the discussion about socially inclusive cities, it can be stated that the programs analyzed here are steps towards inclusion. Their main merit seems to lie in the creation of opportunities for the population as a whole – particularly for the poor – to participate in shaping the municipal policy and building democratic institutions. Both are crucial aspects of the agenda of recently re-democratized countries such as Brazil.[29]

Towards inclusion 3: Technical cooperation - The project PRORENDA Urbano

The programs discussed so far had an eminent political character: they were conceived either as *luta* (struggle) against the political system, or as concessions to the systems. Either way, the technical aspect of implementation and the consequences for managing the programs were given low priority or were being neglected. In 1996, a request for technical cooperation made to the German Government by the State Government of Pernambuco together with the Municipal Government of Recife was analyzed by the *Gesellschaft für Technische Zusammenarbeit* (GTZ) . This analysis was the basis for a project that started in 1998 with the objective to "strengthen the exercise of citizenship of the poorer population living in areas ZEIS in Recife or other settlements in the metropolitan region."[30] This objective was to be achieved by working in principally three areas with the PREZEIS structure:

(1) Revision and optimization of the participatory planning and implementation processes of PREZEIS

(2) Facilitation of the access to the labor market

(3) Strengthening of community organizations in their capacity to undertake self-help activities

In addition, it was proposed to offer an URB and FIDEM assistance in organizational development. This aimed to create administrative structures compatible with the participatory working procedures and to develop pro-

---

[28] See for example Matthaeus.

[29] Souza (2001).

[30] GTZ (1996), p. 47.

posals for the introduction of similar programs in other municipalities of the metropolitan region.

Introducing such an externally financed technical cooperation project into the historical, political and administrative context mentioned above was a challenge. Although the assistance was welcomed, the great achievements obtained through the joint *luta* of NGOs and popular movements against municipal government had created a strong self-consciousness of the involved, and expectations were multiple:

- The URB staff saw the project as the first systematic assistance to deal with the complex issue of participation and shared decision making and expected training and institutional capacity building;
- The NGOs expected financing of their activities related to PREZEIS in general and to the COMULs in particular;
- The popular movement expected principally training and further qualification besides an additional source of financing for projects;
- FIDEM expected, on top of the direct involvement of the project in PREZEIS, an active collaboration in designing an upgrading program for World Bank financing (later called PROMETROPOLE) in the metropolitan area.

The divergent expectations made it difficult for the project to establish clear priorities and a work plan. The decisive starting point was the specific situation of PREZEIS in 1998, that the Fundo PREZEIS had was well stocked and PREZEIS was not able to spend the funds allocated. According to the then president of URB, the internal discussion process on priorities and a lengthy technocratic planning procedure created serious obstacles for the functioning of the system. As an initial response, the project carried out a participatory evaluation of the overall structure of the PREZEIS, where the methodology of Future Workshop was applied.[31]

The result of this Future Workshop was the definition of three main lines of action: elaboration of proposals for the revision of the planning procedures; design of a training program for community leaders (COMUL representatives), NGO and URB staff; and elaboration of proposals for restructuring the administrative procedures within the URB.The proposal for establishing a community self-help fund (Fundo Comunitario) was made by the project, but at that time was rejected on the ground that the communities needed to concentrate on demanding effective actions from the state. The discussion between the communitarian oriented activities of

---

[31] Jungk/Mueller (1973). Matthaeus (2001).

NGOs and the political activists mentioned above was brought to the forefront and was decided in favor of the latter.

Revision of the planning procedures

At the beginning of the project, the elaboration of the upgrading plans followed more or less the traditional lines of planning: detailed socio-economic survey with a registration of all the families living in the area, topographical survey and design of upgrading measures (street widening, resettlement, infrastructure etc.). The COMUL took part in the planning process; there was, however, little methodological adaptation to a participatory process. The documents prepared were heavy, detailed and soon outdated – a situation common in many upgrading projects. The planning procedures proposed by the project were revised by the introduction of Micro Plans. Additionally, the well known Rapid Rural Appraisal was adapted for use in urban areas and was applied in two areas in the city of Olinda. The proposal also suggested splitting the planning process into two phases:

- Initial surveys and documentation of the actual situation together with the formation (or strengthening) of the COMUL, elaboration of a conceptual plan (partido urbanistico),
- Detailed upgrading and land regulation plan only when finance is secured.

The proposal was accepted by the URB under the Magalhães Government but not implemented. Only in the year 2000, the newly elected Municipal Government prepared twenty-five conceptual plans, partially following the projects' earlier proposal. These conceptual plans are now being integrated into development plans for each of the PAR micro regions. The strategy of elaborating "development plans for the micro-regions" seems to be a great step towards overcoming the spatial separation of the ZEIS areas (for which upgrading plans were prepared without major consideration of the spatial context) and the regions in which these ZEIS were located.[32]

The use of the PAR micro-regions for discussing and defining a micro region development plan brings together the discussion of the budget in the PB with the planning area. Hence, it will be possible to integrate plan-

---

[32] In the process of elaboration of the development plans for the microregions the PRORENDA urbano project was not directly involved as the project reduced its cooperation with URB at the end of 1999 and concentrated on the introduction of the Community Fund.

ning and investment processes as well as the integration of different social classes living in the micro regions. Thus, the PREZEIS, with this new concept, overcomes its isolation (and its frequent "tunnel view") and must adjust itself to the discussion of micro-regional issues –d a change, however, that so far has not been completely accomplished.

Training of URB staff and community representatives

The participatory evaluation, using METAPLAN as facilitating techniques and the Future Conference, stimulated the demand for training in the application of these techniques. An intensive program was designed and implemented during the years 1998-2000. It involved all of the DGZ staff, many members of other directorats of the URB and community representatives of the COMULs in which the elaboration of the upgrading plan or improvement works were underway or in preparation. Approximately 200 people participated, some of which attended a series of courses and were trained as moderators.

The course program consisted of three to five days of intensive training/workshops outside Recife. Confining a training center to a number of days of intense interaction between architects, engineers, social workers, sociologist, lawyers, economists and the community representatives created a new basis of understanding and a breaking of class and social status differences.

The training courses started with an introduction to participatory group work (module I), techniques of participation and visualization techniques (METAPLAN). It culminated in the discussion of how to make community meetings more effective. The second module introduced participatory project planning based on ZOPP and logical framework. The third module focused on work plans, project organization and monitoring.

In all of these three modules, participants were identified who had the personal and professional profile as well as the interest in being trained as moderators/facilitators. For this group of approximately twenty-five participants, special courses in basic and advanced moderation techniques were offered.

Introduction of annual work plans and monitoring

The training changed how URB and COMUL staff cooperated and created the need for a more systematic planning of the PREZEIS activities. From 1999 onwards, all of the different elements of PREZEIS (i.e. Coordination and Technical Committees) were used in the preparation of annual work plans and a monitoring system. Introducing them was a major change for PREZEIS. Although plans are still not fully used, they forced the participants to specify their intentions and to document and review them.

The elaboration of the work plans forced the members of PREZEIS for the first time to define their tasks and to define responsibilities more clearly. It was only through this exercise that the PREZEIS started to realize that the actual executing agency (and deciding agency) was the URB with its legal power. The coordination committees and COMULs are in reality advisory bodies that pass motions to be executed (or not) by URB, with the exception of activities carried out by the NGOs with their own budgets.

The work plans turned out to be a great "innovation." Monitoring the plans during the year, as proposed by the project, was agreed, but never systematically executed. The traditional work style of acting spontaneously combined with poor documentation prevailed by and large; however, the plans were used as yardsticks at the end of the year evaluation and their elaboration become a regular exercise at the beginning of the year.

The introduction of systematic programing revealed another interesting fact: the PREZEIS valued much more all the activities directed towards conscious raising and political articulation, expecting that the URB automatically takes over the execution of the planning and implementation process. However, that this process needs careful programing and that it should be extended to the COMUL (and their work plan) was accepted only after long discussions. The elaboration of exemplary work plans or templates in one COMUL led to the experience of integrating all governmental and most none-governmental works planned or carried out in that COMUL, e.g. getting family health care programs to interact with the upgrading discussion, integrating the discussion on places in child and community schools. The elected members of the COMUL in that community became a type of coordinator between programs, and the COMUL assumed a new function.

This experience, however, did not generally apply. It did not lead to new standards and was discontinued after some time. It was realized that introducing this integrated policy approach demanded a high commitment on behalf of the municipal administration and required a reorientation of all agencies involved in working with poor communities. This commitment was achieved during the outgoing Magalhães administration, and the new PT government has not yet taken up this issue.

Community Fund

The experience with work plans on the COMUL level and the attempt by community leaders to do more than "only" represent their community in PREZEIS committees revived the discussion about establishing the community fund and the need for assistance in construction, extension or reformation of the housing units.

The community fund was conceptualized as an instrument to strengthen the project planning and executive capacity of community organizations in supporting small self-help projects directed towards raising environmental consciousness, environmental protection or recuperation. After approval by the Forum PREZEIS, the thirty-five COMULs were invited to present proposals to a steering committee, which was to select five proposals. The criteria for participation and evaluation of the proposals were very basic; however, only nine COMULs submitted proposals within the stipulated period and the selection of the five "winners" was based on criteria considering the consistency of the proposal andcommunity involvement in defining a self-help component. The "winners" received an initial financial contribution of 1,300 for a pilot project and further 3,000 for the main project. Additionally, technical assistance in detailing and implementing the projects, as well as training in project planning, management and accounting are being provided. The funds for these projects came from the state government, the municipality and the GTZ (with a share of one third each).

The proposals selected included:

- cleaning-up the area as part of a sports tournament, linked with workshops on environmental hazards and means how to overcome or minimize them;
- cleaning, fencing and planting of slopes used as garbage deposits, street theaters, the foundation of youth groups top protect the planted area;
- establishing a community maintenance unit of the private sewage connection that was to become self-sufficient by collecting a maintenance fee;
- awareness-raising activities in a community that had access to a natural pond to clean the pond and improve public access to it;
- reorganizing the waste collection system, cleaning informal dumping places and structuring the area as public space (for seating, plantation, waste collection boxes).

All the activities were carried out with great enthusiasm and involved a great portion of the population. They led to a visible change in the areas. Thus far, the impact has been a lasting one. A third phase of the projects is underway, directed towards the creation of permanent structures to maintain and operate the installations and services created. This third phase will also end the direct involvement of the project *PRORENDA urbano*. The five communities are made aware of the fact that after the completion of the project, they will have to find their own financial resources in order to continue it. All community leaders have accepted these proceedings and are working towards this goal.

During the different phases of the projects, the communities mobilized a wide variety of institutional support. The support came from the URB representatives in the COMUL, the NGOs and a variety of municipal and state government units, universities, and research institutes. The projects became their :own" initiatives, and outside influences and interference were kept to a minimum Besides financial resources the project was also provided one (part-time) civil engineer and one social worker for all five areas. The very limited involvement and the permanent awareness that the project was neither run by the government nor by other agencies were fundamental aspects when mobilizing ones own resources and networking with the partners.

The greatest difficulty for initiating the projects was the creation of an executive committee. It involved all (or many of the existing) community organizations, the design of a management system for the funds, which included nominating a treasurer, opening a bank account, and participating in training courses for accounting and simple bookkeeping.

After the first experience in the five areas, the program was extended to three further ZEIS. The total population living in the now eight areas is approximately 50,000 inhabitants. The experiences of the projects and their impacts will be presented to the Forum with the twofold objective of detailing the work of the Coordination Committee and the other COMULs, and discussing how to make the community fund an integral part of the PREZEIS activities, including the allocation of financial resources of the Fundo PREZEIS for this purpose.

The experience of the community fund was analyzed by Schwanz (2002). His principal findings are as follows:

- The Community Fund offers favorable conditions for the promotion and implementation of self-help projects;

- The formal condition for the participation of the community organizations of the ZEIS were realistic, and all groups were able to meet them (with varying degrees of difficulty);
- The project supported immediate and visible improvements and concrete results;
- The community leaders showed high responsibility and motivation in handling the community fund. The possibility to receive further qualification (in project planning and management) was an important reason for the high motivation and engagement;
- A large proportion of the population was mobilized and actively supported the community fund projects; However, the number of directly engaged community leaders was small which led to high demands on the responsible leaders (mainly in terms of time);
- The population identifies (even after the short time of existence) itself more with the community fund projects rather than with the lengthy negotiations of the COMUL; however, the active leaders responsible for the community fund are to a great extent the same ones as the representatives in the COMULs;

In addition, the capacity of community leaders to mobilize wider support for funding community projects demonstrates their experience in political negotiation and mobilization. On the other hand, the lack of basic knowledge in organization and management techniques was surprising, but can be explained by the lack of practice and opportunities. In this respect, the experiences with the community fund are in line with many examples worldwide, pointing in a similar direction.

The present discussion is directed towards an attempt to fundamentally change the relationship between community organizations and the municipality: demands are being raised that the maintenance activities, performed inefficiently and on a limited scale by the municipality, should be handed over to the communities. It is expected that this would lead to a more active involvement of poor communities in the management and maintenance of their local infrastructure and reduce the "demanding" character of ZEIS. The road to this goal is still a long and stony one as extension of the community fund to other areas needs careful monitoring as does the public (municipal) agency dealing with the PREZEIS need substantial reform. As discussed earlier in this article, this could become the most difficult part of the exercise.It seems, however, that the Community Fund could be a very useful instrument to complement the working of the COMULs. Through the Community Fund the population could be mobilized and engaged in concrete small scale improvement projects, whereas the COMUL could work out the long term goals of land regulation and infrastructure improvements.

Towards inclusion 4: Expecting substantial financing through PROMETROPOLE

Although PREZEIS and the PB opened and consolidated political participation opportunities and the Community Fund showed ways of community involvement, it must be remembered that the poor neighborhoods of Recife, with lack of infrastructure and very limited services, affect almost half the population. To overcome this deficiency and to move towards a reduction of the physical divides and exclusion, heavy investment is required.

In an earlier analysis of the poverty regions and regions of major environmental damage, the watershed of the Beberibe River was identified as concentrating a population of approximately 400,000 inhabitants, two thirds of whom live below the poverty line in an environment considered to be of "very low urban quality" (*pessima qulidade urbanistica*).[33] The Beberibe watershed concentrates aproximatley 40% of the metropolitan population living in poverty. The Beberibe River has become an open sewer and pollutes the river system in its lower part, which characterizes the historic city of Recife.

With an investment of 100 Mi. US$ to be provided by the state government and a World Bank loan, the program PROMETROPOLE is suppose to change this situation. Conceptually, the program has incorporated the principles of the above-discussed political participation and the experiences of PREZEIS and PRORENDA *Urbano*.

According to PRORMETROPLE, its guiding principles are:

- Consider the Beberibe watershed as a planning unit and develop an integrated vision for the region;
- Value the natural resources of the river as an asset for the daily life of the inhabitants of the region and use it as a landmark for the restructuring of the urban environment;
- Develop a positive attitude towards the occupation of the hilly region of the watershed and propose solutions technical and social solution for these problems (instead of massive resettlement);

---

[33] PROMETROPOLE, Produto 1, (2000).

- Improve the housing situation, starting from the existing housing stock and avoid a maximum resettlement;
- Refurbish public space and increase the offer for creative activities, which favor the integration of the communities;
- Strengthen the existing participation channels;
- Support local cultural activities;
- Support to local economic activities and example more existing economic potentials;
- Protect the river source and the ground water;
- Value education as a basic key to success in the process of changing socio-economical situation of the population.[34]

These principles tend to strike a balance among participation, sclf-help and governmental action. In addition, the participatory process of project preparation also shows the change in World Bank attitudes and its departure from technocratic planning and openness for suggestions from below. The management structure tries to avoid the PREZEIS system's existing problems without loosing the participatory elements. Local development committees and community offices form the basis, and a special implementation unit will be responsible for efficient management of the project.

The proposal for the PROMETROPOLE project was the basis for elaborating a structural plan of the whole Beberibe basin. Its principals, however, are guiding the housing component of the strategic metropolitan planning in process in collaboration with the City Alliance Program.

The first results of the city alliance discussions in the field of housing and upgrading of slums indicate that the metropolitan region will need investments of around 100 million US$ annually to maintain the existing situation that is, to avoid decline due to population growth and continuous migration. The improvements of all slums and squatter areas of the metro region to a minimum standard of safety and infrastructure services will need investments in the range of 800 Mi. US$.

These figures, of course, raise daunting questions: how will this be financed? And, looking from the angle of social inclusion, can we really advance without these investments? In my conclusion I will link these questions with the experiences of participatory decision making and political participation.

---

[34] PROMETROPLE, Produto 1, (2000).

Conclusions

This paper presented the history of the popular movement of Recife, the introduction of participatory elements in urban politics such as ZEIS, PREZEIS and Participatory Budgeting as well as the building capacity within the framework of the PRORENDA project. All of them showed the progress and obstacles on the way to social inclusion and political participation. These instruments led to a high political consciousness of the population organized around the PREZEIS structure. The Recife experience suggests, however, that efficiency and effectiveness is seriously reduced in the application of these instruments due to managerial deficiencies in the executing agency of the municipality. The lack of financial resources to attack the serious and rapidly growing structural problems in the fields of housing and infrastructure pose additional limitations to further social integration.

There is evidence that the political opening and dialog are not sufficient yet, but solid administrative reforms of the municipal administration and the provision of financial resources need to be in line with the political dialog. This includes more and efficient tax collection (aspects which could not be discussed in this paper), subsidies from higher tiers of government such as the state and federal government (p. ex. PROMETROPOLE), and the exploration of the involvement of the private sector, which so far has been nearly neglected.

To make use of the political consciousness that the popular movement has gained over the last two or more decades, additional instruments need to be designed. The limited experience with the Community Fund in the *PRORENDA Urbano* project seems to be one possibility. It may introduce the engagement of the community organization in terms of more physical output-oriented activities to complement political action. The ability to connect and to articulate networks was a great asset in the project preparation and implementation of the Community Fund projects. On the other hand, experience shows that organizational and managerial capacities do not necessarily develop when interacting within a political environment.

References

Assies, Willem (1992), To get them out of the mud: neighborhood organizations in Recife 1964-1988, CEDLA Latin America Studies: 63, Amsterdam.

Devas, Nick (2001), Urban Governance and Poverty: Lessons from a Study of Ten Cities in the South, University of Birmingham, Urban Governance, Partnership and Poverty Birmingham, UK.

FJP (2001), Deficit habitacional no Brasil, Fundação João Pinheiro, Belo Horizonte.

GTZ (1996), Hauptbericht Projektpruefung PRORENDA Stadtteilentwicklung Recife, GTZ, Eschborn.

Jungk, Robert/Muellert, Norbert (1973), Zukunftswerkstätten, München.

Larangeira, Sonia (1996), Gestão Pública e Participação: A Experiencia do Orçãmento Participativa em Porto Alegre, in São Paulo em Perspectiva 10 (13), p. 129-137.

Lehmann, D. (1990), Democracy and Development in Latin America, Cambridge.

Matthaeus, Horst (1995), Urban Management, Participation and the Poor: Experiences from Porto Alegre/Brazil, Unpublished Ph.D., University of Birmingham, UK.

Matthaeus, Horst (2001), Oficina do Futuro, in Markus Brose, ed., Metodologias Participativas, Editora Tomo, Porto Alegre.

Melo, Marcus (2001), Urban Governance, Accountability and Poverty: the politics of participatory Budgeting in Recife, University of Birmingham, Urban Governance, Partnership and Poverty, Working Paper 27, Birmingham, UK.

Prefeitura (1980), Plano de Desenvolvimento do Recife, Recife, Prefeitura.

PROMETROPOLE (2000), Programa de Infrastructure em áreas de baixa renda da Região Metropolitana do Recife, FIDEM, Recife.

Schroeder, Edgar (2000), Partizipation in den Favelas von Recife, TU Hamburg-Harburg.

SEHDUR-PE (1990), Politica de Habitação Popular em Pernambuco, Recife, Governo do Estado/SEHDUR.

SEHAB/URB (1988), Cadastro das Favelas da Cidade do Recife, SEHAB/URB, Recife.

Singer, Paulo (1968), Movimentos de Bairros, in Paulo Singer and Vinícius Caldeira Brant, eds., São Paulo, O povo em Movimento, Vozes.

Souza, Celina (2001), Participatory Budgetig in Brazilian Cities: Limita and Possibilities in Building Democratic Institutions, University of Birmingham, Urban Governance, Partnership and Poverty, Birmingham, UK.

UN-HABITAT: United Nations Human Settlements Program. Accessed at http://www.unhabitat.org.

Abbreviations and Acronyms

COMUL	Commissão de Urbanização e Legalização da Posse la Terra (Local Commission for Upgrading and Land Regularization)
DGZ	Departamento Municipal de Gerenciamento das ZEIS (Dept. for Special Zones in URB)
FEBAP	Federação das Associaçaões dos Bairros do Estado de Pernambuco
GTZ	Deutsche Gesellschaft für Technische Zusammenarbeit GmbH
NGO	Non-government organization
PB	Participatory Budgeting
PREZEIS	Plano de Regulização das Zonas Especiais de Interesse Social
PRORENDA	GTZ supported project in Brazil
URB	Empresa de Urbanização do Recife (private urban planning office in Recife)
ZEIS	Zonas Especiais de Interesse Social
ZOPP	Zielorientierte Projektplanung (project planning tool used by GTZ)

Poverty and Policies of Social Inclusion in Mexico City – "Mejoramiento de Viviendas" Upgrading Scheme

Alicia Ziccardi and Arturo Mier y Terán

Introduction

One of the principal features of twenty-first century Latin American countries is the growing urbanization of poverty. An increasing percentage of the poor live in urban rather than rural areas. A high number of '*colonias* populares' (working class settlements) – areas of predominantly difficult and deprived living conditions, located in the outskirts of the central city – illustrate this process in Mexico.

The intense urbanization process was originally a product of country-to-city migration, reinforced by high rates of population growth throughout the country over several decades. Undoubtedly the extensive manpower available as a result boosted the industrialization process and therefore the country's continuous economic growth.

The urban population has grown from 10% of the national population in 1900 to 27% in 1950, 54% in 1980 and finally 66% in 2000. The national system of cities consists of 364 cities of more than 15,000 inhabitants. There are different types of urban agglomeration. From a demographic, economic, social and political point of view, Mexico City is the most important one – a mega city with a population of 18 million. It consists of the *Federal District*, with 8.5 million inhabitants, and the thirty-four metropolitan municipalities affiliated to the neighbouring body, the State of Mexico. It is part of a central region into which several cities of different sizes are integrated: Puebla, Toluca, Cuernavaca, Cuautla, Tlaxcala, Querétaro and Pachuca.[1]

---

1 More than 23 million people, a little less than a quarter of the national population, live in the central region. Six Mexican cities have a population of 1 million and more, fifty-six cities have a population of between 100, 000 and 1 million, forty-seven cities have between 50,000 and 100,000 inhabitants and 248 small cities have between 15,000 and 50,000 inhabitants. (See the official website of the National Population Union.)

Despite the persistance of a strong concentration of economic activities and population in the central region of the country, the federal government's decentralization policy and the out-migration of industrial production affects the growth of the number and the population in the metropolitan zones (currently numbering 31) and medium sized cities, currently inhabited by 42m and approximately 18m Mexicans, respectively.

Although twentieth century Mexico changed from a predominately rural country to an urban one, the most evident characteristics of its society, territory and cities are the high levels of poverty and the profound economic and social inequalities prevailing in its cities.

The *Federal District* as the central part of the mega city is the territory in which Mexico's lowest index of social marginalization has been recorded. A high level of poverty can is to be seen among the broad majority of citizens living in its outskirts. This is undoubtedly in contrast to the extremely rich enclaves elsewhere with acceptable living conditions for the middle classes which are comparable to those in any big city in the world. With this in mind, it is obvious from the outset that this urban segregation of the popular sectors is a clear spatial expression of exclusion practices and of the profound inequalities prevailing in this territory.

Considering this, the task of the Government of Mexico City's social policy is to take action in order to guarantee the entire population not only a minimum living space necessary for survival but also act to promote social inclusion aimed at a greater social and urban equality which would give citizens the rights to which their national and local legislation entitles them.

Undoubtedly, this is the main demand of the Government of Mexico City's social policies, and will be analyzed in this paper. However, before presenting the demand's analysis and main components, the concepts of poverty and social exclusion which are the main analytical tools of this analysis will be outlined.

Poverty and social exclusion: an outline

Poverty is a state of deprivation, which is a product of miserable employment conditions and the informality prevailing on labour markets. This brings the workers and their families into a situation of shortage of both goods and basic services – usually assessed as "absolute poverty."

In the beginning of the eighties Amartyna Sen (1983) criticized the notions of simple relative poverty, arguing that there is an irreducible core of poverty determined by hunger and starvation. The perspective opened by Sen is quite original because it is not based on the possession of goods but on the absence of the ability to satisfy basic needs which may vary greatly according to circumstance and different community and social conditions in a society. From this perspective, occupation, income and consumer goods are the means with which to reach a certain standard, while personal characteristics and social context define to what extent these may be transformed into actual assets. Collective housing for the urban poor constitutes a fundamental asset for which lower class families come to live in the precarious conditions of the cities, which exhibit insecure labor conditions and low salaries but access to services and collective facilities.

The circumstances in which the urban poor live are much more complex and the notion of social exclusion contributes to a better understanding of them. This idea was shaped by French urban sociology and was incorporated into the European Union's discourses and social policies in the 1990's. With this in mind, it is a broader notion than just poverty and refers to new economic and social practices which are emerging from new types of employment and social regimes. The same notion describes the general withdrawal of goods and services from workers and their families, resulting mainly from the instability, flexibility and degradation of the urban labour market and from the great restrictions caused by state social policies. In this context, urban poverty is not only an economic exclusion but a social and urban exclusion as well.

The areas which call for action against social exclusion are, among others: access to jobs, loans, social services, justice, education; isolation, territorial segregation, the lack of and bad quality of housing and public services in working class areas; gender-specific discrimination to which women are exposed to at work or in their private lives; political, institutional or ethnic-linguistic discrimination faced by some social groups. All these processes and practices of complex societies are "factors of social risk" – shared by certain population groups (immigrants, dwellers, indigenous populations, disabled people).

In Latin America, however, the notion of exclusion has taken a completely different path in that a situation of insecurity/precariousness and a deterioration of living conditions always had to be accepted by a large part of the population. This has been worsened and intensified by the adoption of neoliberal economic policies. In the sixties theoretical debates over large cities focused on marginalization, attempting to explain the difficulties such societies experienced to establish effective mechanisms of economic and social integration. The right to work, even when recognized by law, has never been guaranteed to all citizens, as is the case with other basic needs. These concerns are not only based on a description of poverty and forms of exclusion but also on the severe processes of economic and social inequality which have lead to a profound division and segregation of our society. In addition to being confronted by the weaknesses of the structural conditions of the labour market and poor living conditions for the majority of people, is subject to a wide range of social practices which generate the discrimination of the lower classes. Therefore the notion of social exclusion, although originating from a totally different economic and social context, allows these topics to be incorporated into a conceptual reflection and into the actions of governments and international institutions.

Poverty and exclusion in Mexico City

The state of poverty and social exclusion in which a large number of workers and their families live, is a product of the country's political history and the economic models adopted in the twentieth century. The city constitutes Mexico's main economic territory not only by being its main internal market, but also by constituting the place where Mexico positions herself vis-a-vis globalization. Its valuable heritage and rich endowment with artifacts makes it Mexico's main cultural centre. It contributes more than any other region to the national gross domestic product (around a quarter of it) and it accommodates millions of Mexicans who have migrated from rural areas or other cities looking for work, guaranteeing them and their families survival and access to goods and basic services. In comparison to other Mexican regions it does not present lowest poverty levels. However, as as will be shown, severe poverty and – above all – social exclusion are a reality for many of its citizens.

The main factors generating poverty are unemployment, informality or insecurity and the low salaries prevailing on the labour market of this big city. What has to be mentioned first is that the two latter phenomena are the main generators of poverty in this urban area, while the so-called open unemployment (occasional unemployment), which is fluctuating at around 3% in Mexico City at the moment, plays a lesser role. The principal cause of the increasing unemployment is that there is more demand for than creation of employment, particularly for adolescents entering the labour market. Hundreds of thousands of young people join the labor market every year. There are not many options for them owing to the restrictions of demand and their limited qualifications for the working world.

It is well known that the economic processes of globalisation lessen the importance of spatial localisation for productive activities. Cash flows and networks tend to flexibilize and de-territorrialize the productive industrial process. At the same time technological innovations and financial capital activites reconcentrate in the metropolitan area. These transformations are found at present in Mexico City's economy but due to the importance of the industrial sector, the city continues to be the manufacturing centre of the country, although beginning to cede its position to the northern region.

As far as the local labour market is concerned, the capital city has been registering a sustained loss of jobs in the industrial sector for the last two decades. The Metropolitan Area of Mexico City (AMCM)'s relative share of manpower in this employment sector declined considerably from 40.4% in 1970 to 22% at the beginning of the nineties and further to 18.3% in 2003 (INEGI, 2003).[2] This drop was substantial not only in the Federal District, but also in the metropolitan municipalities of the State of Mexico and was a consequence of the declining number of establishments and declining gross output (figures: García, B. and de Oliveira, 2000). Another point of consideration is employment in the construction sector which fluctuates at around 5%, in which a high percentage of employees receive very low salaries and have no social benefits or job security.

The loss of jobs due to the competition resulting from free trade is aggravated by the increasing limits imposed by spending habits, which lead to a reduction of the gubernatorial apparatus and, as a consequence, the diminution of employment in the civil service, represented by 6 to 7% of the economically active population (PEA) in the AMCM.

One of the principal characteristics of the urban economy is the expansion of the tertiary sector to which an estimated three quarters of AMCM's PEA belongs at present. The following are examples of such opposing occupations: 1) Information technology services requiring high qualifications and offering high salaries (financial and/or information services, wholesale trade), located in the main corridors of modernity, and 2) The informal tertiary sector, street trading being one of its principal urban expressions. These depict the precarious employment situation, which constitutes one of the most severe urban problems to which we will refer later. It was estimated in 1998 that 46.4% of AMCM's manpower was occupied in the informal sector outside medium sized and large capitalist

---

2 Figures from Instituto Nacional de Estradística Geografpia e Informática website.

establishments.[3] (figure: García, B. and de Oliveira, 2000). This is the consequence of imposed job flexibility, which has caused a decrease in the number of stable and well paid jobs guaranteeing access to social security, health insurance and recreation facilities for workers and their families (e.g. tourist clubs and hotels etc.).

Informality and the precariousness of work mainly prevail on the labour market for working class females, who are primarily occupied in domestic service, low qualified industrial manufacturing (e.g. *maquila*) and formal and informal trade. According to INEGI data, Mexico City has been showing a growing economic participation of women in the past decade. The female occupation rate grew from 35.3% in 1990 to 38.6% in 2003. Independent of qualification, female workers generally have to accept unfavorable salary and stability conditions compared to men, which is a clear indicator of female social discrimination in the city.

Child employment (windscreen cleaners, selling of chewing gum, matches, etc.) to increase the family income is another notorious phenomenon on the streets of cities. This requires abandoning school activities and capacity building at an early age. Its presence is an unquestionable symptom of urban poverty and social exclusion. Borja and Castells (1997) particularly emphasize urban poverty's *"infantilization"* declaring it a flagrant neglect of progress in a global segregated economy. It is estimated that 13,373 street children live in the Federal District, of which 9,165 are boys (Government of the City, 1999). But more important than the numbers are the circumstances which prevent individuals from leaving the poor conditions into which they were born.

Another main reason for the poverty prevailing in the mega city are the low wages and the decline in salaries registered in the last decades. In 2000 it was calculated that 42% of the working population received an income of less than half the minimum wage (Figure: First Report of the Chief Government of the Federal District, 2001) and it is estimated that the accumulated decline of the minimum wage from 1986 to 2000 and from 1995 to 2000 it is 56% and 25.5%, respectively. Furthermore, it is estimated that 78.9% of the PEA gets less than a fifth of the minimum wage, which is insufficient for a family's minimum consumption in the city as elaborated by the Secretary of Employment and Social Welfare.[4]

---

[3] The figure corresponding to the informal sector for the totality of the urban areas of Mexico amounted to 43% in 1997, that is slightly less. Sill (1999), quoting B. García and de Oliveira (2000).

[4] Ibid.

Concerning the magnitude of poverty in Mexico City, Julio Boltvinik has estimated that in the last years of the nineties the percentage of moderate poverty remained the same or decreased slightly, while extreme poverty increased remarkably, growing from 23.9% to 41.8%[5]. According to Federal District Government data, 60.82% of the population, that is more than 5 million people, is in a situation of very high, high or middle deprivation. This index, elaborated by the National Population Board (CONAPO), includes housing conditions, income level and level of education, with the result that practically the entire population of some districts lives under marginal circumstances. This is the case in the south-eastern districts such as Milpa Alta or Tláhuac, where agricultural activities have survived, but also in Cuajimalpa in which Santa Fe, the main real estate development area, which symbolizes entry into globalisation in the past decade, is located. More than half the population of other districts lives under these circumstances as has been observed in Álvaro Obregón, Gustavo A. Madero, Iztacalco, Magdalena Contreras, Tlalpan and Xochomilco.[6]

From a social exclusion perspective particular attention should be given to those parts of the community which are even more exposed to withdrawal, limited access, as well as economic and social discrimination: single mothers, street children, old people, native races, and HIV-carriers. These are vulnerable groups, which need economic support and programs for focussed social assistance. As far as women are concerned, it is estimated that, at a national level, one in almost every five households has a female head of the family, only 10% of them are in a partnership or married and living with their partner, but 80% of these households are located in urban areas. All these social groups have given the Government of Mexico City cause for the design and application of social policies, particularly sub-programs contained in the Program of Territorial Integration to which we will refer later.

Urban segregation as a spatial expression of poverty

Historically, the city has shown remarkable levels of urban segregation. Nevertheless a big rupture in the urban texture and increasing inequality between high and middle class districts and those of the working

---

5 Quote from the Trust of Strategic Studies about Mexico City (Fideicomiso de Estudios Estratégicos sobre la Ciudad de México) (2000).

6 Data of the Government of Mexico City. Planning and Development Coordination (2001), table no. 1.

class have been observed in the last decade. In the twenty-first century there were numerous and extensive wealthy enclaves within the city in which financial corridors with modern high-rise buildings have multiplied as well as commercial mega centres offering luxury goods and/or restaurants and shops belonging to international chains. This leads to a homogenization of the urban landscape in these areas imprinted with the common features exhibited in all big world cities. However, confronting this kind of modernity the city displays an aggravation of urban segregation and the expansion of the impoverished periphery. Undoubtedly, this is also a public investment problem, but at this point it is necessary to consider the urban effects of the economic and social factors generating poverty, which have already been mentioned.

As mentioned before, the decrease in salaries accompanied by insecurity and informality on the labour market produced and/or worsened the circumstances of poverty, which has different consequences on the quality of life of families living in urban areas, such as a diminishing ability of the family to purchase basic goods (nutrition, education, health, culture); an increasing demand for goods within the public sector, parallel to government inability to raise social spending; placing an obligation on families to create different strategies of survival, placing a large number of its members into the labour market, having a considerable effect on adolescents whose consistency and dedication in the educational system decreases, women accepting jobs of lowest productivity and insecure working conditions, and the children of the poorest families being exposed to employment on the streets of the city. The result is that situations of direct social exclusion are increasing.

At the same time Mexico City, as other big Latin American cities, expanded mainly in the form of working class, self-built settlements in which the rural masses found shelter. The city grew along this urbanization pattern. A political deal based on the inclusion of the working class sectors led to the toleration of these settlements. This was due to the fact that they were promoted by leaders connected with the ruling party at that time (Revolutionary Institutional Party – PRI) or due to the battles fought by autonomous social organizations. In both cases the result was an increasing number of *Colonias Populares* on cheap and irregular – from a legal point of view – urban sites, with self-built houses. The autonomous organizations connected to them obtained the supply of the most basic services (fresh water, sewage, public transport). Meanwhile the *vecindades* (vicinities, neighborhoods) in the *Centro Histórico* (historical centre) were already saturated. Working class apartment buildings were not constructed due to rents being frozen for various decades, resulting in the systematic decrease in population in the central area.

At present it is estimated that a little less than a third of the housing units in the AMCM are rented and that the majority of the population lives in self-built *Colonias Populares.* 60% of AMCM's three million units are in *colonias populares,* 15% in *conjuntos habitacionales* (community apartment houses), 12% in middle class residential settlements, 8% in *pueblos conurbados* (incorporated villages), 1.9% in high-class residential settlements, and 1.6% in the *Centro Histórico.* More than 80% do not have a solid floor, 23% have a cardboard, asbestos or metal roofing and high rates of overcrowding, since the average household in the incorporated municipalities has five members and 4.5 members in the Federal District (Alejandro Suárez Pareyón, 2000).

While the precarious conditions of buildings inhabited by the working class is one of the principal indicators of poverty and urban exclusion the deficit and the desolate quality of public services also constitute a clear spatial expression of a denied citizenship. In the Federal District the supply of fresh water and access to sewage covers 97% and 91% of all households, respectively, but the situation in the marginal municipalities constituting the metropolitan area, is alarming: only 91% have fresh water supply and only 72% have access to sewage systems (figures: Merino, Héctor, 2000). Inadequate accessibility is an additional significant factor: due to the settlements' remote location in the poor periphery there is no adequate public transport connecting the population to places of employment or education causing a high loss of working hours on journeys to and from work. Microbuses are the most important means of transport in the metropolitan area, covering 54% of all journeys. These are followed in importance by "route 100" buses, which cover 6.8%, and the subway which covers 15% (figures: Rivera Víctor, 2000). On the other hand, there are approximately 3.5 million individual cars in the city, which are the principal source of environmental contamination and claimed by the city to be the basis of a deteriorating quality of life and health for the entire population.

Perhaps one of the clearest indicators of poverty and urban exclusion is informal trade, which occupies important public spaces (squares and sidewalks) and whose exponential growth in the past decade constitutes a severe urban and social problem. Undoubtedly, the so-called *comercio ambulante* (street trading), is a widespread and insecure form of employment and leads to the occupation of public spaces, particularly in the *Centro Histórico* and in the district centres. In the beginning these workers are illegal, not only for carrying out economic activities without the obligatory authorization but also because in some cases products of illegal origin are sold and taxes are not paid. Thus the informal work within the scope of an urban economy, which does not supply adequte regular employment, challenges the use of public space, impedes circulation and the visibility of established shops, generates waste and creates favorable conditions for an increasing insecurity on the streets. On the other hand, the size already achieved by this group and the social origin of its members create equally serious urban problems. At the same time a potential political electorate is formed, which is undoubtedly very present in the calculations of those who govern when making decisions.

Finally, economic, social and urban polarization generates a favorable climate for the development of insecurity, crime and violence at formerly unknown levels. The population feels threatened each day. People feel forced to increasingly retreat into individuality losing the urban interaction social life in the neighbourhood and in the *colonia* (settlement). National and local governments devote themselves to public security which is becoming the first and foremost demand of the civil community, rather than allocating more budgetary means to social policies. It requires large amounts of public funds without being able to guarantee peace on the streets.

The social policies of the government of Mexico City

The substantive and operative dimension of social policies in the fight against poverty

It has already been mentioned that the role of local governments cannot be reduced to being managers of social policies defined within the scope of national governments. Local governments should give the impetus to a social-economic policy promoting sustainable human development on a local level rather than managing a limited level of survival (Bodemer, Coraggio, Ziccardi, 1999). Under the circumstances of the high levels of urban poverty and social exclusion registered in cities this ambitious goal requires not only large funds but also a profound institutional reform creating a governmental structure capable of implementing such policies. As of yet this has not even been specifically incorporated into Latin American city's agendas.

The political democratization processes of local governments in Mexico City, which began in 1997 when the citizens were given back the right to elect the Head of Government, have not been accompanied by a reform of the inherited organizational structure. It is basically divided into sectors, strongly centralized, exaggeratedly bureaucratic, and it scarcely allows civil participation (figures: Ziccardi, Alicia, 1998). The PRD's (Democratic Revolutionary Party) 1997 election victory in Mexico City provoked a lot of expectations concerning social policies on a local scale, since it is well-known that the triumph of a party with a popular base generates strong social expectations. During Cuahutémoc Cárdena's term of office (1997-1999)[7], the Social Development Authority initiated a public policy intended to reconstruct the social texture, which was severely damaged by the 1995 economic crisis. They incorporated NGOs into the decision-making process and assumed a gender perspective, particularly in reproductive health care programs. Afterwards the health care services were run by the newly created Public Health Authority rather than the Social Development Authority. The Urban Development and Housing Authority gave a push to participative planning processes by realizing 31 Partial Programs of Urban Development in quarters plagued by urban and social problems.[8] At the same time it created the Housing Institute (INVI) and designed a working class housing policy with the participation of NGOs, organizations representing professionals (Chamber of Architects) and social and urban civil organizations from the working class sector.

The policies and programs that were part of the Government of the Federal District's social policies were revised by the second PRD government headed by Andrés Manuel López Obrador. The new government team's decision to place more emphasis on the territorial integration of social programs lead to the creation of the Territorially Integrated Program for Social Development (PIT). This program is granted a territorial privilege to define its intervention areas but it is designed and implemented by the central apparatus of the Government of Mexico City with sparse participation of district and local authorities, which are closest to the citizens. With this in mind it should be pointed out that the majority of the local governments (municipal governments) in Mexico, even in in the context of a democratization process and a strengthening of the local autonomy, have a simple agenda within the scope of socioeconomic policies,[9] which is limited to the provision of goods and basic services, of urban and territorial infrastructure (fresh water supply, sewage, paverment) and, to a lesser

7 The engineer Cuahutémoc Cárdenas left the City Government to be repeatedly appointed presidential candidate of the PRD for the elections in 2000. In his place he appointed Rosario Robles, with previous confirmation of the Legislative Assembly, who is Secretary of the Government until today and politically close to the "Cardenista" group. There were practically no interior changes to social policies during its brief term of office.

8 Figures from Ziccardi (2003a).

9 For the own complex social policies of post industrial societies, see Brugué/Gomà (1998).

extent, activities of communal social welfare, mostly of an assisting nature (support for children, adolescents, old people, women).

In the case of Mexico City social policies are centralised in the executive sphere of the Federal District and in three authorities: Social Development, Urban and Housing Development and Health. These social initiatives concentrate on social well being, urbanity and territorial promotion and are particularly rigorous in the promotion of local economies. Andrés Manuel López Obrador's proclamation "For the well-being of all of us – the poor first."[10] which was part of his inauguration speech, expresses the essence of this social policy. It indicates the government's order of priorities and a style of leadership that is open, direct and accessible to its citizens.[11] Undoubtedly, this behaviour confronts a past in which the authorities of the city were very controlling. The national *secretary of state* and his civil servants had a strong technocratic and authoritarian political profile both in theory and practice. This does not mean that public administration has become more democratic nor that the public has been given more access to decision making. On the contrary, civil participation in central government is still up to the councils (urban development, social development etc.) which are only advisory bodies (Ziccardi, 2003b) and which are made up of people's representatives, frequently elected by the authorities themselves.

A fundamental element of the city government's social policies is that considerable budgetary means have been assigned to innovative social programs in the Territorially Integrated Program (PIT). This is part of an economic strategy aimed at and combating corruption and solidarity, designed by the head executive of the city.

Its principal limitations are that the institutional structure which administers it, is divided into sectors which do not interact. Thus, one of the pending tasks of the present Government of the Federal District is to realize an institutional reform promoting a modernization of the administrative apparatus and the decentralization of budgetary means to the districts. These are local governments whose heads have been elected by the citizens since 2000. Reforms of metropolitan coordination with the authorities of the metropolitan municipalities and of the State of Mexico and more intense civil participation concerning the design, implementation and

---

10 For the substantial and operative dimension of social policies, see Subirats/Gomà (1999).

11 Another message that the head of the government tries to transmit is his attitude towards his job is starting his workday very early. He holds a press conference everyday at 7 a.m. accompanied by his secretaries and his close team that colloquially reports on the most important topics of the day.

evaluation of public policies are also vitally important. At present the 16 districts headed by the local authorities, which are closest to the citizens, receive approximately 20% of the total budget of the Government of the Federal District, a percentage that is very close to the ones of the past.and has not changed substantially with the political democratization of the City Government. Budgetary means are therefore limited, although the districts are the areas in which civil life takes its course and to which citizens come to have their basic needs satisfied. This results in the local government's main social undertakings consisting of the introduction and conservation of basic urban infrastructure (water supply, sewerage).

On the contrary, the centralized administration had approximately 43% of the total budget of the Government of the Federal District at its disposal from 2001 to 2002 and reduced that to 28% in 2003.[12] The rest ist allocated to decentralized organisms or other governmental bodies such as the Superior Law Court of the Federal District, the Electorate Institute of the Federal District, the ALDF, but is also used to pay off previous debts.

As already mentioned above, social policies are the responsibility of three authorities of the central government: Social Development, Health and Urban Development and Housing. Economy, Tourism, Environment and Public Works are also involved in social activities, however, they only have very low budgetary means at their disposal. From 2001 to 2003 the Health Authority more or less stuck to its budget, about 25% of the central government's budgetary means, which was an amount similar to that of the Public Security Authority. The PIT's budgetary means are part of this and are, among other programs, assigned to the economic support for the elderly for nutrition and medication (*Nutrition Support Program for Old People*) and to the improvement of housing (*Mejoramiento de Vivienda*) in working class quarters. The Urban Development and Housing Authority (SEDUVI) has maintained similar amounts in the same years, but only represented 1% in 2003. The housing scheme "*Mejoramiento de Vivienda*" that, from a sectorial point of view, belongs to SEDUVI does not constitute a part of its budget, but is part of the one of PIT..

Both the *Nutrition Support Program for Old People* and the *Mejoramiento de Vivienda en Lote Propio* (House Upgrading on Self-owned Plots) are part of the PIT and Andrés Manuel López Obrador's Economic Program in which budgetary means are assigned to chapter 4000 "The Poor first." The PIT works in areas of middle, high and very high marginalization, applying 13 subprograms aimed at improving the quality of life

---

[12] The total budget of the Federal District in 2004 is 137.707 million Pesos Mexicanos, about 10.050 million Euro, based on an exchange rate of 13, 7 Pesos per Euro.

in working class areas. The PIT's budget for 2004 is 5.938 million Pesos Mexicanos (433 million Euro), of which 48% go to the elderly people's subprogram, which aims to provide 350.000 inhabitants (60 years and older) with a basic pension and 22% go to the program for *Upgrading, Extension and Repair of Housing*, which consists of the granting of 26,368 loans.

Therefore, most of the programs and subprograms aim at social inclusion, mainly working on the poorest sectors of the population, with a combination of both specifically focused and universal criteria. Focused, since in a first step zones of predominantly very high and high marginalization are identified – there are 870 such territorial units out of a total of 1,352 in the city. Inside these units, however, situations of exclusion or social vulnerability are identified – old people, single mothers, unemployed young people – within which and an attempt is made to improve the universal situation for these groups. The selection criteria for housing schemes are different as will be shown further along.

A classification based on Brugué and Gomà's typology (1998) results in the following principal programs and subprograms which can be grouped as follows:

a) Local Economy Promotion Policies:

- Granting productive loans (micro-loans, Loans for small and medium enterprises);
- Promoting employment (capacity building and employment);
- Scholarships for unemployed workers;
- Support for disabled persons.

b) Local Social Welfare Policies:

- Nutrition programs (breakfast for school children and support for Liconsa milk consumers);
- Education (scholarships for children living under poor and vulnerable circumstances);
- Elderly people (economic support for nutrition, medical care and free medication).

c) Urban and Territorial Policies:

- Housing (Upgrading, Extension and Repair of Houses on self-owned plots and Community Area Rescue of the unidades habitacionales, PRUH).

d) Others: Support for rural production (PIEPS, FOCOMDES, ALIANZA)

An innovative urban program of social inclusion: the housing scheme Mejoramiento y Ampliación de Vivienda en lote propio (Upgrading and Extending Houses on self-owned plots)

Due to the quantity of projects carried out and their budgetary importance the PIT's two main (sub)programs are: The Program of *Nutrition Support, Medical Care and Free Medication for People Older than 60 years* and the *Upgrading and Extending Houses on Self-owned Plots Housing Scheme*. Both programs are intended to reduce the poverty and exclusion, which the working class has to bear. Innovative practices are initiated, which, in the former program generate capacities for old people and guarantee free access to health in general and in the latter constitute means of improving the quality of inhabitable space for families, selected in accordance to certain criteria as a first step towards a better urban inclusion. The latter program constitutes an innovative public undertaking aimed at the improvement of the majority of working class areas in the city through social inclusion.

Objectives of the housing scheme

The principal objective of this housing scheme is to create the financial, technical and social conditions to improve the conditions of working class dwellings, initiating a massive social inclusion process. A study on the housing situation in the Federal District was made in 1997. It indicated that 300,000 houses surveyed showed deterioration due to wear and tear, another 300,000 could be considered in bad shape, due to the construction materials used as well as the plumbing.[13] These buildings are the result of massive self-building by the working classes in Mexico City. The housing scheme *Upgrading and Extending Houses* on self-owned plots was designed to support and accelerate these processes individually or collectively. It also aimed to extend, strengthen and consolidate houses in progress, to build up unified familiar networks and to overcome overcrowding by building additional houses on family plots. Likewise, the housing scheme aims to contribute to the consolidation of working class quarters and to avoid a wider peripheral expansion of the city.

---

13 Figure from Eibenschutz (1997).

This public activity consists of granting loans to upgrade or extend adverse housing. An architect who gives specialized technical assistance and advice concerning permits and licenses is assigned to each family. Loans for upgrading are up to 660 times the minimum wage (30,000 Pesos, about 2,200 Euro) and for new houses up to 1,350 times the minimum wage (61,000 Pesos, about 4,500 Euro). The loan is intended for construction materials and labour and the repayment period is eight years. Payments start one month after the completion of the project. As an incentive there is a 15% discount on monthly installments for punctual payment and 5% on advance payment.

According to the 2004 budget 1,318 million Pesos (96.2 million Euro) are assigned to the housing scheme to grant 26,000 loans. The goal is to increase it to about 60,000 between 2004 and 2006, to reach a total of 113,000 loans when the PRD ends its term in 2006. (The monthly minimum wage valid as of January 2004 is 1,376 Mexican Pesos, about 100 Euro.)

The institutional and social actors

The housing scheme is sectorally attributed to the Urban Development and Housing Authority and is carried out under the responsibility of the Housing Institute of the Federal District (INVI). The institute will install modules in the *colonias populares*, to integrate the demand, to carry out socio-economic studies, to lay down the credits by contract, to control repayments and to evaluate the housing scheme.

It has to be mentioned that representatives of Mexican NGOs who are part of the International Habitat Coalition (IHC), a UNO institution, and representatives of the Chamber of Architects of Mexico City participated in its design. Other social organizations such as the Revolutionary People's Union Emiliano Zapata (UPREZ), which shows a strong presence and intense supporting activities among the working classes living in the *colonias* in the Federal District, and a Colombian NGO, called FEDEVIVIENDA, contributed their ideas and experiences. The Mexican People's Savings Bank, a civil savings and loans association with a lot of experience with low-income families, was also involved.

At present, the principal characteristic feature of this housing scheme is that it is a public social scheme that is not only governmental as it works in cooperation with the NGOs united in the IHC, the National Chamber of Civil Engineers and the Chamber of Architects of Mexico City. The team of the latter professional association gave the impetus to include lecturers and young architects from public and private universities i.e. the National

Autonomous University of Mexico, the Metropolitan Autonomous University, the National Technical Institute, the Technological Institute of Monterrey and the Intercontinental University. Therefore, the housing scheme is not based on bureaucratic rules or functions but on a wide network of public and social actors.

The fundamental pillars of this housing scheme are micro-loans and technical assistance granted to the self-builders of houses who are plot owners in Mexico City's *colonias populares*. The borrower receives the money directly and applies it with the help of a professional who accompanies the entire participative design and construction process. The participating architects are trained to realize better rooms, lower costs and higher productivity. Young graduates in the final stages of their university career (architecture, civil engineering and social work) perform their social service or supervised professional traineeship in the housing scheme or write their thesis on it. Every year 230 architects, 170 trainees on social service and twenty professionals from different universities in the field of housing participate in the housing scheme.

Beneficiary selection criteria

A triple territorial focus lays down the selection criteria for loans:

- Territorial units with very high or high marginalization, on regulated urban ground or ground which is in the process of regularization and which are not close to ecologically protected areas or areas of high flood and collapse risk. At the moment, the housing scheme operates in 815 working class quarters of Mexico City, about half of its urban area.
- The head of the household's income must be less than a third of the official minimum wage of the Federal District. The household income, which is the total income of the community of members composing the family, is also considered.
- Not being the owner of another house.

Some results

This upgrading housing scheme assisted about 53,000 families between 1998 and 2003. It is clearly a redistribution scheme that grants financial capacity to social groups with a very low income to improve their housing conditions. It transforms the beneficiaries into borrowers based on confidence and simplifying the procedures, without requiring them to mortgage their property. It also frees them from the inaccessible requirements demanded by banks for a housing loan.

76% of plots are inhabited by more than one family (or domestic group), i.e. these are shared houses. On average there are 2.9 families per plot in the central areas of the city, 2.2 in the intermediate areas and 1.6 families in the outskirts. Thus the housing scheme hits at the heart of the problem by improving housing conditions.

Furthermore, labor and construction materials are purchased in the housing areas themselves, strengthening the quarters' economies and generating employment, mainly in the construction industry.

The housing scheme creates institutional networks and networks of solidarity and mutual support. It encourages savings of money and the like, incorporates the local workforce, promotes the participative administration of the recipient and strengthens the local economy. It also distributes financial resources in the working class quarters through the employment of labourers, the purchase of construction materials and the contracting of work to local workshops.

The housing scheme targets a significant percentage of the population inhabiting the *colonias populares*, granting between thirty and 100 credits for upgrading and extension in each of the 815 quarters in which it is active. One of the urban effects is that the already upgraded houses start to be a positive reference to the neighbours and stimulate the demand for the integral upgrading of the entire quarter's services and infrastructure. This is a challenge which still appears difficult to achieve but which is part of the urban transformation horizon planned from the beginning by those who designed the program.

Perhaps the most fundamental feature of this program is to set up a network of cooperation between public (INVI, UNAM, UAM), private (Chamber of Architects of Mexico City, the Iberian American University, the Autonomous Technological Institute of Monterrey, the Intercontinental University) and social (NGOs, neighborhood organizations) institutions. This breaks with the bureaucratic hierarchy which is to be found within the government. It requires that the program's own actors become active in a democratic administrative culture, in a project that is transforming the relationship between government and local society. The obstacles caused by traditional practices, whose bureaucratic lethargy is a source of conflict, have been circumvented so far. An evaluation of present practices and the experience gathered therefrom should be carried out without delay.

Finally, this housing scheme is widely accepted by the working class sectors. One of its principal characteristics is its striking difference to the federal government's housing policy which is based on the private estate development of new or finished houses and complemented by a limited offer of subsidized houses. It is also important to mention that in 2002 the housing scheme "Upgrading and Extending Houses on self-owned plots" won the National Housing Award for the best practices.

Conclusions

Considering the high poverty and social exclusion levels in Mexico City the Federal District's urban social policies can be characterized by the design and implementation of programs that are mainly targeted to satisfy the basic needs of the poorest sections of the population, who inhabit the *colonias populares* and, to a lesser extent, the *vecindades* (neighborhoods) of the city centre. They are part of what Brugué and Subirats (2003) call "policies of need," whose objective is redistribution in order to generate more social and urban equality and achieve more social inclusion. These complex policies of budgetary distribution require the articulation of different activities, networking, the creation of a new type of relationship between government and citizens and policies incorporating the *barrios populares* into the urban texture, which should be institutionally consolidated in the next few years.

The social policy is based on institutional discrimination in favor of the poorer sectors, which grants privileges to territories by assigning budgetary means to them. It seems appropriate to select homogeneously poor areas of the city according to territorial features, particularly because the city is characterized by a striking social segmentation and urban segregation. However, the program remains less effective than it could be due to the fact that it has been designed and is carried out by a central administration, which is divided into separate sectors.

New forms of public administration, embodied in a network can already be seen within the present housing scheme. These are continuously faced with the obstacles imposed by a central administration, operating vertically and inefficiently. This impedes the creation of new, more effective and democratic administrative forms in the city. Efforts should be concentrated on evaluation of and proposals for modifications of the institutions belonging to the Government of Mexico City.

The head of the city government is trying to create a *new type of proximity in the relationship between authorities and citizens*, which is reflected in the very high popularity that it enjoys at present. The governmental motto "The Poor First" and Andrés Manuel López Obrador's open approach to applying budgetary means in an economical way and fighting corruption in the governmental apparatus generates widespread political sympathy. Undoubtedly, the redistributive capacity of these social public activities is a merit of the present administration and an important step towards facing the poverty, exclusion and inequality in this mega city. The programs, however, have some weaknesses due to the fact that they operate within an institutional structure, which has the same values and practices of the past and is working with a budget, whose amount and permanence are not fully guaranteed.

References

Barnes, Matt (2002), Social exclusion and life course, in Matt Barnes, et al, Poverty and exclusion in Europe, Gran Bretaña, p. 1-23.

Bodemer, K./Coraggio, J.L./A. Ziccardi (1999), Las política sociales urbanas en el inicio del nuevo siglo, Documento de Lanzamiento de la Red n 5 de URBAL Políticas Sociales Urbanas, Montevideo.

Boltvinik, Julio (2000), Los métodos de medición de pobreza. Conceptos y tipología, in L. Gallardo and J. Osorio, Los rostros de la pobreza. El debate tomo III, U-Iberoamericana, sEUIA/ITESO, Limusa, Noriega Editores, México, p. 17-116.

Brugué, Quim/Gomà, Ricard (1998), Las políticas públicas locales: agendas complejas roles estratégicos y estilo relacional, in Quim Brugué and Ricard Gomà, Gobiernos locales y políticas públicas, Barcelona, p. 25-56.

Brugué, Quim/Gomà, Ricard/Subirats, Joan (2002), De la pobreza a la exclusión social. Nuevos retos para las políticas públicas, in Revista Internacional de Sociología, tercera época, n 33, septiembre-diciembre, p. 7-45.

Concha, E./Alberto, Fernando Carrión/Cobo German, eds. (1994), Ciudad y violencia en América Latina, in Serie de Gestión Urbana, vol. 2, PGU-LAC, Programa de Gestión Urbana, Quito, Ecuador.

Cordera, Rolando/Ziccardi, Alicia, coordinator (1999), Las políticas sociales en México al fin del milenio, descentralización diseño y gestión, IIS-Facultad de Economía, UNAM, México, in press.

Damian, Araceli (2000), Pobreza Urbana, in Gustavo Garza, coordinator, La Ciudad de México en el fin del segundo milenio, El Colegio de México, Gobierno del Distrito Federal, México.

Eibenschutz, Roberto (1997), Bases para la planeación del desarrollo urbano en la Ciudad de México, Miguel Angel Porrúa, México.

Fainstein, Susan/Gordon, Ian/Harloe, Michel (1992), Divided cities, New York and London in the contemporary world, Blackwell, Oxford, Cambridge.

Fideicomiso de Estudios Estratégicos sobre la Ciudad de México (2000), La Ciudad de México, hoy, México.

Fitoussi, Jean-Paul and Pierre Rosanvallon (1997), La nueva era de las desigualdades, Buenos Aires.

Garza, Gustavo, coordinator (2000), La Ciudad de México en el fin del segundo milenio, El Colegio de México, Gobierno del Distrito Federal, México.

Gobierno del Distrito federal (1999), Información estadística del sector social, México.

Gomà, Ricard/Subirats, Joan, coordinators (1999), Políticas públicas en España, Barcelona, 1st reprint.

Instituto Nacional de Estradística Geografia e Informática. Accessed at http://www.inegi.gob.mx.

Islas Rivera, Víctor (2000a), Red Vial in Garza, Gustavo, coordinator, La Ciudad de México en el fin del segundo milenio, El Colegio de México, Gobierno del Distrito Federal, México.

Islas Rivera, Victor (2000b), Transporte metropolitano de pasajeros, in Gustavo Garza, coordinator, La Ciudad de México en el fin del segundo milenio, El Colegio de México, Gobierno del Distrito Federal, México.

Merino, Héctor (2000), Sistema Hidráulico, in Gustavo Garza, coordinator, La Ciudad de México en el fin del segundo milenio, El Colegio de México, Gobierno del Distrito Federal, México.

National Population Union. Accessed at http://www.conapo.gob.mx.

Quinti, Gabriele, Exclusión social: sobre medición y sobre evaluación, in Menjívar, Larín Rafael, opcit. pp. 71-93.

Rosanvallon, Pierre (1995), La nueva cuestión social, Buenos Aires, Argentina.

Sen, Amartya (1984), Poor, relatively speaking, in Amartya Sen, Resources, values and development, Cambridge, Massachusetts.

Suárez Pareyón, Alejandro (2000), La situación habitacional, in Gustavo Garza, coordinator, La Ciudad de México en el fin del segundo milenio, El Colegio de México, Gobierno del Distrito Federal, México.

Subirats, Joan/Gomà, Ricard (1999), Políticas públicas: hacia la renovación del instrumental del análisis, in Ricard Gomà and Joan Subirats, coordinators, Políticas públicas en España, Barcelona, 1st reprint, pp 21-36.

Subirats, Joan/Brugué, Quim (2003), Políticas sociales metropolitanas, IGOP, Barcelona.

Ziccardi, Alicia (1998), Gobernabilidad y participación ciudadana en la Ciudad Capital. Miguel Angel Porrúa, México.

Ziccardi, Alicia (2001), Las ciudades y la cuestión social, in Alicia Ziccardi, coordinator, Pobreza, desigualdad social y ciudadanía. Los límites de las políticas sociales en América Latina. CLACSO-FLACSO-México-IISUNAM, March, Buenos Aires, Argentina,.

Ziccardi, Alicia, coordinator (2003a), Planeación participativa en el espacio local, 5 Programas Parciales de Desarrollo Urbano en le D.F., IISUNAM, Posgrado en Urbanismo, PUEC, UNAM.

Ziccardi, Alicia (2003b), La demora de la democracia local: el difícil tránsito de vecinos a ciudadanos, in Revista Iberoamericana, n 11, Universidad de Hamburgo.

Melrose Commons, South Bronx – A Community's Fight for Inclusive Planning

Christoph Stump

Introduction

The existing political and bureaucratic planning procedures as well as public dependency on fiscal budgets restrict urban planning mostly to feeble short-term strategies of doubtful success bound to election periods. Urban poverty and isolation are often even a result of a top-down planning approach that intends to relieve socially and economically stressed neighborhoods. A community-based approach organized with a view towards developing a strong and cohesive civil society seems to be much more effective in the long-term perspective. Crucial to an inclusive strategy is not only a trouble-free cooperation between planning officials, their agencies and politicians; also, for a sustainable planning effort, community activists and local organizations are needed with a long-term commitments to the community.

A most promising example of such planning cooperation between city and community in the United States is the Melrose neighborhood in New York's South Bronx. Considered as a number one location for urban decay, drug and gang crime worldwide, we are now witnessing a time- and resources-consuming renaissance here, despite the struggle against prevailing prejudices and ignorance. The author of this case study was interned at the Office of Bronx Borough President Adolfo Carrión, Jr. in 2002 and met several times with Yolanda Garcia, executive director of the local Community Development Corporation *Nos Quedamos*. This case study uses this experience by providing insights into the historical background of the South Bronx and its planning patterns up to 1990, into the action taken by the local community, and into what followed as an inclusive planning procedure. Finally, the temporary results of the effort are presented.

The 'urban blight' of the South Bronx

The phenomenon of "urban blight" in the South Bronx is based on the political and economical breakthrough of the automobile in the 1940's and of the top-down planning policy of the city administration. For the development of the Bronx as a favorable extension for the housing needs of New York's fast growing population, the new possibility of mass transportation by subway raised the pressure on denser development in the beginning twentieth century, for access to mid- and downtown Manhattan was quick and affordable even to the working class. The result was a rather densely built neighborhood with 4-5 story tenement buildings and lot coverage of 70% to more than 80%. The open space was mostly reduced to the minimum requirements of the "back yards," and the extremely narrow courts at the side of each building. Density already reached the average of the Lower Eastside of Manhattan, which was considered a slum at that time. In seventeen census tracts, the density exceeded 500 inhabitants per hectare, in a few other ones even 700, and 80% of the families lived in the approximately 18,000 apartment buildings.

Fig.1: Apartment Buildings of 1920-1930 at Courtland Avenue and East 150th Street, Christoph Stump, October 2002

Few major factors led to the downturn of the borough: the coming of the automobile, the chief planner Robert Moses' plans for express- and parkways and the so-called "Manhattanization." The latter meant subsidized housing production in the borough's outskirts. "For many, The Bronx had been a way station; it was where you went, when your economic status improved, but you left as soon as that status improved even more."[14] The first major influence on the borough's social fabric was the availability and affordability of the automobile to the middle classes in the 1930's and 1940's and the advancing of large-scale production of traffic infrastructure in the 1940's and 1950's in New York City. Automobilization prompted soon the stabilizing, mostly white mid-income population of the too densely built and populated neighborhoods in the South Bronx to move further to the north and even to the nearby Westchester and White Plains counties. New immigrants took the place of the lost residents. Within only one or two decades, the ethnic composition had changed from a mix of white Protestant Americans, German immigrants and African Americans to a mix of African Americans and immigrants from the Caribbean and Latin America.

The *New York State Limited Dividend Housing Companies Law* from 1926 had similar consequences. It enabled housing companies to condemn rights and local tax abatements when producing housing for a limited dividend of 6% when providing restricted rent schedules and selecting low-income households. This law was meant to increase the low-income housing stock and to bring down the density in the slum-like areas. Several huge projects established, always pushing the reinforced development northwards to the still cheaper and undeveloped land. Thus, the old apartment buildings from around the turn of the century became less and less attractive for high- and mid-income households. The new generation of buildings was even equipped with elevators, since law permitted self-operation from 1920. Indeed, the new housing production in the north allowed many people to move away from the South Bronx. However, and against the expected effect, the density did not decrease in the endangered neighborhoods. Quite contrary, the substitution of the mixed-income neighborhood by mostly low-income immigrants caused even more people to live in the same area. Double-ups and triple-ups were no rarity, and the landlords were not able to maintain the overcrowded buildings with the obtained rents. Most landlords were hoping to be able to raise the rents, after the Depression. But the lacking maintenance of the buildings expedited the neighborhood's decline. Eventually, many building owners de-

[14] The Bronx Museum of the Arts (1986), p.28.

cided to give up their property, gain as much rent as possible and stopped investing in the housing stock.

In these difficult times, Robert Moses' controversial decision to build the Cross-Bronx Expressway (1946-1963) destroyed the once lively and thriving, if somewhat shabby, lower mid-income neighborhood East Tremont, north of Melrose. The new highway construction cut right through its heart in order to connect the George Washington Bridge with Long Island and New England.[15] The eleven kilometer-long, six-lane expressway required the demolition of buildings and hundreds of businesses and thousands of families to be displaced. An alternative route would have affected only six buildings. But it was completely ignored by the master planner, although public officials and community groups opposed the route forcefully. Long before the construction, it had been obvious that the expressway would not contribute positively to the economic state of the Bronx; however, the highway cut off the borough's poorer south from the mid-class neighborhoods in the north and led the southern community into urban isolation.

Figure 2: Cross-Bronx Expressway at Hugh Grant Circle. View to the southeast with East 177th Street IRT station. Source: Stern, Robert A. M.; Mellins, Thomas; Fishman, David, p. 971. Source: The New York Times, New York, New York

[15] Stern, Mellins, Fishman (1995), p. 971ff.

But such ruthless transportation planning does not completely explain the urban blight in the South Bronx. Reference should also be made to Camilo José Vergara's studies in "The New American Ghetto." Here, Vergara observes the South Bronx among other emerging ghettos over two decades: very often, either lacking maintenance of the heating system or illegally improvised room heating caused fires, especially in overcrowded or partly vacant old apartment buildings. Fires are extremely dangerous for buildings built at the beginning of the twentieth century and earlier. The New York City Building Code required the four and five story apartment buildings to have only a fireproof construction on the ground floor; six story buildings had to be fire proof up to the first two floors. Another problem with old apartment buildings is their extremely high density. The courts along the side lot lines, which are mostly shared with the neighboring building, are often as narrow as just over one meter with opposite window-openings. Another source of fire were definitely arsons committed by the building owners.

Figure 3: Abandoned and boarded-up apartment building at Melrose Avenue and East 160th Street (Christoph Stump, October 2002)

Figure 4: Vacant land along Melrose Avenue north of East 156th Street (Christoph Stump, October 2002)

If the building's rent couldn't guarantee a minimum interest for proper maintenance at least the owner wanted to claim their insurances premium. Vacant apartments and vacant, deteriorated buildings are a safety threat to the entire community, since not only homeless people take over the accommodations, but also especially drug dealers and criminals use the space for their businesses.[16]

Within only a few years between the late 1960's and mid 1970's, the South Bronx became symbol of a deteriorated, isolated and very dangerous ghetto, where even the police only dared to patrol during daytime. While the community experienced a time of crime and disinvestment, many businesses and public services moved out. Discriminatory mortgaging played an important part in real estate development. Norman Krumholz reports a case from Cleveland, Ohio, where a Community Reinvestment Act had to push lenders to extend their credit engagement in disinvested, formerly so-called "redlined" districts, where banks and insurances denied or made it harder to get credits for residents, only because of their living environment or their ethnicity.[17] A nationwide study of 1991 confirmed that New York

[16] Tolchin (1973a).

[17] Krumholz (1997), p. 66.

performed worst in a housing bias ranking, especially regarding Hispanics and African Americans, the prevalent population of Melrose.[18]

The result to the community was a rapidly decreasing attractiveness. In consequence, the rents dropped dramatically. Finally, most landlords had no interest in their real estate anymore. Along with the fading revenues for the property owners, the payment moral for the property taxes diminished. The legislator then enacted a law that provided the city with condemnation rights on property in tax debt for more than twelve months. Thanks to this law, the city took title of a fair number of lots. In the South Bronx the proportion of condemned property to private property exceeds fifty percent in some blocks. The city demolished burnt-out buildings and boarded up abandoned property. Thus, entire blocks were cleared and would have given parts of the community an almost suburban touch, had the vacant land not been used as illegal dump.

High-rise urban renewal projects

The consequences of disinvestments, crime and isolation in the borough's south were so grav, that the city decided to launch large-scale housing investments. They are also known as *urban renewal projects*. One such project in Melrose was simply added to the existing housing stock: it did not take a parcel that might have had to be cleared. It is located on top of a commuter's railroad track and is thus called Air Rights Buildings. The logic of the project neither demanded nor provided any open space, let alone parks or public service facilities. The first projects were an answer to the huge demand for accommodation by those caught in mostly economical hardship – especially single parent households and elderly citizens. They were considered to be in a transitional state of need: they had just dropped out of a well functioning society, had special problems because of extraordinary circumstances, but would soon restabilize and find their way to an ordinary sustaining life again. Thus, the urban renewal projects intended to put up people with special needs rather than to provide decent housing.

Later urban renewal projects, the Melrose Houses or the Andrew Jackson Houses for example, occupied entire blocks. They had to be cleared of the still-existing and inhabited left-over apartment buildings and townhouses that had escaped earlier demolition.

---

[18] Lueck (1991).

Figure 5: Air Rights Building at Park Avenue and East 159th Street, Photo: Christoph Stump, October 2002

The "block clearing" strategy had several major impacts on the very weak, but nonetheless extant community. One impact was the unavoidable loss of those units that had to be demolished. The new projects did not provide housing units for the displaced residents if they did not correspond to the new project's occupancy restrictions. The South Bronx thus had to fight even more homelessness. Also, the block clearing forced several local businesses to either move or close; local employment was becoming rare. The new developments flooded the entire neighborhood with newcomers. The Melrose community was clearly overburdened to deal with such an increase of the socially problematic population.

The urban renewal projects themselves generated problems that were mostly new both to the inhabitants and to the neighborhood. Besides the fluctuation problematic of subsidized housing, the buildings provided only one entry for 147 units in the Melrose Houses and one entry for 204 units in the Andrew Jackson Houses. Given these circumstances a building or even a floor community could hardly develop. The projects' anonymity, their architectural designs of dark, windowless corridors and slow elevators and the lacking social mixture provided an ideal breeding ground for burglary, drug dealing and rape. Some members of the Melrose Community held the urban renewal's residents responsible for spreading general crime in their neighborhood. A fair amount of the vacant building stock invited criminals to use the space for drug abuse, drug dealing and as refuge.[19] In 2001 the most pressing problems still emerged from the vandalized vacant buildings. With fire, health and safety hazards and the insufficiently maintained NYCHA (New York City Housing Agency) projects, the area became drug- and crime-ridden.

Top-down planning 1960-1990: The urban renewal era and its outcomes

The results of disinvestment, arson, abandonment, dislocation, crime, and substance abuse became evident to everyone in the city when the New York Times published the existing circumstances in the South Bronx on the title pages of four successive issues in 1973.[20] But the inhuman living conditions of this fatal environment were also nationally recognized when President Jimmy Carter visited the devastated Charlotte Street in 1977, only a few blocks northeast of Melrose. The following announcement of $1.5 billion investment in the area had a tremendous effect on the mass media. One year later New York City's Mayor Edward I. Koch offered the chair of the South Bronx Development Office to experienced urban-renewal specialist and former president of the New York State Urban Development Corporation Edward J. Logue. By 1979, however, the plan's $1.5 billion budget already had been whittled down step-by-step to only $400 million in 1979. When an internal quarrel with the Board of Estimate emerged, the Mayor ordered a new plan from Logue.[21]

The new urban-renewal plan was released in 1980 by the City Hall in order to get approval in public hearings by the affected residents, and by city officials.[22] The costs for the 25,000 new and rehabilitated, mostly owner-occupied housing units, the 10,000 to be created jobs, the 450,000 m^2 industrial and commercial space and the 193 recreational spaces and community facilities were estimated to cost $200 million each of the seven proposed years. Once more the budget posed a problem. The city and the state had shifted the finance burden to the Federal Government, since it was President Carter who had promised to invest in the large-scale development. Finally, between 1978 and 1986 a mere $250 million were spent in government housing funds with 36,863 renovated and 12,780 units

---

19 New York City Department of City Planning (2001), p. 12,13.

20 Tolchin (1973a); Tolchin (1973b); Tolchin (1973c); Tolchin (1973d).

21 Goodwin (1980a).

22 Goodwin (1980b).

built, mostly before 1983, when in the Reagan era Federal housing funds ran out.[23] But one year later, the first real sign of a new urban-renewal strategy was set in Charlotte Street, where ninety ranch-style houses were completed by the South Bronx Development Organization and sold for less than $50,000 with state-subsidized mortgages to families earning less than $25,000 per year.[24] The new strategy proposed owner-occupied housing, because owners were more likely to protect their property than tenants.

In 1984, the Bronx industry seemed to recover when new sites in Morrisania north of Melrose and in the north Bronx were available. Hunt's Point at the southern tip offered a primary access to the country's mainland with the new rail connection.[25] But the Bronx obviously did not receive a share of the economical rise caused by the promising service industries proportionate to other outer boroughs. Lucrative businesses avoided the northern borough; the Manhattan-bound companies preferred to locate their back-offices in the emerging downtowns of Queens and Brooklyn.[26] The only "back-office" building in the Bronx built at that time was the Fordham Plaza building in the middle of the borough, with the city administration as tenant. But many, above all the Borough President Stanley Simon, recognized a slow recovery of the Bronx. Developers were coming back and land values rising; however, Hispanics and African Americans were benefiting in neither an economical nor a social way.[27] Neighborhood housing experts already feared a new crisis, because serious land speculation evolved in certain areas.[28] Some developers even urged the administration to rename the South Bronx, for even the name then internationally connoted urban blight and decay.[29]

In 1986, a huge corruption scandal shattered the borough's administration. The Bronx county leader was arrested for twelve years and his entourage of administration officials, including the Borough President, were forced to resign.[30] As it turned out, a greater number of board members of several agencies did business with a view to political loyalties to certain local leaders. The successor of the Bronx Borough President be-

---

23 Chavez (1987).

24 Shenon (1984).

25 Wedemeyer (1985).

26 Chavez (1987).

27 James (1986).

28 Chavez (1987).

29 Verhovek (1988).

30 Lynn (1987).

came Fernando Ferrer after the communities and minority leaders demanded an African American or Hispanic as their advocate in the city administration.

The city's planning for the Melrose Commons urban-renewal plan had only just started[31]: The New York City Department of City Planning studied the East 161st Street-Corridor for a possible redevelopment of a Bronx downtown.[32] This new input led to a low-rise housing plan for Melrose with 4,000 units for mid-income families in thirty blocks of small, attached houses, headed by Director of the Bronx Office of the Department of City Planning Bernd Zimmermann.[33] Zimmermann was later in 1988 appointed Director of Planning and Development for Bronx Borough President Ferrer's office.

Ferrer managed to set up an unstained crew for a new approach in borough politics and successfully merged the different ethnic interests. It was his office that commissioned the Regional Planning Association to initiate a planning process for the entire borough. The report of 1991 included several recommendations that were later incorporated into the Bronx Center Plan.[34] The plan asked for 2,600 units as vital part of the Melrose community being the largest municipally owned stretch in the city (55% of all property and 85% of the vacant land belonged to the city).[35] The Bronx Center Plan also provided 23,000m² commercial space, a centrally located 1.5 hectares park and the realignment of a clear-cut diagonal street strip around the old courthouse at the northeast of the later Melrose Commons Plan into the 90° street grid.[36] The plan's objectives to establish a police academy for $160 million and an expansion of the existing Bronx Museum of the Arts to nurture education and jobs to the neglected neighborhood fell victim to budget cuts.[37] The Bronx Center Plan, covering a 300-block area in the borough's south, was thus envisioned to be a long-range plan and provided four nodes: [38]

(1) A civic center around the county building on Grand Concourse with restored building and surrounding parks, an expansion of the Bronx Museum of the Arts, a 3,700 m² ten-story office building, new court-

31 Planning 9/1991, p. 15:2.

32 Rothstein (1994).

33 Chavez (1987).

34 Planning 9/1991, p. 14.

35 Rothstein (1994).

36 Planner's Network website.

37 Planning 9/1991, p. 14.

38 Golden (1990).

houses and Concourse Plaza at East 161st Street, a shopping mall accompanied by office space, and an entertainment center;

(2) An institutional center around Hostos Community College, which received a $200 million extension, the police academy, Lincoln Hospital, several public schools, and the landmark post-office;

(3) An economical development around The Hub, the still existing second largest commercial strip in the Bronx at the crossroads of East 149th Street and Third Avenue;

(4) Melrose Commons, a moderate-income housing development, reaching north of East 154th Street to East 163rd Street approximately between Park and Third Avenues. The expected costs of the now proposed 2,600 units would exceed $400 million until 2002.

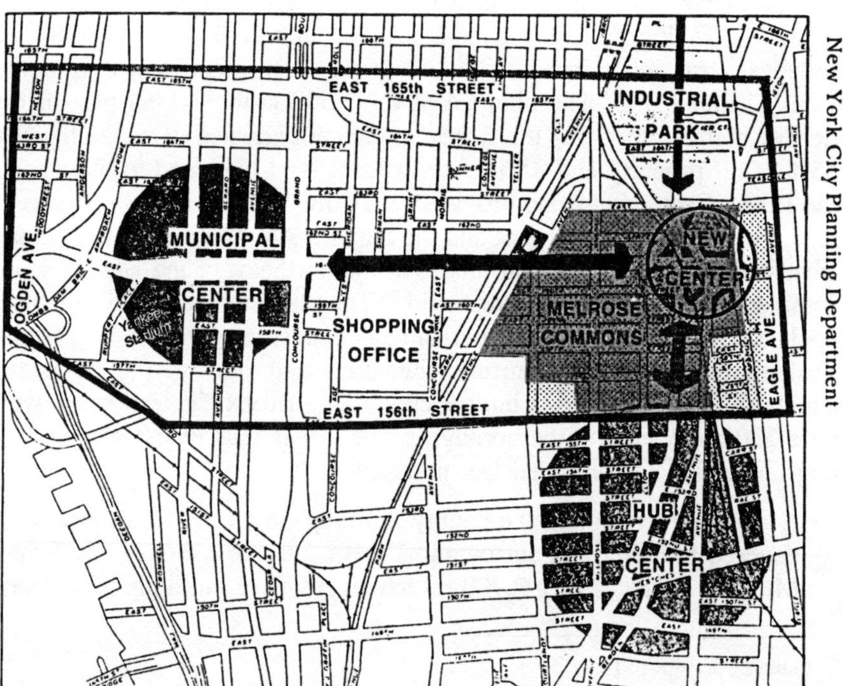

Figure 6: Concept Map of the Bronx Center Plan, 1991. Melrose Commons and an expanded community college ("new center") form two eastern nodes, upgraded court facilities near Yankee Stadium form the western node, and a retail center ("the Hub") forms the southern node.

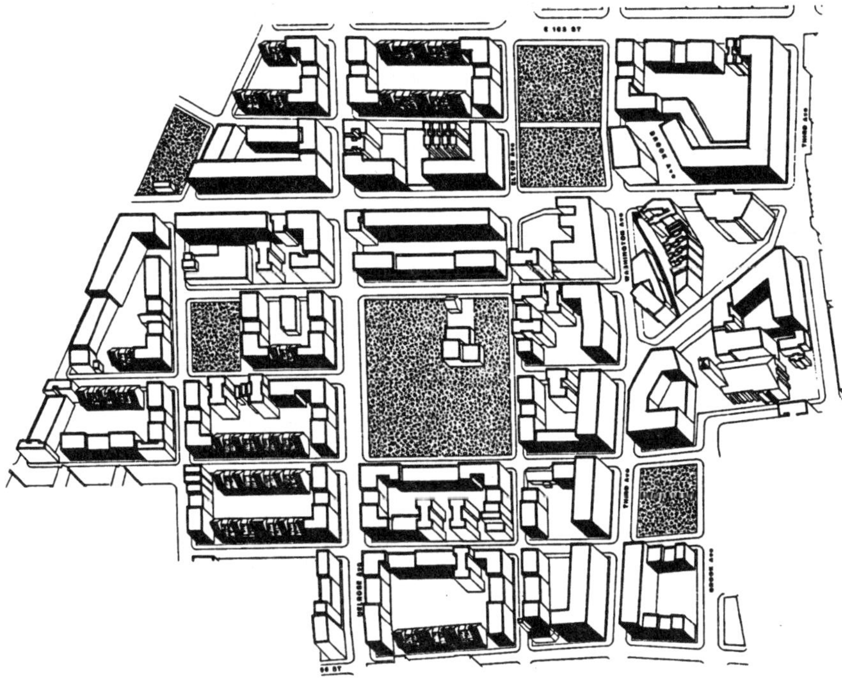

Figure 7: Axonometric view of the proposed Melrose Commons site in 1991 before community participation. Source: Planning 9/1991, p. 15

Especially the last node had wakened skepticists. It was not clear whether private developers would succeed in drawing better-off homebuyers to the site, even though the city's development subsidies were estimated to amount to $100 million. They argued that middle class homebuyers would not accept a neighborhood surrounded by vacant city-owned lots or areas of high unemployment rates.

A project, probably similar to the proposed Melrose Commons development, advanced east of Third Avenue in March 1993 as Melrose Court with 263 heavily subsidized condominiums in attached four-story townhouses.[39] The mega-block development provided two secured wide streets for parking and private backyards with entries for the two upper units per building. The very idea of townhouses sold to a homeowner, who could rent out the other two units in his building was not considered to be feasible by banks. They feared that homeowners might have difficulty in finding enough renters at suitable prices in the area. Another project was finished around the intersection of East 155th Street and Elton Avenue earlier

[39] Oser (1991).

in November 1992. Here, 26 brightly colored, subsidized two-family homes were sold for less than $150,000 to buyers earning $30,000 to $52,000.[40] The houses provided a rental unit on ground floor and an owner's duplex above.

Figure 8: Melrose Court at St. Ann's Avenue and East 157th Street. Photograph: Christoph Stump, October 2002

Towards Inclusive Planning

To advance the Bronx Center Plan, the Borough President Fernando Ferrer appointed a Steering Committee in May 1992 composed of political, civic and community leaders as well as an Advisory Council. Also, in a kickoff conference in June the Mayor's Office expressed its will for cooperation. The Advisory Council was opened to any interested member of the community. High Bridge is a neighborhood in the northwest of Melrose where residents would not have been affected by the relocation requirements the plan asked for Melrose Commons. During that summer, a Melrose resident ran into a city worker, who was picking up notes for the already advanced Bronx Center Plan.[41] Word spread quickly and the com-

---

[40] Color Them Brightly (1992).

[41] Rothstein (1994).

munity found out that they had not been informed about the city's considerations for the neighborhood – particularly that so many residents and businesses should be relocated once again. According to the plan's Draft Environmental Impact Statement, 78 homeowners, 400 tenants and 80 businesses and their 550 employees located in that area were to be displaced. The standard procedure for the planning efforts would have stipulated a public hearing at a certain point, usually including politicians, developers and architects lined up against neighborhood activists watching their own energy disperse in rancor.[42]

The Bronx Center Project organized a second forum on November 12, 1992 at Lincoln Hospital to learn about public concerns about the Bronx Center Plan. The discussion was this time located in the immediate neighborhood of the proposed Melrose Commons urban renewal area. Taking the opportunity, the chair announced that the urban renewal plan was about to being certified.[43] Melrose residents protested on the spot and articulated that they had no interest in being relocated.[44] A series of questions was also raised concerning the affordability of the proposed development, the advantages for the existing businesses, the missing provision health care in the community, the inappropriateness of the designated open space in the plan, the realignment of the street grid being used differently as proposed, the need for sufficient density to sustain local commercial activities and social institutions, and the building construction and materials.[45] At that time, the Melrose community was the home of approximately 6,000 people and had a median family income of under $12,000 a year.[46] The Steering Committee was clearly faced with a cohesive community – a fact not considered yet at all.

Yolanda Garcia, whose family owned a carpet store on Third Avenue, and other affected community members started to lobby in Melrose and distributed flyers to inform as many community members as possible. They later formed the community group "We Stay/Nos Quedamos" in February 1993.[47] The group became a Local Development Corporation (LDC) and in 1999 a Community Development Corporation (CDC) and elects its board members once a year. This time, the community felt, those who stayed with the neighborhood through times of decay and crime

---

[42] Muschamp (1993).

[43] Planner's Network website.

[44] Rothstein (1994).

[45] Planner's Network website.

[46] Municipal Art Society of New York website (2003), Map ID# BX5.

[47] Waldman (1997).

should be part of the planning process. From then onwards, the Melrose neighborhood activists met at St. Peter and Paul's Church at the intersection of St. Ann's Avenue and East 159th Street every second week and initialized a quantitative study about the willingness of the residents for the proposed relocation. The survey of several thousand residents in the neighborhood found only three residents who wanted to move as proposed by the city's plan.

The study helped enlist the support of local officials, above all the Borough President Fernando Ferrer, and put pressure on the then Mayor David N. Dinkins, who happened to face reelection. The Borough President convinced city officials to postpone the certification of the plan for six months.[48] Obviously, Ferrer welcomed investment in his borough, but he was also painfully familiar with the kind of projects that, while physically located in a community, contributed little value to it[49] – if streets and parks were planned by professionals, who may have had good abstract ideas about places, but little knowledge of what it's like to live in this particular one; if housing projects displace people from existing buildings and shred the urban fabric; if office buildings generate jobs for which local residents lack adequate skills; if, last but not least, architecturally impressive buildings provide temporary construction jobs but no long-range economic stability for the residents.

The Bronx Center Project

Having now realized the residents' interests, the Bronx Center provided two community organizers.[50] At a space at Courtlandt Avenue and East 158th Street donated by a long-term resident, the community group *Nos Quedamos* held biweekly meetings to discuss aspects of the plan with representatives of the Departments of Housing and Urban Development, City Planning, Housing Preservation and Development, Environmental Protection, Parks, Transportation and other city agencies, including the Mayor's, the Congressman's and Bronx Borough President's Offices. The group made clear that its members, and not the bureaucrats, knew better, what was best for their neighborhood. *Nos Quedamos* steadily sent faxes to the affected officials to inform them about the planning progress and, at the same time, informed the residents and discussed the ongoing planning with them at St. Peter and Paul's Church.

48 Planner's Network website.

49 Muschamp (1993).

50 Rothstein (1994).

The negotiation process took six months to redraw the Bronx Center Plan for the 300-block area, roughly bounded by East 147th and 165th Streets, Harlem River and St. Ann's Avenue.[51] In May 1993, the Bronx Center Steering Committee finally submitted a report of the planning results in English and Spanish languages to the Borough President Fernando Ferrer, who spearheaded the entire community-based, volunteer-planning effort. The Bronx Center engaged and brought together the energies and imaginations of Bronx citizens, institutional and political leaders, city officials, community activists, academicians, professionals and youths. The process was guided by the Bronx Steering Committee, the Advisory Council and five working groups. The Municipal Arts Society, the Pratt Institute Center for Community and Environmental Development, along with the Bronx Borough President's Office provided staff assistance. Partially sponsoring were the New York City Economic Development Corporation and New York State Urban Development Corporation. "Effective and meaningful planning must be product of a 'bottom-up' community-based process. Planning based on this principle holds the most promise for long-term benefits for all members of the community," says the preamble.

Four guiding principles embodied the values, desires and hopes of the community members and thus influenced the entire planning effort. These principles were (1) Bottom-up planning promising long-term benefits for the residents, (2) interdisciplinary, comprehensive and integrated planning at every stage, guaranteeing a holistic renewal, (3) economic and social revitalization triggering an economical engine to the planning area, the borough and city, providing education, training and access to capital, and delivering health and human services along recreational and cultural opportunities, and (4) continuation to anchor the Bronx Center on a participatory planning process developing civic responsibility and civic life.[52] Ongoing regular participation of the residents through the Bronx Forum was ensured the long-term success of the effort.

The five working groups deliverd proposals for developing future images of economic development, health and human services, education and culture, housing and urban design, as well as for transportation. These proposals did not suggest a full-blown plan, but served rather as platform for further discussion:

(1) *Economic Development*: The priority concern was to enforce the economical situation of the area's residents as workers, entrepreneurs and investors by improving the job supply and job training opportunities.

---

[51] Bronx Center Steering Committee (1993), p. 14.

[52] Bronx Center Steering Committee (1993), p. 7-8.

Proposed projects were Job Training; Technical assistance for contractors; local hiring agreements to ensure local residents preferred in job offers; community banking to improve access to basic banking services and capital; hub retail development; Yankee Stadium/Waterfront Triangle to redevelop a major recreational and business complex along the Harlem River waterfront and to renovate the Bronx Terminal Market neighborhood; and finally the Morrisania Industrial Park to establish a residential/light industrial mixed use zone.

(2) *Health and Human Services*: Both human services and health care should empower people to help them move from poverty toward financial self-sufficiency. Services were to be client-centered, comprehensive, accessible, affordable and available in English and Spanish. The working group focused on a Community Resources Development Bureau to help not-for-profit service providers address their services to the needs of local residents; service clusters to concentrate services in at least three places; filling service gaps to face needs concerning prenatal and reproductive health (teenage pregnancy prevention, AIDS prevention and treatment, mental health, treatment for substance abusers); computerized management to improve coordination of service delivery; and college programs to stimulate interest in human services careers.

(3) *Education and Culture*: All projects should enable lifelong learning and training, stressing diversity and inclusiveness using creative and performing arts, and should be expanded beyond the bounds of schools, high schools and colleges. The working group demanded schools as community centers; the Police Academy; the New Court complex including educational facilities for law and criminal justice; an education consortium coordinating resources; an arts development consortium; and arts-related industries.

(4) *Housing, Open Space and Urban Design*: The community-participatory development of new and rehabilitated housing for residents of all income-levels, first of all for those living in or nearby the Bronx Center area, had major importance. It was very important to the community that, if possible, no one should be dislocated against his will, and, in an unavoidable case, should receive a benefit package, including the right to return to affordable housing in the neighborhood. Public-private funding was encouraged to respond to the existing housing needs that would be identified through a comprehensive planning approach. Also a matter of concern was the clean-up of existing vacant lots, up to that time mostly used as garbage dumps, and a possible use as parks, community gardens and certainly for housing. Zon-

ing was recommended to allow both commercial/social services on ground floors and residential on upper floors. Projects included Melrose Commons request that the existing plan of 2,600 housing units to be reviewed and redesigned by area residents, preparation of use, bulk, affordability and design guidelines, and a density of 150-250 residential units per hectare for appropriate community services; Infill Housing to enliven community and streetscape as well as other projects.

(5) *Transportation*: The work group stated that fluid and safe access to and from the area was critical to the economic and social development of the Bronx Center area. Proposed projects included the Bronx Center Link, an additional public transportation system running along 161st and 149th Streets, Grand Concourse and Third Avenue; Gateway Stations showcasing the latest transit design; Upgraded Stations; Parking Task Force; and Neighborhood Traffic Studies.[53]

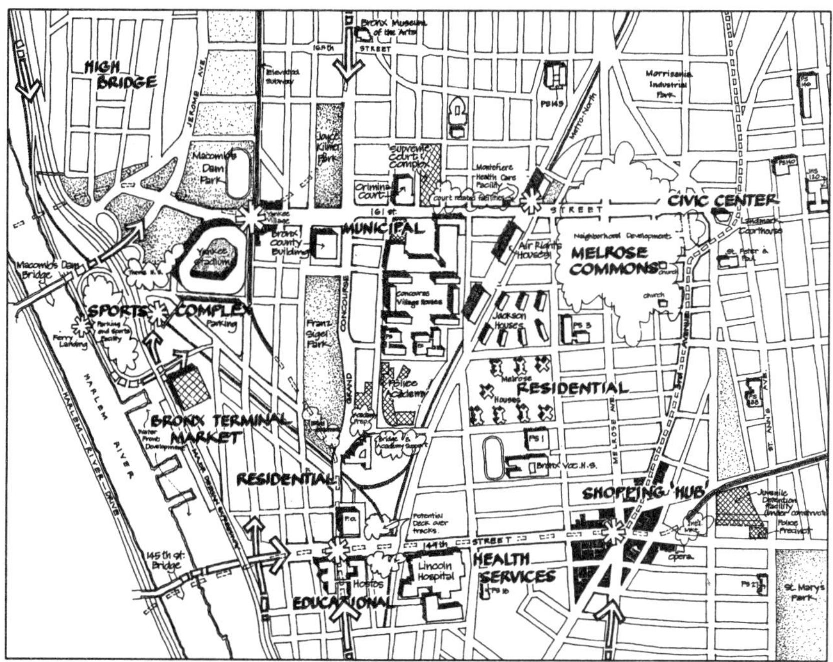

Figure 9: The final Bronx Center Plan in May 1993 after community participation. Source: Bronx Center Steering Committee, p. 19]

[53] Bronx Center Steering Committee (1993), p. 8-13.

The Melrose Commons Urban Renewal Plan

The working groups' proposals for the Bronx Center Project led to a series of results within the following decade. The powerful force of the community group *Nos Quedamos*, together with dedicated voluntary architects and planners, affected city agencies and with the support of the Borough President, created the development plan for Melrose Commons, a central 33-block project of the Bronx Center's Housing, Open Space and Urban Design working group. The plan was certified by the Department of City Planning in late November 1993 and approved for a final review by residents and elected officials.[54] The urban renewal plan was expected to go through the process without major problems, because the plan already was developed by a comprehensive task force of all affected parties.

In late April 1994, a City Planning commissioner submitted amendments to the Melrose Commons plan without any public hearings. He declared that the amendments would accelerate the review period for "minor" modifications, after the ULURP conclusion.[55] ULURP (Uniform Land Use Review Procedure) provides community participation in the review of an urban renewal plan. The modifications targeted the density and the urban design controls, because there were fears that construction restrictions could prevent the city, state, Federal government or private developers from financing within a reasonable time frame.[56] As a result of citywide pressure from the community, the Borough President and City Council members, the City Council dropped the amendment before finally approving the plan less than one year later on June 16, 1994.

Melrose Commons is probably the most ambitious project of the whole Bronx Center Plan because it needed immense external funding and was not designed for the funding requirements of minimum standard in material and appliances. Therefore, this part of the plan required distinct negotiation efforts and the long-term commitment of the community. Learning from that incidence, *Nos Quedamos* set certain principles:

"In order to ensure adherence to plan guidelines (both HPD/DCP[57] requirements and community standards), allow flexibility in interpretation as the physical developments evolve over time, develop phasing strategies that permit residential and business relocations to occur properly, and enable local preference (job training, contracting, vending opportunities), it

---

[54] Muschamp (1993).

[55] Planners' Network website.

[56] Rothstein (1994).

[57] NYC.gov website (2003).

will be necessary to develop a mechanism by which the community can be involved in both the development of RFP/RFQ's and their review and selection. *Nos Quedamos* believes that true community planning is a partnership defined by a community's ability to co-sponsor a project.

The community:

- sponsors: design reviews, the selection of contracts, the selection of contractors,
- participates in marketing,
- selects buyers and renters,
- participates with the "partnership" in monitoring meetings and briefings, drawings, designs, construction quality, environmental issues, marketing materials (for local vendors, etc.),
- provides funding for said community monitoring" [58]

While ostensibly an urban renewal plan, the route taken by the Melrose Commons Urban Renewal Plan more closely resembled that of a Section 197-A plan.[59] However, the Melrose Commons Plan along the guidelines of the Bronx Center Project reduced the proposed housing units from 2,600 to 1,700 in mostly townhouse-like developments and some focus buildings along Melrose and Third Avenues, which were considered main roads by the planning team around *Nos Quedamos*.

The urban renewal plan recommended building approximately 1700 new housing units, creating 23,000 m² of commercial space, 23,000 m² of community facility space, and 1.6 hectares of open space distributed across 63 development sites.[60]

Housing was thought to be woven into the fabric of the existing community; varied types of buildings allow different scales to be developed. Housing units are to include off street parking but not between homes and the public sidewalks/streets. The plan recommended forty units of new rental housing in Los Jardines, sixty units with community health facility on ground floor in La Puerta De Vitalidad, 85 units, eight-story senior citizens residence in HUD 202, La Casa De Felicidad, 36 new three-family houses in La Plaza de Los Angeles, mixed-use residential and commercial

---

[58] Planner's Network website.

[59] City Charter Section 197-A is a provision that permits a local community board to develop a long-range neighborhood plan that can be adopted as policy by the City Planning Commission. Once adopted the plan can serve as a legally binding guide for future growth and development within the community.

[60] Municipal Art Society of New York website (2003), Map ID# BX5.

building, as well as other mixed-use development in Melrose Arms, Townhouse and Co-Housing Development in *Nos Quedamos*.

The plan also proposed the restoration of two abandoned landmark courthouses as town centers for new civic, community, educational, and cultural uses: the former YMCA containing a swimming pool, running track, and playing surfaces should be returned to community use; close sections of Brook Avenue and East 162nd Street should be closed to vehicular traffic to provide sufficient land mass to create a pedestrian mall and plaza to encourage new community, educational, cultural, and entertainment uses.

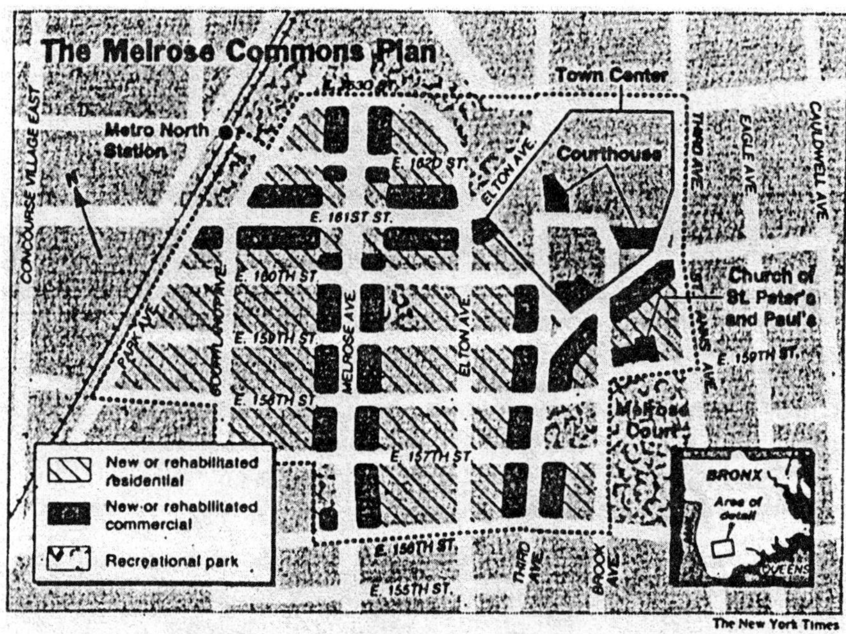

Figure 10: Melrose Commons Urban Renewal Plan as approved on 16 June 1994. Source: The New York Times, 10 July 1994, IX 8:3

Outcomes of the community-based planning effort

A short-term improvement for Melrose Commons was the provision of vacant land for community use. This could be brought into life quickly but also called for the neighbors' vigilance and action. The city converted own property acquired through land banking (property condemnation after defaulting property tax payments) into so-called "Green Thumb" lots for gardening or community interim use. The lots were cleaned-up and later fenced. But soon trucks came to knock down the fences the city just had erected in order to dump on the land once more.[61] The Sanitation Department stated it would no longer replace the fences. So the community identified the dumpers and called the sanitation police, who confiscated the trucks. Finally the fences were replaced, and residents began to till the land as community gardens.

Figure 11: Community garden at Elton Avenue and East 160th Street. Christoph Stump, October 2002

The first project of the reconfigured Melrose Commons Plan commenced in late 1998, delayed partly because the city failed to complete the condemnation of property on time.[62] The Plaza de Los Angeles consists of 35 three-story townhouses, with a total of 105 housing units for an average of $225,000 along Elton Avenue between East 156th and 159th Streets. The $11 million project allows the owner, whose income may not exceed $71,000, to live in the three-bedroom duplex apartment and rent the two one- and two-bedroom simplexes to help pay the mortgage on the property. City and state subsidies are estimated to approximately $95,000 per

61 Waldman (1997).

62 Garbarine (1998).

home and provide tax abatements of another $800 per year. The proposed design-guidelines resulted in brownstone-like facades, with red and beige bricks and sand-colored cast stone and brick sidings, instead of the vinyl typically used for affordable housing in the South Bronx. Parking spaces, rather than being in front of the houses, are at the property's rear.

Figure 12: La Puerta de Vitalidad at Third Avenue and East 158th Street. Christoph Stump, October 2002

According to plan, *La Puerta de Vitalidad* opened as the first apartment building in October 2002.[63] Located at Third Avenue between East 158th and 159th Streets, the seven-story building serves a mixed population of 49% low-income families and 51% formerly homeless families in fifteen one-, forty two- and six three-bedroom rental units.[64] Fronted on Third Avenue by a multi-hued brick facade, the building also includes a retail outlet and 600 m² on the ground floor slated for a child care center. The $14 million project was funded through the 85/85 Program, sponsored by the New York State Housing Finance Agency and the NYC Department of Housing Preservation and Development (HPD), and equity was raised

[63] At Melrose Common Project (2002).

[64] NYC.gov website (2002).

through the Low Income Housing Tax Credit Program. The building constitutes a key step toward revitalizing the Third Avenue Corridor.

Finished in the same month, Melrose Commons II, also known as Sunflower Way II, was completed as second townhouse development.[65] The thirty three-family homes are similar to the *Plaza de Los Angeles* project. They provide a duplex for the owner and two simplexes on the upper floors for renters, who help pay the mortgage. Unique to Sunflower Way II are energy efficient features that enabled the development to receive "Energy Star" certification and the 2003 Northeast Green Building Award.[66] The townhouses of the $12 million project between East 158th and 159th Streets and Elton and Melrose Avenues were sold for an average of $289,000 to families earning between $41,000 to $75,000. Funding came from the NYC Housing Partnership and HPD. In all of these construction projects, another important part of the Bronx Center has been carried out: the contractor used local workers for the developments, fulfilling the Local Hiring Agreement of the Economic Development working group.

A project of the transportation working group asked to upgrade the public transportation stations around Melrose. The earlier described Metro-North rail station underneath of one of the Air Rights Buildings was studied for possible future improvement.[67] In fact, the station was short-term upgraded with new signs, additional lighting, some stair and platform repairs and a freshly painted wall; however, it still remains a place hardly known to residents because of its isolation and poor signage. It still definitely is not a place where people feel safe.

The entire Bronx Center Project was recognized as a new strategy of urban renewal planning nationwide. Thus, several side effects emerged, like a general optimism concerning the borough's future. HPD started to advertise guided tours in the New York Times, which offered the exploration of Melrose for interested citizens.[68] In September 1998, the Bronx Borough President's Planning Office published a community-based proposal for a new Yankee Stadium environment called "Safe at Home – Yankee Stadium in the Bronx" due to the Bronx Center guidelines.[69] It gave an idea of the two major activity nodes, the sports and recreational surroundings of the stadium and a retail complex at the Bronx Center Market site. And finally, the office also submitted a plan for the Hub, the

---

[65] At Melrose Commons Project (2002).

[66] Northeast Sustainable Energy Association website (2003).

[67] Buckhurst Fisch and Jaquemart, Inc. (2001).

[68] e.g. Walking Tours (2002).

[69] Ferrer (1998).

commercial strip around the intersection of Third Avenue and East 149th Street, to improve commercial business and reinforce economic development based on the ideas of the Bronx Center.[70] Recommendations included primarily pedestrian and public transportation traffic improvement, better access and renovation of upper stores for back office use and design guidelines.[71] The big national lenders now looked at the Bronx without prejudices and discovered strong occupancy, retail and transportation affecting an increase of private investment of up to 400% between 1997-1998.[72] Experienced borrowers in the South Bronx even got loans comparable to those in other regions, dealing now without the risk penalties applied to those buying in the Bronx.

Problems with the implementation of the Melrose Commons Urban Renewal Plan

Grass-roots democracy is a difficult effort. Melrose Commons is a case in point to prove the community's fight for using vacant city property. The new community gardens played an important role in passing down responsibility to the local residents and in creating a community's identity. In fall 2002, there were not less than nineteen "Green Thumb" gardens in the Melrose Commons Urban Renewal area. One garden serves as well-known and significant refuge for Puerto Rican culture.[73] The garden, called *Rincon Criollo* (the name means down-home corner), was founded already in 1979. But the Urban Renewal Plan, developed with community participation, calls for the relocation of most of the gardens. In order continue the urban renewal, the community developer *Nos Quedamos* wants to move *Rincon Criollo* one block for further development.[74] However, the neighbors protested against the intention of the CDC to move the garden. In 2001, a lawsuit by the state attorney general, has blocked sale or destruction of any community garden without an environmental impact study, arguing that gardens older than twenty or thirty years have in essence become public parkland. But eventually the gardeners had to move.

One of the most annoying developments occurred to a former, now landmarked old courthouse, at the northeastern corner of Melrose Com-

---

70 Municipal Art Society of New York website (2003), Map ID# BX9.

71 Caplan (2001).

72 Hall (1995).

73 Raver (2001).

74 Critchell (1999).

mons. The Bronx Center Plan as well as the Melrose Commons Urban Renewal Plan considered the courthouse as new public heart of the community. Here, a planning center was supposed to be established as a meeting place for Bronx residents so that they could learn about and actively participate in the ongoing planning and implementation of the Bronx Center projects.[75] A renovated portion of the landmark abandoned in 1978 could have provided a welcoming atmosphere for broad interaction among community members and the various agencies that operate programs in the Bronx Center. A 1992 estimate put the cost of restoring the courthouse at $43 million, but *Nos Quedamos* developed a plan to restore it piecemeal as funds materialized.[76]

Figure 13: The boarded-up landmark courthouse at Third and Brook Avenues. Christoph Stump, October 2002

The CDC organized $900,000 to start the job and began negotiations with the city about a lease. Mayor Rudolph W. Giuliani and the Landmark Preservation Commission awarded a citation to the president of the Urban Assembly, who played a major role in the Bronx Center as head of the

[75] Bronx Center Steering Committee (1993), p. 44.

[76] Halbfinger (1998).

Steering Committee for his work on the courthouse plans in 1994.[77] But in 1996, the city administration abruptly ended the negotiations with the CDC and sold off the courthouse to an electrical contractor for $130,000 in early October. *Nos Quedamos* then tried unsuccessfully to sue the city to stop the sale; one year later, the contractor defaulted on his payments and the courthouse once more became city property.

In March 1998, the city organized the next auction for the building, after *Nos Quedamos* had urged the city in tough negotiations to repair the roof for $300,000, to seal the windows and bolt its doors to protect its interior.[78] This time the CDC had not only raised $6 million to support a library, a small museum and after-school programs, but also managed to mobilize private financial support. However, the community was outbid by a real estate broker in the end. He bought the courthouse for $300,000 considering a restoration for $12 million as a department store or medical offices. When confronting him with the community's concern, the broker promised to meet with them and find a solution. But once more, the broker failed to restore the courthouse with its ornate interior, terrazzo floors, marble staircases and granite facade.[79] In March 2000, he put the building on the market for $1.8 million, also considering a lease to TV stations to use it for New York-based dramas, or to rent it as warehouse. The Borough President Ferrer criticized both city and broker for failing to live up to their promises that the building would be restored and reopened. Ferrer had asked the Giuliani administration several times to lease him part of the courthouse for his headquarters. That way, the whole Third Avenue Corridor would have experienced a revival with coffee shops, restaurants, dry cleaners, and other services the people needed.

Future Developments

The hard work of *Nos Quedamos* and its supporting planners led to three very successful, completed developments: *Plaza de Los Angeles*, consisting of the 35 three-units townhouses, *La Puerta de Vitalidad* offering 61 rental units in a seven-story building and Sunflower Way II with another 30 three-family homes. But more projects are in the pipeline. Excavation already began for *Villa Hermosa*, an 80-unit development in cooperation with South Bronx Churches,[80] and a nine-story elevator building

---

77 Gonzales (1996).

78 Halbfinger (1998).

79 Siegel (2000).

80 Steven L. Newman Real Estate Institute website (1999).

between East 156th and 157th Streets and Melrose Avenue, the *Palacio del Sol*, is already under construction. [81] It will provide 123 units of rental housing for low-income families including a community room for meetings and a 1,000 m^2 ground-floor commercial space facing Melrose Avenue. In the rear of *Palacio del Sol* will be space for 47 cars and a landscaped area.

La Casa de Felicidad is an 85-unit senior housing project designed for independent living low-income senior citizens.[82] To be located at the intersection of Third Avenue and East 158th Street, the project sits at the eastern edge of the Melrose Commons neighborhood. The *Melrose Commons Urban Renewal Plan* includes design guidelines that determined the building massing and street frontage. The building runs almost the entire block from East 158th Street south to East 157th Street, as well as 30 m along East 158th Street. Just opposite *La Puerta de Vitalidad*, these two projects will form a gateway to the transformed Melrose Commons neighborhood. The project is a joint venture of *Nos Quedamos* and Phipps Houses, the oldest non-profit housing developer in New York City. The building is designed with community spaces on the street level. The majority of the resident apartments live on the six upper floors. Street level community spaces face Third Avenue as well as a landscaped rear yard. A garden space for the building residents with raised planting beds is planned.

A further look into the future of the Melrose Commons Urban Renewal Area is not easy. Most recent major budget cutbacks force the borough presidents to reduce their planning capacity considerably. Thus, the borough administration is often bound on short-term, low-cost contributions; planning is centralized at the mayor's office. But hopes of the community developers are high that the plan will not get divided up into little pieces to shortsighted profit developments. As long as each project rises with a comprehensive approach, considering the site as part of the entire community and city, the core of the planning intention is met.

Conclusion

Melrose Commons is an example of a community's self-inclusion into an otherwise top-down planning process. The Bronx Center Project, which finally led to the legally binding Melrose Commons Urban Renewal Plan, was based on two strong feet, a willing and open administration and a

---

[81] NYC.gov website (2003).

[82] Larson Shein Ginsberg Snyder website.

strong, cohesive community. Most of those parts of the plan that are already in the process of completion have either been planned for a long time as public projects, like the renovation of the County Building and its surrounding parks and the civic center around the Criminal Courthouse at East 161st Street, or they are products of the neighborhood's long-term effort for Melrose Commons. Without the community as the driving force, the area's renaissance would not have been possible. Nevertheless, a visionary Borough President and many voluntary helping hands helped the activists' protests to produce a respectable result.

Today, Melrose is still faced with serious problems. Some are health-related like asthma and AIDS, others are connected to education, e.g. teenage pregnancy and school dropout. Substance abuse, which is still a threat to many, has now led to a phenomenon called "missing generation," for the addicted are not in the physical and psychological state to care for their children or their aging parents. The physical and economic foundation of Melrose Commons though has been greatly strengthened. Certainly the most important effect of the revitalization project has been to restore the people's sense of community and civic responsibility. Throughout its work, the community developer *Nos Quedamos* has established and maintained a unique collaboration between institutions of higher education such as Columbia University, Pratt Institute, and Hunter College; city and private sector planners; architects; businesses; and local, national and international nonprofit and non-governmental organizations. This sustained and diverse collaboration has produced an unprecedented level of sharing information and resources, benefiting all involved.

References

Note: New York Times articles are quoted according to the following pattern: date, section (e.g. A, B, C... or I, II, III), page: column.

At Melrose Commons Project (2002), 61-Unit Rental In South Bronx, October 13, XI 1:4.

Bronx Center Steering Committee (1993), The Bronx Center, A Report to Bronx Borough President Fernando Ferrer from the Bronx Center Steering Committee, May.

The Bronx Museum of the Arts (1986), Building a Borough, Architecture and Planning in the Bronx 1890-1940, Exhibition Catalog, New Jersey.

Buckhurst Fish & Jaquemart Inc. et al (2001), Metro-North Railroad Melrose Station Study, Final Report, New York, NY.

Caplan, Paula Luria (2001), CityWide Growth: The Hub, December 14. Accessed at http://nynv.aiga.org/pdfs/NYNV_CGO_BronxHub.pdf, 2003.

Chavez, Lydia (1987), From Ashes, Bronx Faces Uncertain Future, The New York Times, June 14, 1:1.

Color Them Brightly (1992), The New York Times, November 8, X 1:1.

Critchell, David (1999), A Group Named 'We Stay', A Garden That Must Depart, The New York Times, December 19, XIV-CY 14:5.

Ferrer, Fernando with Beyer Blinder Belle Architects & Planners LLP (1998), Safe at Home – Yankee Stadium in the Bronx, September.

Gallagher, Mary Lou (1991), The Bronx Is Up, Planning, September, p. 14f.

Garbarine, Rachelle (1998), Neighborhood Rises in the South Bronx, The New York Times, December 25, B 7:1.

Golden, Tim (1990), In the Ravaged South Bronx, a Camelot Is Envisioned, The New York Times, December 17, B 1:2.

Gonzales, David (1996), A Civic Heart Is Sold Off In 'Bake Sale', The New York Times, October 5, I 25:1.

Goodwin, Michael (1980), 'Mr. Urban Renewal' Acts to Rebuild His Image, The New York Times, May 10, X 25:2.

Goodwin, Michael (1980), New Plan, Dependent on U.S. Aid, Is Offered to Rebuild South Bronx, The New York Times, July 20, 1:1.

Halbfinger, David M. (1998), Auction Ends 5-Year Dream in 5 Minutes, The New York Times, March 20, B 3:4.

Hall, Trish (1999), A South Bronx Very Different From the Cliché, The New York Times, February 14, XI 1:5.

Hernandez, Raymond (1993), Melrose Commons Nearer Start, The New York Times, December 5, XIII-CY 11:1.

James, George (1986), For the Bronx, A New Image Is a Tough Shell, The New York Times, June 10, B 4:3.

Krumholz, Norman (1997), in Willem van Vliet, et al., Affordable Housing and Urban Redevelopment in the United States, Urban Affairs Annual Reviews No. 46, Thousand Oaks, CA.

Larson Shein Ginsberg Snyder, LLP (n.y.), Project description of La Casa de Felicidad for Nos Quedamos/Phipps Houses/HUD 202. Accessed at http://www.lsgsarchitects.com/display.asp?code=513, 2003.

Lueck, Thomas J. (1991), New York Ranks High in Housing Bias, The New York Times, November 3, X 1:2.

Lynn, Frank with Michael Oreskes (1987), in Bronx Politics, Signs of City's Future, The New York Times, June 15, A 1:2.

Municipal Art Society of New York. Accessed at http://www.mas.org/ContentLibrary/Bronx_Plans2.pdf, 2003.

Muschamp, Herbert (1993), Slouching Towards Utopia in the South Bronx, The New York Times, December 5, II 44:1.

New York City Department of City Planning (2001), Community District Needs, The Bronx, Fiscal Years 2002/2003, New York City Department of City Planning, New York, NY.

Northeast Sustainable Energy Association (2003), 2003 Northeast Green Building Awards. Accessed at http://www.nesea.org/buildings/buildingawards/Melrose.pdf, 2003.

NYC.gov (2003), City Planning Commision in the matter of an application submitted by the Department of Housing Preservation and Development (HPD). October 8. Accessed at http://www.nyc.gov/html/dcp/pdf/cpc/030533.pdf, 2003.

NYC.gov (2002), Phipps Houses and Nos Quedamos open first apartment building in Melrose Commons. Accessed at http://home.nyc.gov/html/hpd/html/hpd-archive/phipps-houses-pr.html, 2003.

Oser, Alan S. (1991), Higher Density Goal Spurs New Designs, The New York Times, November 10, X 5:2.

Planner's Network (n.y.), Melrose Commons: A Case Study for Sustainable Community Design. Accessed at http://www.plannersnetwork.org/htm/pub/case-studies/melrose.htm, 2003.

Raver, Anne (2001), New Hope for Community Gardenders, The New York Times, March 29, F 12:1.

Rothstein, Mervyn (1994), A Renewal Plan in the Bronx Advances, The New York Times, July 10, IX 1:2.

Shenon, Philip (1984), 'Pioneer' Settler Bring Glow to South Bronx, The New York Times, January 14, I 1:3.

Siegal, Nina (2000), Hall of Justice, Source of Conflict, The New York Times, March 21, B 1:2.

Stern, Robert A. M./Mellins, Thomas/Fishman, David (1995), New York 1960, Architecture and Urbanism Between the Second World War and the Bicentennial, New York, NY.

Steven L. Newman Real Estate Institute (1999), Leveraging Rebuilt Communities: Affordable Housing for the Emerging Middle Class, Day Two of The New York Real Estate Forum 2001 City Roundtable "Bronx Reborn: Developing Regional Real Estate Assets," March 30, Conference Transcripts. Accessed at http://www.baruch.cuny.edu/realestate/bronx_transcripts2.htm, 2004.

Tolchin, Martin (1973a), Future Looks Bleak for the South Bronx, The New York Times, January 18, 1:4.

Tolchin, Martin (1973b), Gangs Spread Terror in the South Bronx, The New York Times, January 16, 1:7.

Tolchin, Martin (1973c), Rage Permeates All Facets of Life in the South Bronx, The New York Times, January 17, 1:6.

Tolchin, Martin (1973d), South Bronx: A Jungle Stalked by Fear, Seized by Rage, The New York Times, January 15, 1:3.

Vergara, Camilo José (1999), The New American Ghetto, New Brunswick, NJ.

Verhovek, Sam Howe (1988), Many No's to Parting 'South' From Its Bronx, The New York Times, August 1, B 3:1.

Vliet, Willem van, et al. (1997), Affordable Housing and Urban Redevelopment in the United States, Urban Affairs Annual Reviews No. 46, Thousand Oaks, CA.

Vogel, Carl with Suzanne Boothby and Amanda Bell (1999), Melrose's Thorny Predicament, City Limits, September/October, p. 13-15, 33.

Waldman, Amy (1997), How To Fight City Hall, The New York Times, November 9, XIV-CY 1:3.

Walking Tours: New York City Department of Housing Preservation and Development (2002), The New York Times, October 18, E 42:2.

Wedemeyer, Dee (1985), Q. & A. With Bronx Planning Chief, The New York Times, July 21, VIII 12:1.

Durban's Local Agenda 21/Local Action 21 Program – A Vehicle for Social Inclusion?

Debra Roberts

Introduction

Durban's Local Agenda 21 (recently renamed Local Action 21) program has been at the forefront of the Local Agenda 21 movement in southern Africa since the mid-nineties. This chapter describes the first five phases of the program (1994 to 2003) and the opportunities and challenges encountered in localizing the sustainable development concept in Durban. Key amongst these was the initiation and development of the program during a period of local government restructuring. While this process of transformation has allowed new ideas to be introduced and debated, it has also created a decade-long period of institutional uncertainty. The perception that Local Agenda 21 has a 'green' focus and is 'anti-development' (due to its location within an environmental line function) has also been significant, resulting in an initial lack of proactive and sustained political and administrative support for the concept. More recently this situation has begun to change as the importance of environmental issues and the links with sustainability have become better understood by the city's decision-makers. A further problem encountered has been the limited human and financial resources available in local government, a factor that has restricted the program's capacity to build support and consensus among stakeholders. Despite this, Durban's Local Agenda 21 program has been successful in helping to keep sustainable development on the city's agenda and has contributed significantly to its eventual incorporation as a core objective in the city's recently released Integrated Development Plan. It has also provided a mechanism through which local stakeholders can interact with local government around environmental management issues. The chapter concludes with a section on the lessons learned and factors required to ensure future progress.

Driving forces for change

In 1994, Durban became the first city in South Africa to accept the Local Agenda 21 mandate as a corporate responsibility. Since then, Durban has been at the forefront of the Local Agenda 21 movement in the country. In order to understand this experience, it is important to understand the context within which the process evolved. Three drivers are of particular importance. Firstly, at a global level, the 1992 Rio Earth Summit and Agenda 21 mainstreamed the concept of sustainable development and prioritized the importance of local action in realizing this goal. In South Africa, this paradigm shift was accompanied by a process of post-apartheid[1] democratization which created a nation-wide 'window of opportunity' for new concepts (such as sustainable development) to be debated and accepted by previously conservative governmental structures. Finally, at a local level (i.e. in Durban) these national and international trends were accompanied by the establishment of an Environmental Management Branch, which became the Local Agenda 21 champion within the city.

In working towards the globally articulated objective of achieving sustainable development through local participative action, Durban's Local Agenda 21 program has faced a series of key opportunities and challenges. The visible and vocal role played by the Environmental Management Branch has strongly influenced the program's successes and failures. It has, for example, helped keep Local Agenda 21 and sustainable development on local government's agenda, but it has also contributed to a situation where a strong, dedicated and identifiable political[2] champion has not yet emerged. This situation has been exacerbated by the perception that Local Agenda 21 is a 'foreign' concept largely concerned with 'green' issues. This lack of 'political mainstreaming' poses serious challenges to the program's long-term sustainability. At the same time, however, the role played by the Branch in championing sustainable development has resulted in increased support for the concept amongst the administrative[3] structures of the city. This has culminated in the inclusion of the concept

---

1 Apartheid policies created a society divided along racial lines and exacerbated the economic gulf between the wealthy, advantaged minority and the poor, disadvantaged majority.

2 Elected officials.

3 Non-elected officials.

as a core, overarching objective within the city's recently released Integrated Development Plan (IDP)[4] (2003-2007):

> *There has been unanimous support from IDP workshop participants (from sectors throughout the city), senior management, politicians and other key stakeholders not to conceptualize 'sustainable development' as something that must be treated separately from, or as an add-on to our current IDP strategy that drives this IDP. This it is argued defeats the very purpose and intent of ensuring that every action is sustainable. More importantly, by re-thinking the way we have approached our revised IDP, we are now ensuring that sustainable development forms the 'life breath' of our IDP...We contend, in this revised IDP, that sustainability is not just about environmental protection...The balancing of social, economic and environmental needs...will emphasize the efficient usage of all our resources and therefore ensure that all forms of development occur within the carrying capacity of our natural surroundings (eThekwini Municipality, 2003).*

The more holistic and long-term focus of the IDP can also be attributed to the appointment of a new City Manager (in 2002) who has become an influential champion for sustainable development and has helped prioritize environmental concerns alongside social and economic considerations.

Another important factor influencing the development of Durban's Local Agenda 21 program has been the fact that South African local government has been in a state of transformation since 1994 (a process that is only likely to be completed in 2004). While the restructuring process has opened a 'window of opportunity' in terms of the ability to transform previous structures and governmental systems, the high levels of uncertainty associated with this process have impacted on the development of Durban's Local Agenda 21 program and necessitated a phased approach to implementation. To date, four phases have been completed and a fifth implementation phase is in progress (see Fig.1).

Phase 1: Assessment and prioritization (1994 – 1996)

The primary aim of Durban's Local Agenda 21 program is the development of an environmental management system (EMS) (see Fig. 1) which will ensure that social, economic and ecological concerns are inte-

---

[4] The Integrated Development Plan is a requirement of the Municipal Systems Act (2000) and is the principle planning instrument that guides and informs all planning and development in a municipality.

grated into all planning and development processes within the city. From the outset it was clear that the lack of information on the city's environmental status was an obstacle to realizing this goal. The preparation of Durban's first State of the Environment and Development Report (SOE&DR) was therefore undertaken as the first step in EMS development.

A participative approach was employed in the planning and execution of the SOE&DR project. This included the establishment of three participative forums to engage communities, business and industry and local government stakeholders in discussions around the project; and the initiation of case studies in selected local communities to probe environment and development priorities. The findings of the case study interviews undertaken during the SOE&DR project in communities with different racial and socio-economic profiles challenged the widely held assumption that given choices between environment and development issues, the poor would prioritize development while the affluent, having met basic development needs, would give greater weight to environmental needs. The study suggested that there is a far more complex understanding of the inter-dependencies of environment and development issues amongst local communities in Durban. It appeared that the wealthiest and the poorest share an awareness of the need for environmental protection, the former because they have met other needs, and the latter because so few of any of their needs have been met. This awareness was found in all the communities studied and was present in the thinking and views of both leadership and residents. Several community leaders acknowledged that environmental issues had been severely neglected in the past due to the need to focus on political change, but that with the new prioritization of development needs the importance of environmental issues had become increasingly clear. This perspective was not, however, uncontested as many people from all sectors continued to stress the dichotomous relationship between environment and development, with development being regarded as of greater importance than environmental issues.

The completed State of the Environment and Development Report highlighted the sustainability challenges and opportunities in 17 key environment and development sectors[5] in the city. These were prioritized through a community-based process, which resulted in five environment and development issues emerging as the top priorities amongst Durban's communities:

---

[5] Terrestrial resources, atmospheric resources, fresh water resources, marine resources, urban form, housing, transport, water supply and sanitation, waste, energy, economy, education, health, violence and peace, governance, city finances and the legal framework.

- promoting peace, safety and security in the metropolitan region;
- improving water and sanitation management;
- developing an integrated housing policy;
- establishing a structure to coordinate land use, transportation and environmental planning in the metropolitan area;
- institutionalizing the Integrated Environmental Management procedure of the national Department of Environmental Affairs and Tourism.

Phase 2: Policy formulation and action planning (1997 – 1999)

A cluster of projects was initiated during Phase 2 of the Local Agenda 21 program to begin addressing the priorities identified during Phase 1. These projects focused primarily on policy formulation and planning, and aimed to develop a framework within which stakeholders could act or contribute towards improved sustainability.

Durban Metropolitan Environmental Policy Initiative (DMEPI): New legislation[6] promulgated as part of the local government restructuring process assigned the coordination and planning of environmental management in Durban to metropolitan government, and implementation to local level authorities. This acknowledged (for the first time) the need for a strategic and coordinating environmental management function that was distinct from the already existing operational activities of local councils and their line functions. The emergence of this new, strategic metropolitan level environmental management function (together with increasing legislative requirements contained in emerging national and provincial environmental and planning law) made it clear that a restructuring of the environmental function within the city was necessary. In order to initiate this process, the Durban Metropolitan Council approved the development of Durban's first Environmental Management Policy and related Institutional Framework. The development of the Policy represented the first building block of the city's EMS and informed the thinking around options for an appropriate and supportive Institutional Framework. Both the policy and associated institutional framework were developed in consultation with representatives drawn from a broad range of stakeholder groups throughout the city.

---

6 Schedule 2 of the Local Government Transition Act (No. 209 of 1993).

Strategic Environmental Assessment (SEA) of the Durban South Basin: The Durban South Basin is a metropolitan environmental 'hotspot' containing areas of heavy industry and residential development located in close proximity to one another in a topographically contained region. It is the economic 'heartland' of the Durban and South Africa's second most important manufacturing center. Over the past several decades the South Basin has become a focal point for community mobilization around environmental quality and justice issues. The aim of the SEA was to develop sustainable development guidelines to address existing problems and to guide future development in the area. The study examined potential short-term and long-term development scenarios for the South Basin and evaluated them against sustainable development criteria. The findings of the evaluation process suggested that the area was likely to retain an industrial character well into the foreseeable future and that the resources (i.e. financial and technological) required to address environmental quality issues were linked to the need to attract new industrial investment into the Basin. The extensive public participation process undertaken during this project included an environmental education and capacity building component. Although much time and effort was spent on this element of the project, it had a limited impact due to the heightened tensions that existed between local government and local communities as a result of the study's finding that certain future development options could result in the loss of existing residential areas.

Durban Metropolitan Open Space System (D'MOSS) Framework Plan: This project focussed on the design of an open space plan to protect and guide the management of the city's natural resource base. A review of the role of open spaces in meeting the needs of a growing African city showed open spaces to be a key service provider providing goods and services (such as water supply and pollution control) that are vital in meeting the basic needs of urban residents, particularly poor, conventionally unserviced communities. In Durban the total replacement value of these open space services was estimated – using international research in the field of resource economics – at R2.24 billion per annum ($1 = R7). This figure excluded the value of Durban's tourism sector, worth approximately R3.5 million per annum. This project provided the opportunity to test the usefulness of tools such as resource economics in raising the profile of 'green' issues on the political agenda.

Community Open Space Development: In order to demonstrate the practical advantages of improved environmental management to local communities, a project was undertaken to create usable open spaces in high density residential areas that would contribute to the ecological functioning of the open space system. This project was also intended to address community priorities such as poverty alleviation, improved quality of life, equal access to resources and job creation. The key problems encountered included the lack of maintenance funds, vandalism, wasted resources, poor project management, and the discontent of local communities at not being involved in the maintenance of the project areas. Successful projects were characterized by active councilor and community involvement, however, even in these areas problems such as vandalism and lack of adequate maintenance funding limited the success of the intervention.

Education and Outreach Initiative: The lack of understanding amongst all stakeholder groups regarding the importance of environmental management, sustainable development and Local Agenda 21 prompted the initiation of an education and outreach program. The initiative included the production of media materials, capacity building and training opportunities and the use of innovative tools such as street theatre. 'Green Bafana', for example, was a street theatre performance involving a trio of Zulu free-lance actors which was developed to bring sustainability issues to life. In the Zulu language and culture ‘Bafana’ means ‘the boys’, but it also has an attached connotation of popularity. The key theme of the play was that individual actions have an environmental impact, either positive or negative. The play also celebrated the positive actions being taken by local government and communities to improve quality of life and sustainability in Durban and was primarily targeted at school groups, local government officials and councilors.

Phase 3: Transition and review (1999 – 2000)

Following the completion of Phase 2 it became apparent that there would be a significant transition period as preparations began for the establishment of the Durban Unicity[7]. It was decided that the most strategic use of this time would be to consolidate work already done and to lay the foundations for future program development.

Cities Environmental Reports on the Internet (CEROI) Project: South Africa’s four largest cities participated in this international project[8]. The aim of the CEROI project was to facilitate comparative global reporting through the development of a simple and easily understood State of the

---

[7] The merging of a seven (previously fifty-two) local government administrations into one Unicity administration.

[8] The CEROI project was conceived and coordinated internationally by UNEP / GRID-Arendal (United Nations Environment Program / Global Resources Information Database) in partnership with the ICLEI Cities 21 Campaign.

Environment Report template for the Internet. This represented an opportunity for Durban to increase the accessibility of the information collected within its Local Agenda 21 program to a broader range of local, national and international stakeholders.

Documentation of Durban's Local Agenda 21 Program as an International Case Study: European Commission funding from the International Institute for Environment and Development (IIED) facilitated the documentation and publication of Durban's Local Agenda 21 program and created the opportunity to formally record and evaluate the work undertaken during the first seven years of the program. This documentation process has been critical in developing an institutional memory in a situation where staff turnover levels are high and where institutional restructuring is a highly disruptive force.

Awareness and Preparedness for Emergencies at the Local Level (APELL) Project: The SEA project recommended the initiation of UNEP's[9] APELL program in order to better prepare Durban for technological and industrial accidents in the South Basin. Although a launch workshop was held, this project could not be formally initiated as a leading community-based organization in the Basin withdrew from the process because of APELL's association with the SEA project. A subsequent mission by an overseas conflict resolution expert established the conditions to be met if APELL was to be successfully undertaken in Durban. Although all three stakeholder groups (local government, business/industry, local communities) expressed their qualified commitment to these preconditions, the international funding organization who sponsored the mission declined to fund the Durban APELL project. The reasons given were that the expected project budget exceeded its financial means, the project would deviate from its core business and its national government's policy for South Africa had shifted to priorities other than environmental protection and resource management. Although this organization offered to assist Durban in obtaining alternative sponsorship, this setback effectively resulted in the demise of the APELL initiative in Durban.

Education and Outreach Initiative – Promotional Event: Following a spate of staff resignations[10], the Environmental Management Branch suspended the Education and Outreach Initiative. In order to ensure that the impact of the Initiative was not entirely lost, a promotional event was held to focus the attention of key local government officials and politicians on

---

[9] United Nation's Environmental Program.

[10] This was largely due to the high workloads, poor salaries and limited opportunities for advancement in the under-resourced Environmental Management Branch.

the achievements of the program. A series of posters and a video profiled the work undertaken during the first six years (1994-2000).

Creation of an Interim Environmental Management Structure: Following approval for the interim restructuring[11] and expansion of the Environmental Management Branch flowing from the DMEPI process, approval was received in 2001 for the filling of seven of the 19 new posts created. A review of critical posts throughout the Council, however, led to this decision being revisited and only two of the new posts being approved for advertisement. This effectively left the Branch under-resourced, and in a reactive rather that proactive mode.

Phase 4: Preparing for the Unicity (2000 – 2002)

The transition from apartheid to democracy in South Africa has brought with it changes to the size and nature of many of the country's larger metropolitan areas. In Durban there has been a metamorphosis from a municipal area of 300 km^2 (pre-1996) to a transitional metropolitan area of 1366 km^2 (1996-2000) finally culminating in a Unicity[12] (post 2000) of 2297 km^2. This has resulted in large areas of peri-urban, rural and tribal land being included within the city's boundaries. 60% of Durban is currently considered to be peri-urban and rural in nature. The projects initiated during Phase 4 were a response to the required transition from a metropolitan to Unicity administration.

Review of Environmental Performance in Local Government: A review of local government's performance against the requirements of the Durban Metropolitan Environmental Management Policy was identified as the next step in the development of in the city's EMS. This process identified six key projects that could assist in meeting the sustainability objectives of the city's Long-term Development Framework (see Fig. 2). The resource limitations of the Environmental Management Branch have restricted the extent to which it has been possible to address these needs. 'Standard Environmental Management Plan and Revegetation Specifications for Civil Engineering Construction Projects' have, however, been completed and are in use, and the training of relevant line-function staff in the use of these guidelines has also been completed. Some exploratory

---

[11] Recommendations for final restructuring in the new Unicity Council were also made, but it was acknowledged that these would only be addressed in the medium to long term. The interim restructuring was a short-term measure to address immediate capacity shortages in the environmental management function.

[12] Now known as the eThekwini Municipality.

work has also been undertaken (post-Phase 4) in investigating the requirements associated with three of the remaining five projects i.e. environmental by-law reform, development of environmental indicators for the city score card and the development of a cleaner production centre.

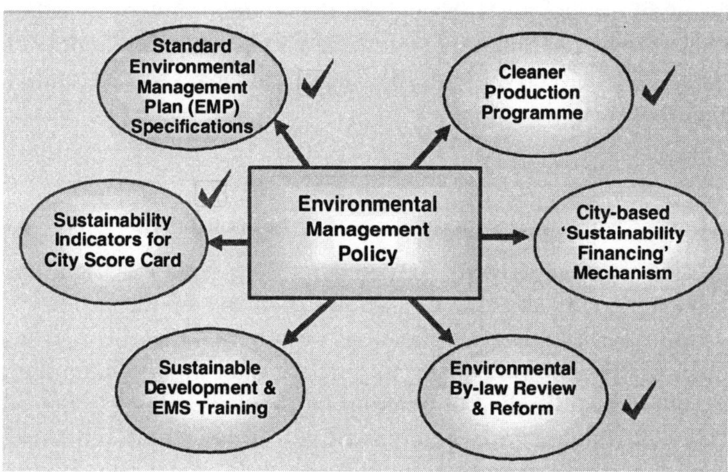

Preparation of the eThekwini Environmental Services Management Plan (EESMP): This project focused on the extension of the metropolitan open space plan to the new Unicity boundaries. The Unicity plan differs from the previous metropolitan plan in that it includes only those areas considered to be critical to the sustainable provision of open space services. The metropolitan plan, however, included all areas considered to contribute to the ecological viability of the open space system. This change in design approach resulted in a substantial reduction in the spatial footprint of the Unicity plan. The replacement value of the open space services provided by the Unicity open space system has been estimated at R3.1 billion per annum. Financial and legal tools were also investigated with a view to ensuring that important open spaces in private ownership are not lost because the owner's financial inability to maintain them, or through the implementation of existing, inappropriate development rights. Although the project was completed in June 2001, the Environmental Management Branch continued to refine the EESMP during the remainder of Phase 4, producing a more accurate and updated version of the plan in March 2002. This revised plan was accepted by eThekwini Council in

April 2003 as the guide for the future planning and development of the open space system within Durban.

Cities for Climate Protection Project: Concerns linked to open space planning and air quality management in Durban suggested that there was a need to consider both the local and global implications of these problems. 'Climate change' provided a useful umbrella under which the global impacts of these local problems could be debated. A subsequent Bilateral Grant Agreement between the national Department of Environmental Affairs and Tourism (DEAT) and USAID (US Agency for International Development) to implement a South African program to address global climate change (with a specific focus on eight South African cities) has provided funding and technical assistance for the initiation of a climate protection project in Durban.

Phase 5: Prioritizing implementation (2002 – onwards)

At the completion of Phase 4 it became apparent that while important progress had been made in developing the policy and strategic planning framework of the city's Local Agenda 21 program, there was an urgent need to focus future resources on implementation. This pre-empted the World Summit on Sustainable Development (WSSD) – held in Johannesburg (South Africa) in August/September 2002 – which similarly emphasized the need for a renewed global focus on the implementation of sustainable development. Ten years after the 1992 Earth Summit, the international mandate of WSSD was to identify areas where more efforts and action-oriented decisions were needed, and to adopt concrete steps and quantifiable targets for improving the implementation of Agenda 21 and the other Rio agreements. At the Local Government Session of the Summit this need was echoed in the call for a move "from Agenda to Action" and culminated in the launch of the new 'Local Action 21' program. Local Action 21 is envisaged as the new, action oriented phase of Local Agenda 21 that will facilitate the accelerated implementation of sustainable development in the decade following WSSD. In line with this approach, the eThekwini Council resolved in April 2003 that the name of the municipality's Local Agenda 21 program should be changed to 'Local Action 21'.

This name-change has been accompanied by a reorientation in the activities of the Environmental Management Branch towards more implementation-focused projects, for example:

- **Ethekwini Sustainability Partnership (ESP) Program**: This research project was initiated in order to identify high profile, showcase projects and programs that would deliver on a triple bottom line (i.e.

ensure returns on financial, social and natural capital). Such projects could be used to demonstrate the value of sustainable development by providing direct benefits to citizens and by developing the municipality's reputation as a partner in sustainable development initiatives. The ESP program ideally seeks to provide tangible examples of the benefits of sustainable development through building public-private-community partnerships. Nine projects were identified and documented during the course of the project. It is the intention that this work assists the new institutional structures responsible for the future development and implementation of the city's Sustainability Management System, in identifying priority action areas. The Geographic Information and Policy Unit has already begun work on the one of the identified projects i.e. the development and integration of sustainability indicators into the performance management system of the eThekwini Municipality.

- **Cities for Climate Projection Project**: Following the completion of the energy and emissions inventory for local government operations in Durban, projects are being identified that will contribute to a reduction in greenhouse gas emissions. The most significant of these involves a landfill gas-to-electricity project at three of the city's landfill sites. This will be South Africa's first Clean Development Mechanism project and, when fully implemented, will result in a reduction of 3.8 million carbon equivalent tons of green house gas emissions.
- **Regular State of the Environment Reporting/Portfolio of Sustainability Best Practice**: Regular State of the Environment (SOE) reporting (both web-based and hard copy format) has recently been initiated as part of the city's performance management system. It is intended that the full SOE report will be updated every three years, while the headline indicators required for the city scorecard will be updated annually. The State of the Environment Report will also include an updated version of the eThekwini Municipality's Portfolio of Sustainability Best Practice, produced for the first time in 2003. This document identifies specific projects being undertaken by local government (either exclusively or in partnership) which contribute to social, ecological, economic and institutional sustainability, and communicates this work and its benefits to the broader Durban population.
- **EThekwini Environment Services Management Plan**: Following Council approval of the eThekwini Environment Services Management Plan, an implementation program was developed. This included motivating for and acquiring capital monies from the Council budget in both the 2002/2003 and 2003/2004 financial years (R2.5 million

and R1 million respectively) in order to begin the acquisition of environmentally sensitive land that is under threat from development. Information sharing sessions have also been held with planning and development management staff in the city, in order to build capacity and understanding of the importance of the open space system in achieving long-term sustainability. This has resulted in better coordination across the line functions and helped to ensure that natural resource considerations are factored into the evaluation of development applications. A video is also being developed in order to facilitate future discussions with tribal leaders regarding the importance and protection of tribal land within the city's open space system.

- **Sustainable Procurement Program**: Given the significant sustainability opportunities offered by local government's role as a procurer of goods and services, the possibility of initiating a sustainable procurement program is being investigated. The outcomes of various international funding applications are currently being awaited.

Durban's sustainability roadmap

In reviewing Durban's experiences, UNESCO's (United Nations Educational, Scientific and Cultural Organization) 'wise practice' framework has provided a useful tool for highlighting the sustainability lessons learned that may be of general applicability to other local authorities considering the initiation of a Local Agenda 21/ Local Action 21 (LA 21) programs. These lessons are summarized in the following figure.

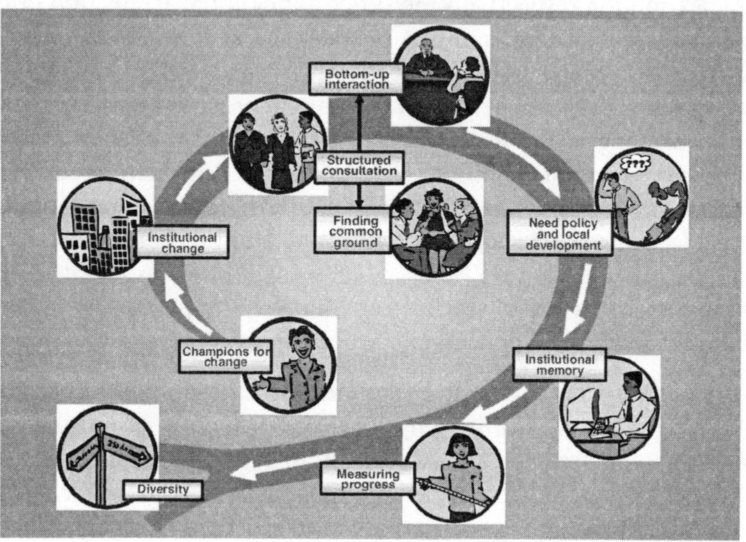

1. Ensure Long-term Benefit
Benefits of the activity will be evident years from now and will improve environmental quality.

Need for change

Durban has shown that LA 21 is not a pseudonym for 'business as usual'. It is a call for long-term change in all sectors. For government this could mean changing its structures to ensure a critical mass of people and resources to work towards sustainability, or facilitating the involvement of local stakeholders in decision-making processes. For business and industry it could mean changing modes of production to become responsible contributors to local and global sustainability rather than just a vehicle for economic gain. For communities it could mean replacing activism with a willingness to sit at the bargaining table to discuss new and difficult issues. Because LA 21 programs will have to mediate these processes, they must be flexible enough to meet the expectations of the different stakeholder groups and responsive enough to react to the new priorities and needs that will emerge through time.

Ripple effects

LA 21 processes are slow to unfold and require time to become well rooted in local administrations and political structures. Changes in attitudes do not occur instantaneously. Because of the evolving nature of these processes it is possible that decisions made at one point will have consequences later on in the process. This 'ripple effect' needs to be managed, and the possible long-term consequences of all decision-making critically evaluated.

2. Capacity Building and Institutional Strengthening

The activity should provide improved management capabilities and education for the stakeholder groups as well as knowledge and efforts to protect the local environment.

Need for capacity building

Because the concept of sustainable development is so complex and the terms 'Local Agenda 21' and 'Local Action 21' foreign to so many, capacity building and education are critical elements of any LA 21 program. This capacity building must be an ongoing process, rather than a once-off exercise. Capacity building must also be a priority task rather than the first program element to be sacrificed when resources and skills are scarce. In order to be successful, LA 21 programs must also acknowledge the capacity mismatch that exists between stakeholder groups. This is an important consideration, as these programs seek to create partnerships for local action under conditions where each partner will usually have different skills and capacity building needs. One size does not fit all! Capacity building is also important in ensuring that processes are not dominated by the agendas of gatekeeper groups.

Need for a critical institutional mass

There is a need to establish a critical institutional mass to sustain momentum and ensure delivery. This is necessary as LA 21 programs require widespread networking and partnership development, a process that cannot be undertaken successfully by one or even a few people. Where this critical institutional mass is not achieved, there is a danger that there will be too strong a reliance on program champion(s). Under these circumstances, program sustainability becomes strongly aligned with the commitment and energy of individuals, a situation that is highly unsustainable.

3. Sustainability

The activity adheres to the principles of sustainability (the extent to which the results will last and development will continue once the project/program has ended).

The need for mainstreaming

Working towards greater sustainability in the urban environment is a complex task involving the coordination of stakeholders, resources and priorities. Because it will never occur spontaneously it must be planned for. For this reason it is imperative that LA 21 programs are mainstreamed (i.e. prioritized within the strategic planning processes of local government) in order to ensure broad scale commitment and involvement. LA 21 programs in the developing world particularly need to have a strong developmental focus and must demonstrate how sustainability can help meet people's basic needs and improve quality of life. Location within an environmental department therefore brings with it the danger that these processes will be seen as 'green' or anti-development.

Need for adequate resourcing

Human and financial resource limitations will have severe impacts on LA 21 programs. This ranges from the inability to undertake work, to the need to curtail or stop successful initiatives. Preventing the wastage of human and financial resources will require that LA 21 programs are adequately resourced from the beginning. This is important, as stakeholder expectations are raised through involvement and the inability to complete the project or implement the resulting recommendations creates mistrust and reduces commitment to future projects.

Grab opportunities

LA 21 programs should make use of 'windows of opportunity'. This does not mean that programs should be deliberately opportunistic in nature, but rather that they should be able to use changing circumstances (e.g. political transformation) to their advantage. The drawback is that the change and uncertainty that often characterize these 'windows of opportunity' can have equally negative consequences for the LA 21 process, making it difficult to plan proactively and impacting on the motivation and commitment of staff.

Catalysts and implementers

There is a division between role players that act as 'catalysts' and those that act as 'implementers' in any LA 21 program. Typically 'catalysts' initiate new projects, promote new ideas and seek out new problem solving techniques. Every 'catalyst' must, however, be partnered by an accompanying implementing agent to give effect to these new ideas. Unless both capacities are present in local government, many sustainable development initiatives are unlikely to move from the drawing board.

4. Transferability

Aspects of the activity can be applied to other sites, in or outside the country.

No carbon copies

LA 21 processes are not standardized and the individual needs and priorities of each city should be used to craft a city-specific program. Although key principles and methodologies may be transferable between cities, in each case these have to be applied or used by people and institutions with a deep knowledge of the local context.

5. Consensus Building

The activity should benefit a majority of the stakeholder groups, whilst bearing in mind that in some cases certain under-privileged groups may need to be treated as special cases.

Need for compromise

All too often the notion of sustainable development is taken to imply a 'win-win' scenario. This is misleading, as there are likely to be instances where the move to greater sustainability produces situations that are regarded by some stakeholder as 'win-lose' scenarios. This implies that LA 21 programs will be arenas for difficult decision-making and that they will have to rely on strong and visionary leadership to ensure that the best long-term decisions prevail. Particular care must be taken where potential losers belong to vulnerable or disadvantaged groups to ensure that improved sustainability for the many does not further peripheralise the few. These groups must be fully engaged in determining and overseeing the change process.

Conflict management

Where competition exists between well-established and entrenched power bases, new integrative initiatives such as LA 21 may be seen as threatening, signaling the emergence of a new competing power base, or as an attempt to control existing ones. LA 21 practitioners should not think that because they advocate a better, more sustainable future, that this idea will be readily accepted or embraced by other stakeholder groups. Some stakeholders could have vested interests in perpetuating unsustainability for short-term gain. LA 21 programs can therefore be highly conflictual in nature and this must be planned for through the establishment of conflict management processes and structures that regularly bring together different stakeholder groups and power bases for debate, dialogue and capacity building in order to build trust and new partnerships.

6. Participatory Process

Participation of all stakeholder groups – where the intentions of all groups are known – and the involvement of individuals, is intrinsic to the process.

Champions

The scale and complexity of the global environmental crisis often serves to trivialize the role of the individual. In LA 21 processes a single person or small groups of people can and do make a difference. LA 21 programs must therefore make space for more than just stakeholder groups, they must facilitate action by highly motivated individuals, particularly those that will act as champions. Champions are important as they provide continuity when interest wanes amongst other stakeholders, help brand processes, provide a rallying point for people with similar interests and are often instrumental in unblocking stalled or difficult processes. Without hard working and committed champions, no LA 21 program can hope to succeed or survive in the long-term. At the same time there are potential pitfalls associated with too strong a reliance on champions. There is the danger that when a champion moves on (either geographically or in terms of interest) that the program will lose momentum or collapse entirely. This does not mean that champions are irreplaceable but that Local Agenda 21 programs should work towards the identification of a range of champions amongst all stakeholder groups (e.g. amongst city administrators in different line functions, politicians, community groups and NGOs) and help build their capacity to ensure the continuity and sustainability of the program.

7. Effective and Efficient Communication Process

A multidirectional communication process involving dialogue, consultation and discussion is needed to attain awareness.

Consultation

The success of the consultation and participation processes within any LA 21 program is often the best barometer of overall sustainability. Effective participation and consultation requires the creation of small, committed and accountable stakeholder groups that can play an integral role in the planning and implementation of projects. A structured approach to participation (i.e. clear objectives and rules for interactions, defined roles and responsibilities) also provides a mechanism for addressing the distrust that can exist between stakeholders. By working together in an agreed on format, new understandings and friendships are developed.

8. Culturally Respectful

The process values local traditional and cultural frameworks while also challenging their environmental validity.

The challenge of cultural diversity

In a culturally and politically diverse society, LA 21 programs must employ different tools and approaches to communicate ideas to stakeholders in terms that are meaningful to them.

9. Gender and/or other Sensitivity Issues

The process accounts for the many aspects of gender and/or other sensitive issues.

The silent constituency

To date, Durban's LA 21 program has not focused specifically on gender-linked or other sensitivity issues or problems. This is not a result of a lack or awareness but rather the result of focusing limited resources on issues that are perceived to have greater developmental and political significance. This demonstrates how easily this aspect of sustainable development can be overlooked. Mechanisms will have to be found to mainstream gender and other sensitivity concerns, particularly in the cities of the developing world. This will require a diversity of interventions e.g. training of local government officials, the establishment of specific institutional structures to deal with gender and related issues, and for these issues to be incorporated into performance management systems.

10. Strengthening Local Identities

The activity provides a sense of belonging and self-reliance at various levels.

A cocktail of action

LA 21 projects that focus on policy development or planning are unlikely to change the attitudes of local communities. For any Local Agenda 21 program to survive it must appeal to grass-roots stakeholders as well as policy makers. It is difficult for most stakeholders to sustain interest and involvement in high-level processes that appear to have no direct benefits. This suggests that Local Agenda 21 programs must link planning and policy generation with local development projects in order to ensure sustained buy-in from the broader community.

11. National Legal Policy The activity adheres to current government environmental, economic, legal and social policies.

12. Regional Dimension

The activity should embody the regional, economic, social and environmental perspective

From the bottom – up

Compliance with national and regional policy and law is a critical element in ensuring long-term sustainability. There will, however, be instances where local processes highlight the unsustainability or unsuitability of these higher order requirements. Under these circumstances local needs should be used to inform and motivate for changes in these broader frameworks.

13. Human Rights

The activity should provide freedom to exercise fundamental rights.

Providing a platform

LA 21 programs must provide a platform for all stakeholder groups to exercise their fundamental rights and to lobby for change where these rights are compromised through unsustainable development

14. Documentation

The activity and the lessons learnt have been well documented

Creating institutional memory

The complexity and dynamism of many LA 21 programs mean that many important processes, experiences and decisions are not adequately documented due to a lack of time and resources. The net result is that no permanent institutional memory is created and valuable lessons are lost. Time and resources must be found in all LA 21 programs to document sustainability experiences.

15. Evaluation

The activity has been tested to determine the extent to which wise practice characteristics have been utilized.

Measuring Progress

It has been internationally recognized that a system for measuring achievements and monitoring the implementation of LA 21 programs is important. This need is, however, often overlooked due to the lack of appropriate human and financial resources and the fact no measurable objectives were specified at the beginning of the process. This means that those involved directly in the program are not be able to realistically assess the level of success and that the progress made will often be obscured by the difficulties associated with the process. The need for monitoring also underlines the urgent need for accurate and comprehensive databases to be developed in all key sustainable development sectors to establish the baseline state and evaluate future progress.

Informal Areas and Strategies of Inclusion in the Context of an Urban Development Project in Cairo

Monika El Shorbagi

Introduction

Present urbanization patterns as well as the structural heterogeneity of formal and informal economic spheres in many countries in the South continue to increase disparities and aggravate the social and environmental problems of the urban poor. Development discourse and practice has been searching for some time to identify appropriate strategies and mechanisms to address urban poverty and the resulting problems of marginalization and exclusion. In recent years, a shift has taken place to incorporate local communities as active partners into urban upgrading and development interventions. Their empowerment is believed to be crucial to tackle the root causes and not only the symptoms of poverty. This entails the acknowledgement of the capacities and efforts of community organizations, networks and individuals. Instruments are being developed to promote and strengthen local communities through pro-active, positive approaches, capacity-building measures and the establishment of functioning linkages among community networks as well as between communities, governmental and non-governmental development agents.

The following article presents the experiences of the Participatory Urban Development Project Manshiet Nasser in Egypt. The project tries to identify and demonstrate mechanisms and solutions for the manifold and interrelated problems of the so-called informal areas, i.e. settlements which have been founded and developed illegally over the past decades. They constitute the majority of poor urban areas in Egypt, particularly in the large urban agglomerations of Greater Cairo and Alexandria. The article will give an overview of informal residential development and the dominant socio-economic features of informal areas, followed by a brief presentation of the strategies, areas of action, problems and potentials of the project.

Residential informality in Greater Cairo

According to the last census in 1996, Egypt's urban population accounts for 42.6% of all Egyptians, whereas the underlying definition of "urban" is purely administrative and not consistently based on population numbers.[1] With its roughly 14-16 million inhabitants, Cairo hosts in 2002 more than 20% of Egypt's total population of about 69 million.[2] According to an extensive study which has been conducted in 2000, around 62% of the Greater Cairo population live in so-called informal settlements covering 52.8% of the total residential built-up area.[3] Residential informality is thus the dominant type of living in Greater Cairo. The majority of the residents of informal areas, i.e. 91%, are living in informal settlements on privately owned agricultural land which has been illegally subdivided, informally sold and illegally built upon. The remaining 9% are living in squatter settlements, mainly on desert land owned by Cairo governorate.[4]

Informal urbanization of agricultural land started on a larger scale in the mid-1960's, in most cases around existing village settlements or large public sector factories. During the same period, squatters encroached on state-owned desert land, usually around quarries, military camps or cemeteries. The high pressure for housing due to high population growth rates of around 3% p.a. resulted in rapid price increases for building land which soon exceeded the profits gained from agriculture and further encouraged illegal urbanization of agricultural land.

---

1 Some settlements which are administratively defined as cities have less than 10,000 residents and some large residential agglomerations in the Delta and on the periphery of Cairo with more than 100,000 inhabitants are defined as rural villages. If international definitions were applied, i.e. if all settlements with more than 10,000 residents were considered as urban, the percentage of Egyptians who live in cities would increase to 66.8%. Denis (1999), p. 31.

2 Greater Cairo consists of the governorates of Cairo, Giza and Qaliubiya. Cairo is purely urban; Giza and Qaliubiya encompass both urban districts and outlying village administrative units. Estimates of the inhabitants of the Greater Cairo metropolitan area vary considerably according to the definitions of its boundaries

3 Sims (2000). The study was carried out on behalf of the Institute for Liberty and Democracy and the Egyptian Center for Economic Studies

4 Growth rates are higher in informal than in formal areas, which adds more to densification than to further expansion. Sims (2000). Contrary to wide spread assumptions, these growth rates are mainly due to inner-city migration rather than to net-in migration from rural areas and provincial cities. Denis/Bayat (1999), p. 9 and 10.

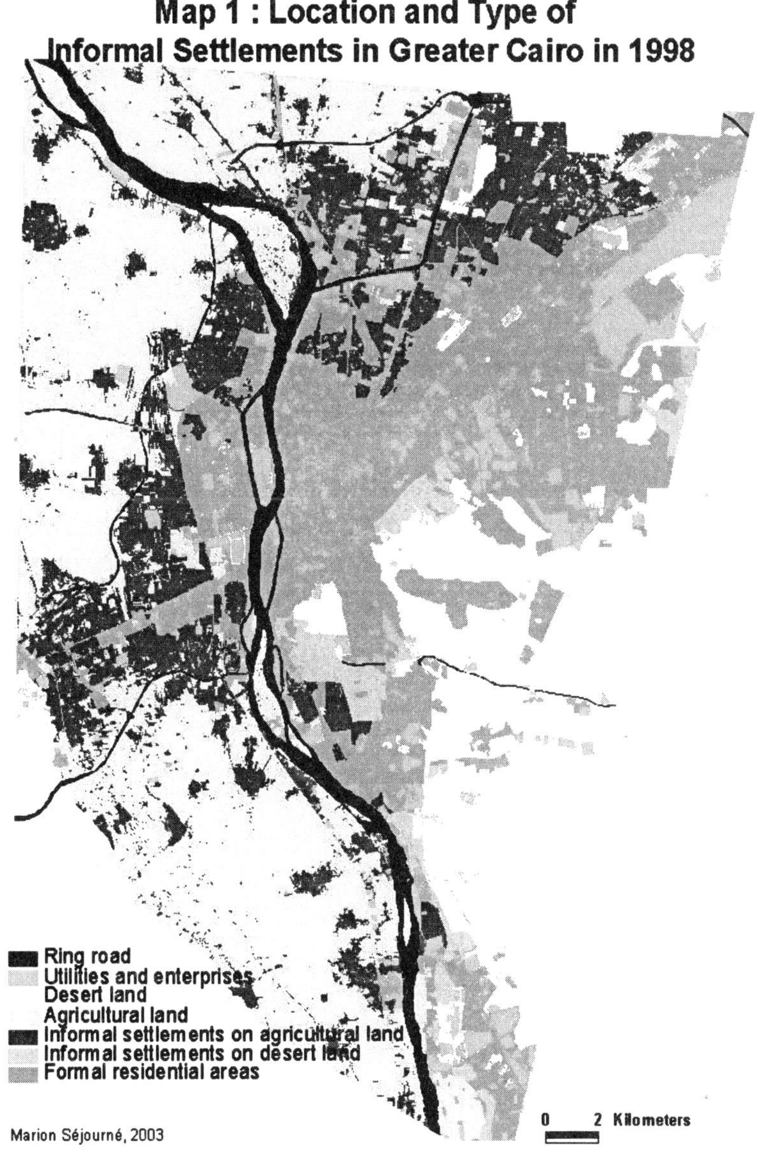

Map 1 : Location and Type of Informal Settlements in Greater Cairo in 1998

The boom of informal urban development started in the mid 1970's and lasted until the mid 1980's. During this period, millions of Egyptians migrated to the Gulf states and invested major portions of their lucrative salaries in real estate and construction. Land prices were cheaper in informal areas, and the absence of effective state control allowed for modifications of building standards and maximum exploitation of the plots for construction. Building costs could thus be minimized, and housing proved to be a profitable investment. Most investors are owner builders who live in the house with their families and rent out every square meter which they do not need themselves. Many use the rent to finance the gradual reinforcement of the structure or the extension of the building for their growing-up offspring to marry.[5]

The state was not able to capitalize on the enormous investment capacity of the informal sector, e.g. by providing serviced sites which are affordable to the poor. Public housing projects could by far not satisfy the need, and the rent control law discouraged legal investment in housing for rent so that no legal markets were available to meet the growing demand for housing. When the Egyptian government became finally aware of the phenomenon of informal settlements, it started to issue a series of decrees and orders to stop further illegal urbanization, with little real impact however, except for the increasingly prevailing system of *ikramiyat* (bribes) for state employees to turn a blind eye on construction. Finally, two decrees were issued in 1996, which made illegal construction punishable under military law. These decrees slowed illegal urbanization considerably, at least in some areas and for some years. The government's alternative to informal settlements was the construction of satellite cities to direct the growth of urban centers to the desert. Despite enormous investments, however, only a fraction of the expected population did move to the new cities, and some of them are virtually empty. The State failed to integrate the by then well-established socio-economic mechanisms of the informal sector, and the urban poor simply can not afford to live there since no secondary jobs are available, the costs of living are too high and social networks are weak.

Poverty and marginalization in informal areas

Most informal settlements in Egypt are not synonymous with shantytowns or slums. Due to the relatively high degree of investment security in informal areas on privately owned agricultural land, the quality of construction does not differ significantly from that in formal areas. The socio-

---

[5] Until a new law was issued in 1997, rent control made it virtually impossible to increase rents in accordance with inflation rates. House owners had also no possibility to terminate rent contracts which could be inherited by several generations. As compensation, house owners used to demand high up-front payments (*khiluw*), usually amounting to half of the total amount of the rent for 15 to 30 years. In some cases, these up-front payments were not substantially lower than the purchase price would have been.

economic spectrum of inhabitants is relatively diverse and encompasses a considerable number of middle class residents. Land in squatter areas is much cheaper but entails also a higher risk of eviction, thus discouraging substantial investments. The housing stock in squatter settlements tends to be of lower quality and includes dilapidated buildings and extremely precarious structures, particularly in areas which are not yet consolidated. However, both types of settlements have a number of pressing problems in common: serious infrastructure deficiencies, insufficient social and community services, difficult vehicular access and serious environmental problems. Residential densities are extremely high in many areas, particularly in older, consolidated settlements. The incidences of underemployment, youth unemployment[6] and illiteracy rates tend to be higher than average, as is the percentage of the poor and ultra-poor.

There is a serious lack of in-depth analysis of urban poverty in Egypt. Poverty studies rely almost exclusively on governorate aggregates. This conceals considerable variations within the urban governorates which is particularly distorting for Greater Cairo where the bulk of the country's rich and wealthy families are living. According to the 1997/1998 Egypt Human Development Report (EHDR), the overall percentage of urban poor (22.5%) almost matches that of rural areas (23.3%).[7] A representative sample survey carried out in 1998[8] found that the monthly income of 68% of all households in Greater Cairo was less than LE 500 (at the time ca. 139 US $ per month or 1.14 US $ per day) which is roughly the poverty line used in the 1997/1998 EHDR.[9] Several studies assume that, in abso-

---

6 Although the population growth rate of Greater Cairo is currently estimated at 1.9% p.a., the labor force is estimated to be growing at over 3.0% p.a., due to large numbers of youth in the population pyramid now reaching working age

7 Institute of National Planning (1998), p. 142. Some poverty estimates, particularly those calculated on a headcount basis in studies on consumption poverty, are significantly higher See for example Handoussa (1999), p. 3-4. The considerable variances in poverty estimates are partially due to the fact that a large number of Egyptian households are clustered around the poverty line. Consequently, even minor differences in definition or methodology can yield major differences in results.

8 Nassar (1999), p.22-23.

9 The EHDR uses the lower income poverty line calculated 1996 by El Laithy/Osman (1996). It was set at LE 4,438 p.a. for urban households, at the time roughly 1,305 US$ per household p.a. or 0.88 US$ per person per day. The upper poverty line was estimated at LE 6,082, roughly 1,789 US$ per household p.a. or 1.21 US$ per person per day. Lower poverty line means that *all* household expenditures are equal to the food poverty line. Upper poverty line means that *food expenditures* are equal to the food poverty line.

lute terms, the incidence of poverty and ultra-poverty is much higher in informal and other types of poor urban areas than in any other category.[10]

If asset poverty and capacity poverty are taken into account, the picture may be even more dramatic, given the comparatively higher and increasing demands of skills in urban labor markets such as computer literacy and foreign languages. Several studies describe the correlation between poverty and the high drop-out rates (51%) of children from poor families from primary education.[11] Many of them are working in small and micro enterprises in informal settlements. The number of working children between 5-14 years is estimated at 1.5 Mio. representing 12.5% of the population at this age.[12] The main assets of the poor in urban areas are housing with secure tenure and productive assets such as workshops, shops and stalls, simple machinery and craftsmen tools and household appliances. In times of crisis, families tend to sell some of these assets which often solves the crisis in the short term but aggravates poverty in the longer term. Families with illiterate household heads, high dependency ratios or families depending on casual labor, women-headed households and physically and mentally handicapped are more likely to be poor and more vulnerable to crisis. Street children and children of poor families are likely to remain poor when they grow up.

However, informal areas are by no means homogeneous, neither in terms of income, assets and socio-economic status nor in terms of education. Many State employees, successful traders and small entrepreneurs of the lower middle, middle and occasionally even wealthier classes are living in informal areas. There are also a remarkable number of professionals coming from poor families who have managed to escape poverty due to their family's investing every spare penny in their education, often with tremendous sacrifices. In general, however, it is true that poverty tends to be passed on from one generation to the next since children of poor families are more likely to drop out of school and poor families depend more often on self-employment and casual labor and are thus highly vulnerable to crisis.

Despite the considerable socio-economic variances, many informal settlements have the general reputation of being hotbeds for criminals, Islamic extremists and all sorts of socially unaccepted behavior. Informal

---

[10] Assad/Rouchdy (1999), p.17. Table 3 and following pages from Datt/Gaurav/Dean (1998).

[11] El Baradei (1995), p.28 and p.64. Fergany (1995), p.23. In some areas, the percentage of children who have never be enrolled is much higher than the drop-out rate, e.g. in Manshiet Nasser 62% versus 7% drop-outs.

[12] El Baradei (1995), p.16. Zibani (1994), p.150 and 152.

areas are called *'ashwa'iyāt* – i.e. random, unorganized areas – and the inhabitants are generally considered as being at the receiving end, i.e. passive, needy and powerless. Although they might be consulted and involved in the execution of development programs, they are rarely perceived as partners and even less as potential initiators of actions.

Mechanisms of exclusion and inclusion

Mechanisms of exclusion operate at different levels: the political and administrative level, the level of public discourse and society at large and the level of the community itself. Dimensions of exclusion encompass budgetary discrimination, political exclusion, exclusion from public life and public services, lack of protection by the law as well as individual and collective disempowerment. The different levels and dimensions are intertwined in many respects.

The predominant perception of informal areas as potential security threats obstructs effective community participation in upgrading and development interventions. Control has been the ultimate objective of the State for a long time. Elected bodies of community representation such as the Local Popular Councils are often used as instruments of control rather than as channels for participation. These bodies are usually dominated by members of the ruling National Democratic Party, the key figures of which are chosen carefully at higher party levels. Local elections are usually reproached with numerous irregularities. If any, women play only a marginal role in these bodies.[13]

The neglect of informal settlements for decades led to a serious lack of information. Sometimes even the boundaries are not known to government planners. Many laws and procedures concerning building codes, planning standards and business registration are not applicable, which obstructs upgrading and legalization. There is a considerable lack of understanding of the peculiar problems and their interrelation, and almost no instruments are available for systematic approaches and realistic solutions. Together with the lack of true representation and lobbying power, this translates into continuous discrimination in State budget allocations. In addition, many government employees regard their being transferred to informal settlements as a punishment or they consider these areas as unprotected by the law where extra-legal fees can be conveniently imposed

---

[13] Although these mechanisms of exclusion are typical for Egypt in general, they tend to be stronger in informal areas since the government feels even more need for control.

for any kind of services and licenses. Patrimonialistic attitudes and top-down approaches prevail and services are often ill targeted and ineffective, which leads to the paradox that even insufficient services are frequently underused. Lack of adequate services means more capacity-poverty, less resources, information and access to support programs, aggravation of environmental problems, more child labor and less bridges into formal job markets, less escape channels from poverty, more frustration and less ability to envisage and actively shape the future, thus continuously increasing existing disparities and dynamics of marginalization and exclusion.

The stigmatization of informal areas translates into frequent discrimination in labor markets, institutions of higher education and social marginalization. Residents of informal settlements are often referred to as "al-nas duwl" (those people) as if they constitute a different species of human beings that do not fit into modern life and concepts of civilized behavior. The social marginalization has a negative effect on the self-perception of the residents. Many individuals try to distance themselves from their neighbors and communities suggesting that this is not really an appropriate place for them to live. Others try to conceal their addresses when they study or work outside the area. Community members are often quite cynical about outside perceptions and, occasionally, there is an underlying tone of aggressiveness and defiance.

Much has been written in recent years about neighborhood solidarity, revolving credit and saving clubs (gamaʿiya) and extensive clientele and solidarity networks in urban low-income areas to counter the dynamics of marginalization and exclusion.[14] These networks are based on kinship relations or the exchange of loyalty with access to jobs, resources and services. One author argues that "these networks represent a pervasive organizational grid" which can "infuse and penetrate different constituencies in Egyptian society" and thus give the needs and preferences of the poor and popular classes an indirect voice. Informal networks "connect households and individuals with communal and national institutions...(and) are effective precisely because they are designed to function within a formal system pervaded by informal structures and processes".[15] However, the underlying traditional social ties of networks and social solidarity schemes are slowly eroding in the face of increasing prevalence of nuclear families and material consumption.

In the 1990ies, post-development theories have discovered the informal sector as an area of refuge for those who are marginalized or excluded

---

14 See for example Singermann (1997) and Hoodfar (1999).

15 Singernmann (1997), p. 269-270.

from the modern economy and consumer culture.[16] According to the representatives of this discourse, the economy of the informal sector is being re-embedded into the social sphere. Economic activities emerge from and are restricted by social relations. Revenues which are not needed for survival are often invested to strengthen social relations and to build up social capital. Thus, investment decisions follow a social rationality and the logic of securing survival in the framework of socio-cultural norms and relations rather than the capitalist logic of profit maximization and accumulation. However, these theories run the risk to romanticize coping strategies which are not chosen voluntarily and tend to ignore power relations and mechanisms of exclusion which do also exist inside informal communities. The poor and ultra poor, for example, have less social capital and are therefore less integrated in extensive informal networks. Children of women-headed households and orphans are often discriminated in the "marriage market," divorced women and widows are often looked at with suspicion. Domestic violence against women and children is rampant, particularly if male household heads are unemployed or depend on casual labor. Restriction of women's movements and women's exclusion from the public sphere are particularly strong in areas where most residents come from Upper Egypt, especially from rural areas.

Nevertheless, solidarity mechanisms do exist and have probably prevented thousands of vulnerable families from falling into absolute, long-term poverty or even destitution in times of crisis. The extent of social solidarity varies considerably according to the age and consolidation of an informal settlement as well as the inhabitants' areas of origin and the resulting level of organization and social coherence.

Introduction to Manshiet Nasser

Manshiet Nasser is the largest squatter settlement in Egypt. Its about 420,000 inhabitants represent roughly 7% of the total population of Cairo governorate. It covers an area of 1,731 feddans (7.27 km^2). Densities are extremely high, probably among the highest in the world. Net residential densities reach 2,200 persons per hectare or 220,000 per km^2 in some areas.

Manshiet Nasser occupies a central position within Cairo, stretching along the base of the Moqattam Hills, directly east of Fatimid Cairo and the associated cemeteries of Qait Bey and Sultan Barquq. It is well con-

[16] See for example Latouche (1993).

nected to central Cairo. Due to its proximity to the main arterial corridors of the Autostrade and Salah Salem Road, Manshiet Nasser enjoys also good access to the northeast (to Madinet Nasr and Heliopolis) and south (to El Khalifa, Maadi and Helwan). Connections further to the east are blocked by the Moqattam Hills and a number of military camps.

Map 2 : Location of Manshiet Nasser

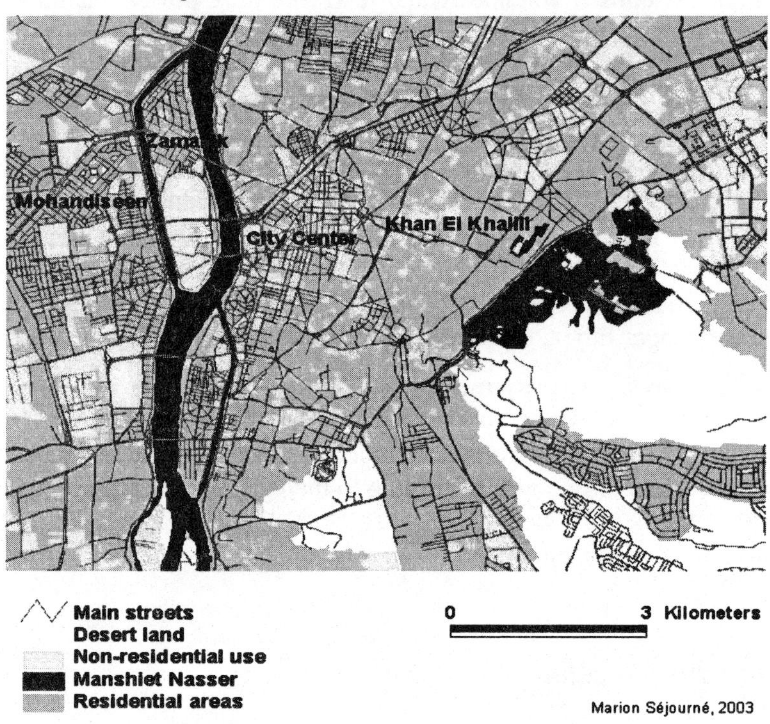

Settlement activities started in the mid 1960ies, mainly by unskilled construction workers from Upper Egypt who had previously settled in tin shacks on the site where the Azhar hospital is located today. For many centuries, the area has been used as a lime quarry and the early settlers had to undertake considerable ground leveling before they could start with construction. Many claimed larger plots than they needed and sold part of them at nominal prices to kin or fellow citizens coming from the same area of origin. The construction of buildings was carried out gradually, according to financial means. Informal development along the same patterns is ongoing to date in the valleys to the east towards the Moqattam Hills.

Today, 57.2% of the residents are tenants. In some areas, more than 30% of tenant families live in one single room, sharing toilets. Most house owners occupy several housing units in the building together with families of relatives. Absentee owners are extremely rare. The families of 75.8 % of household heads came from Upper Egypt which is reflected in patriarchic family structures, conservative social values and relatively strong social cohesion. The percentage of Christians and Muslims corresponds to that of the national level (5-10% Christians) with the exception of the *Zabaleen* area where Cairo's largest garbage collector community is living who are almost exclusively Christian. There is no discrimination based on religion or area of origin.

The average household size according to a survey of the Ministry of Social Affairs in 1998 is 4.4 as opposed to 4.06 for all Cairo governorate according to the 1996 census. A sample survey of the National Center for Social and Criminological Studies reported household sizes of 5.1 to 6.0. Birth and fertility rates are presumably much higher than the city-wide average as, according to the 1996 census, 39.1% of the population of Manshiet Nasser is younger than fifteen years compared to 30.6% in Cairo governorate as a whole. With 52%, illiteracy rates (above 9 years of age) are twice as high as in all of Cairo for which the census reports only 24.2% illiterates. Female illiteracy rates are even more dramatic, i.e. 59.6%. Current enrolment rates in the overcrowded, poorly equipped schools in Manshiet Nasser reach only 38% at primary school level and 33% at preparatory school level implying a growing illiteracy rate for both sexes. Many children work in local workshops in often hazardous working conditions, some of them start as young as six years of age.

According to the survey of the Ministry of Social Affairs, stated monthly household incomes are as follows: 25.3% below LE 150 (roughly US$ 44.1 at the time of the survey), 37.1% between LE 150 and LE 300 (US$ 44.1 – US$ 88.2) and 37.7% above LE 300. For comparison: average city-wide monthly household incomes are estimated at LE 705.[17] Although it can be assumed that at least some of the reported incomes are understated, anecdotal information confirms that income levels are in fact very low and are often based on casual labor and thus extremely unstable. Underemployment is more prevalent than unemployment which is most wide-

17 Nassar (1999), p.22-23.

spread among technical secondary school graduates and youth entrants into the labor market. According to the 1996 census, 12.9% of the working population is employed in government or State enterprises compared to 41.1% in all Cairo. About 16% are working in the private sector and ca. 65% are self-employed, many of them depending on unstable or marginal activities. As many as 55.9% of the local workforce are working inside Manshiet Nasser.

Many problems in Manshiet Nasser are representative for similar informal areas. Only problems related to the hilly topography and the dangers posed by the many cliffs in the area are more or less unique. Other problems vary in degree but less in nature. They are mainly related to the lack of or insufficiency of utilities and social infrastructure, particularly water, wastewater and schools, the scarcity and difficulty of securing land for public facilities, the poor quality of existing services, difficult access and internal circulation, insecure land tenure and environmental hazards which are mainly due to the absence of a functioning garbage collection system and environmental problems related to recycling activities of the garbage collectors as well as polluting small industries. Poverty and numerous social problems such as domestic violence, youth delinquency and low levels of general life skills and awareness aggravate the situation.

The political and administrative framework

Governorates are the main entities of local administration in Egypt. As there is no macro-administrative structure for the Greater Cairo metropolitan region as a whole, Cairo governorate is the principal executive body responsible for Manshiet Nasser. It has to approve development plans, budget requests and the legalization of squatter areas. The governor has considerable executive powers, he is appointed by central government and has the rank of a minister. He can, for example, declare an area as a special development zone which allows for applying modified conditions for legalization regarding planning and building standards or licenses for businesses. Although budget requests are processed through the governorates to the ministries that control national investments (mainly the Ministries of Planning and Finance), national budget allocations are channeled through the sectoral directorates in the governorate which are attached to the respective line ministries. The Governor receives only a budget for administration and has very limited possibilities to create own revenues.

The districts are the implementing agencies in cities. They have also the mandate to conduct needs assessments and prepare budget proposals, although they have rarely the capacity to fulfill this role. Cairo governorate has 26 districts, one of them is Manshiet Nasser. Their structure reflects that of the governorate with most line ministries having sectoral departments at district level. District administrations are headed by the district chiefs who report directly to the governor, in the case of Cairo governorate via one of the four vice governors for Cairo West, East, North and South. District chiefs are also appointed by central government. Most district chiefs (and many governors) in Egypt come from the army or the security forces.

The Ministry of Local Development (MoLD) is insofar important for informal settlements as it commands resources in addition to the regular State budget allocations, i.e. the National Fund for Urban Upgrading. These funds are mainly used for utilities and physical infrastructure. The MoLD is also the head of the Council of Governors and can thus execute influence on the Governor of Cairo.

In the case of Manshiet Nasser, the Minister of Housing (MoH) is another important player since he is the elected delegate for Manshiet Nasser in parliament. He has established a permanent office in the area and shows considerable interest in development measures. Two agencies under the MoH are directly involved in upgrading efforts in Manshiet Nasser: (1) the Department for the Greater Cairo Region within the national-level General Organization for Physical Planning which drafted the Master Plan for Manshiet Nasser and (2) the Greater Cairo Reconstruction Agency which is responsible for the implementation of a number of infrastructure and public housing projects, funded by the MoH and the Abu Dhabi Fund, which are currently being carried out in an extension area adjacent to Manshiet Nasser. Finally, there are certain service authorities (e.g. water and wastewater) which cover Greater Cairo as a whole and are involved in infrastructure projects in Manshiet Nasser.

The legal framework offers a number of channels for community participation in local development. Local Popular Councils (LPC) are elected as representatives of the local population. They exist both on district and on governorate level. They have to approve development plans and budgets. Boards of youth centers and Parent Teachers Councils (PTCs) in schools are also elected. The population is entitled to form NGOs or community development associations (CDAs) which are entitled to carry out development activities.

However, community participation is obstructed by a number of legal and political obstacles. LPCs are nationwide completely dominated by the ruling National Democratic Party and have little practical power and influence. Female membership is extremely rare. During the past elections, a female candidate has won for the first time a seat in Manshiet Nasser. Positions in PTCs and the boards of youth centers are often regarded as a potential jump start into a political career in the local National Democratic Party with the result that these bodies are not really representative and often quite ineffective. Cultural centers and other community services are operated without any formal community involvement altogether.

Contrary to hopes of NGOs and donors alike, the new NGO law No. 84/2002 has not really solved the problems that obstruct the work of NGOs. The law does not clearly define which activities and actions are permitted or prohibited, the registration of new NGOs is still very burdensome and the Ministry of Social Affairs continues to have extensive possibilities of interference. It can even dissolve the board or the NGO altogether. All donor funds channeled through NGOs have to be approved upfront by the Ministry of Social Affairs with hard punishments imposed in case of non-compliance. Particularly smaller, grass-roots NGOs with little influence or political clout have to be very enduring in order not to give up in front of the complicated procedures or indirect requests of extra-legal fees for facilitation.

The Participatory Urban Development Project Manshiet Nasser

The Participatory Urban Development Project Manshiet Nasser (MN project) has started in 1998 in the framework of bilateral cooperation between the Arab Republic of Egypt and the Federal Republic of Germany with Cairo Governorate as the counterpart and the district of Manshiet Nasser as the executing agency. The ultimate objective of the project is the improvement of the living conditions of the local population. The project is also envisaged to contribute to the development of better policies for informal areas and to poverty alleviation strategies. During its first phase, the project has focused on the physical upgrading and social development of Ezbet Bekhit as a pilot area in Manshiet Nasser with roughly 38,000 inhabitants. During its second phase, the project has extended its activities to all of Manshiet Nasser. On behalf of the German Ministry for International Cooperation (Bundesministerium für wirtschaftliche Zusammenarbeit und Entwicklung – BMZ), the German Agency for Technical Cooperation (Gesellschaft für technische Zusammenarbeit – GTZ) provides the technical assistance to the project and the German Bank for Reconstruction (Kreditanstalt für Wiederaufbau – KfW) is financing the needed technical infrastructure, mainly water and wastewater in Ezbet Bekhit.

The MN project is part of the GTZ Participatory Urban Development Program (P.U.M.P.) which consists of four projects: the MN project as an example for an informal squatter settlement, another project in an informal settlement on privately owned agricultural land in Boulaq El Dakrour (BED) in Giza, the Policy Advisory Unit (PAU) and the Local Initiatives Project, both in the Ministry of Planning. The MN and the BED projects are supposed to develop and test mechanisms to solve the most pressing problems in the two dominant types of informal areas and feed these experiences through the Policy Advisory Unit up to the policy level. The LI project is envisaged to develop and establish on a national level mechanisms for the direct engagement of local communities in participatory development from below which draw on experiences with local initiatives made in the MN and the BED projects. The P.U.M.P. is currently the only donor program in Egypt which has counterparts at the micro, meso and macro levels, i.e. districts, governorates and ministries. The MN project is the only project which is directly located at the lowest level of administration in cities, i.e. the district, which is responsible for day to day administration. It is currently also the only German project in Egypt which combines both financial and technical cooperation.

Strategies and approaches of the project

The project's purpose is to create experiences and develop mechanisms to address the multiple physical and socio-economic development needs which can be replicated beyond Manshiet Nasser. In doing so, the project has developed links with sector agencies on all levels from the district through the governorate to a number of ministries. It supports the formation of networks of committed employees in and among sectoral agencies as well as between different administrative levels to test innovative solutions and promote their adoption as standard practice. This is particularly important regarding planning mechanisms and alterations of planning standards, securing of state land from further encroachment, infrastructure provision as well as provision and improvement of services.

An example of proposed solutions is the establishment of service campuses on the few existing empty plots of land with community involvement in service delivery. If schools, youth and cultural centers can be used intermittently for different purposes from morning to evening, building standards for schools can be reduced and extra-curricular activities can take place in other facilities. This allows to provide more student places on less land with de facto more space to be used by students. Proposed mechanisms of community participation in the management of services are important to ensure maximum use and efficacy. Equally important is the proposed creation of revenues for some services and their professional, self-sustaining management on the local level, e.g. for computer centers or a community cinema, since experience shows that if services have always to wait for allocations from central budgets, activities tend to break down due to lack of funds for maintenance. Revenues can also be used to finance additional services which cannot be provided on a purely voluntary basis.

The MN project follows a bottom-up, process-oriented approach and has enjoyed remarkable flexibility to plan its interventions and the allocation of resources gradually, allowing for high levels of community participation. The community has contributed three main principles to the project's approach and strategies: the necessity to resettle families whose houses have to be demolished due to cliff dangers or infrastructure works on-site, in a new housing project which is currently being built in an extension area adjacent to Manshiet Nasser. This is contrary to previous practice of the governorate that used to resettle families in public housing projects at the periphery of the city. By being resettled on-site, the affected families can retain their jobs and social relations which is particularly crucial for the poor who cannot afford transportation from remote areas and who depend heavily on social solidarity networks. Another concern of the community is the combination of physical upgrading measures with socio-economic development interventions since building a school or a health center does not yet solve problems related to the quality of services. Finally, community members have insisted on being involved in every step of socio-economic development interventions and not only in the execution of more or less ready-made programs designed by experts or professional NGOs.

Community development is the area which allows for the most direct and intensive participation of community members and has thus been conceptualized as the main channel for empowerment. However, as in many informal areas, community representation and organization are very weak in Manshiet Nasser. Although a large number of community development associations (CDAs) are found in the area, they did not prove to be very dynamic. Except for two CDAs, membership is restricted to residents coming from the same Upper Egyptian areas of origin as the founders, women are excluded altogether and youth are de facto excluded from any decision-making. Activities are very limited and traditional and so are ambitions.

Therefore, the project has worked intensively with informal community groups of youth, women and young professionals who proved to be much more active and ambitious. Many of them are connected to schools, youth and cultural centers, literacy classes and kindergartens. The project responds directly to their ideas. It provides technical assistance, co-finance and training to implement small-scale upgrading and socio-economic development activities, build up capacities and stimulate collective action and organizational processes. A considerable part of training is provided as on-the-job training, often carried out by local residents who have the required skills and capacities. This proved to be crucial to increase the community's sense of capability and self-reliance.

Activities and actions

As already mentioned, both KfW and GTZ as the two arms of financial and technical German development cooperation are involved in Manshiet Nasser. The bulk of the KfW financial contribution is spent on providing water and wastewater, the key priority of the community, in the pilot area of Ezbet Bekhit. Considerable additional resources are available due to favorable exchange rate developments. Their allocation is currently being planned according to community priorities to improve access to services. This can imply building stairs to provide easy access to areas where services are located, cliff treatment to allow for the use of empty land under the cliffs, street lighting to increase security for women and children, extending utilities to allow for the re-opening of schools on a site which has been flooded by leaking sewage or building transfer stations to establish a functioning garbage collection system with community involvement under the new, privatized solid waste management scheme of Cairo governorate.

The main tasks of GTZ technical assistance are to support the district and the community in planning and implementation of upgrading and legalization. A detailed plan has been developed for the pilot area of Ezbet Bekhit which is based on the principle of maximum preservation of the existing investments in housing while providing for infrastructure upgrading and minimum requirements of circulation and security from dangers posed by cliffs. The plan has been legally approved and provides a model for further detailed planning. Upon request of the Egyptian counterparts, a Guide Plan has been prepared for the upgrading of all of Manshiet Nasser by a joint team made up of Cairo governorate, the Ministry of Housing, community members and the project team over the period of February through October 2001. The Guide Plan is based on the same principles applied in Ezbet Bekhit and represents the strategic framework for upgrading and development. It proposes an integrated upgrading concept with physical upgrading measures complementing social and economic development interventions. The success of the concept depends largely on coordinated multi-actor contributions and the active participation of the local community which is supposed to play a lead role in the development process.

A GTZ financial contribution is used to build two community centers in Ezbet Bekhit, an area with no community facilities at all. Another relatively small financial contribution has been set up as a Local Initiative Fund (LIF) to co-finance small-scale upgrading measures proposed by the community. The LIF is used as the main instrument to demonstrate innovative solutions to problems related to service delivery as proposed in the Guide Plan as well as for socio-economic development, community capacity-building and the stimulation of organizational processes in the community. 19 local initiatives and four major training programs have been implemented or planned. The majority of the upgrading initiatives are concentrated in an area which hosts most of the existing community services to demonstrate the feasibility of integrating services into a campus with multi-purpose use of facilities, community involvement in the management of services and the creation of locally managed revenues to ensure the sustainability of the services.

Examples of completed or planned initiatives are the construction of an open-air cinema and theatre in the cultural center, the upgrading of sports fields and the establishment of a women's sports area in the youth center, the upgrading of the access street to the service campus, the reconstruction of schools desks and chairs with broken wood by an NGO, the construction of sports and recreational areas in schools, a summer program with awareness-raising, sports and cultural activities schools, youth and cultural centers, a training and action program to improve pre-school education, the upgrading of roofs to be used by local kindergartens which are squeezed into tiny apartments, a business information center to facilitate licensing and access of local businesses to existing credit and business support services as well as access to youth employment opportunities, the establishment of a community computer and technology access center, a training program to establish a community-based rehabilitation scheme for the handicapped, the establishment of a community-based well-child checkup system and a health education and action campaign.

All initiatives and interventions have been planned and executed by community members with technical assistance and training provided by the project. Active community members organized themselves in committees around the individual initiatives. They negotiated contributions from government agencies, NGOs and universities, the community and the local private sector. Community members contribute mainly with labor and efforts, the local private sector provided much of the needed equipment and material at cost or for free. The efforts and achievements exceeded by far the project's initial expectations. However, the process of planning and implementation also involved numerous problems, among others conflicts of interests, lack of conceptual and management capacities, attempts of political hijacking, personal sensitivities, time-consuming approval procedures and promised contributions which did not materialize. Nevertheless, experiences to date show considerable impacts: all external agencies that have been involved in actions have expressed acknowledgement and recognition of the community's abilities and efforts. Government agencies have increased budget allocations and community members have acquired considerable skills, are much more able to act collectively and to develop long-term visions and strategies. The demonstrative effect of achievements proved to be very important in the ongoing dialogue with governmental agencies to obtain approvals for modified construction standards for schools as well as the proposed new management models for services.

Another important area of action with regard to strategies of poverty alleviation and inclusion is the development of instruments that can increase budget allocations to informal areas and simultaneously rationalize state investments. Without any redistribution of public funds in favor of poor areas as well as an increase in cost efficiency and cost effectiveness, the dynamics of marginalization and exclusion are likely to deepen and no meaningful extent of poverty alleviation can be achieved. Based on the strategic planning framework of the Guide Plan as well as previous needs assessments, a first exercise in participatory budgeting has recently been carried out for the coming fiscal year within the current five-year plan of central government. The exercise was supported with technical assistance by the MN project team and the PAU on behalf of the Ministry of Planning which prepares State investment plans and approves budget requests.

The requested budget has been prepared by representatives of all sector departments as well as the community and the local private sector. For the first time, investments have been planned as complementary measures. The budget includes also proposals for contributions of the community, the private sector, as well as other donors and development agencies. Physical investments are to be complemented by "soft" development interventions. If approved, it will be the first time in Egypt that a district has an own budget and does not depend on piecemeal allocations for individual sectoral investments. This allows for more cost efficiency and efficacy as well as for synergy effects through integrated approaches and multi-actor coordination.

Experiences and potentials

Strategies of inclusion have been successfully incorporated in the project's approaches and actions in a number of ways: The preparation of detailed legal plans for upgrading based on the principle of preserving existing housing investments has led to the recognition of the area and prepared the ground for legalization. On-site resettlement prevents further social marginalization. Community involvement in guiding the ongoing informal development makes it possible to secure land for the future provision of utilities and social infrastructure. Community participation in all planning activities, small-scale upgrading projects and socio-economic development interventions has empowered the community and led to increased recognition of their efforts and capacities, not only by governmental actors but also by professional NGOs and development agencies such as the Social Fund and the National Council for Childhood and Motherhood. Women have made outstanding efforts in all community initiatives and their important role is meanwhile widely recognized in the community. Women were also instrumental to include poor community members in activities, e.g. by inviting active but illiterate individuals to meetings and activities, explaining written material with remarkable patience.

The bottom-up, process-oriented approach to community development proved to be crucial for strategies of inclusion since it provides non-discriminatory channels for engagement and gradual building up of capacities. It gives also utmost flexibility to compensate for time constraints, avoid social restrictions and stimulate solidarity and cooperation. The involvement of informal community groups and local professionals such as teachers, service employees and businesspersons proved to be very successful. Many of them belong to the first generation of poor families who enjoyed a medium or higher education. They are well aware of the sacrifices of their families and feel responsible to invest their capacities for the development of their community. Many are very concerned with providing equal opportunities to other community members and their ambitions extend well beyond the areas of their professional specialization. For many youth and women, development activities represent an opportunity to escape social constraints and get access to new experiences and contacts.

Although considerable further inputs are still needed, there is a potential to build up capacities which can sustain an ongoing development process without dependency on intermediaries to initiate action. However, one has to bear in mind that community involvement in management, service delivery and socio-economic development activities requires professional skills and considerable efforts which cannot be provided on a purely voluntary basis. On the other hand, there are considerable returns for society at large. With the wealth of their experience, community groups and associations in Manshiet Nasser could also play an important role in mobilization and capacity-building for communities in other similar areas. Combining technical skills with a profound understanding of the dynamics and needs of poor communities, they could be valuable partners for development agencies and professional NGOs.

Challenges and risks

The bottom-up, process oriented approaches in all activities of the project did succeed in breaking the ground for new and more realistic strategies and actions to solve the most pressing problems in informal settlements. However, most areas of action are far from being consolidated. The proposed strategies and solutions need more capacities as well as better organization, coordination and cooperation of all stakeholders. As in all development projects, the main challenges are sustainability and replicability. With capacities in local administration being extremely low, corruption rampant and the salaries of government employees among the lowest in the world, it is difficult to conceive how the complex process of integrated upgrading and development can be managed without consultants or without intensive training and incentives for government employees.

Either option requires additional budget allocations which will not easily be provided in times of continuing deterioration of the national economy. Moreover, recent international and regional developments are likely to reinforce the government's primary concern with stability with independent civil society efforts being primarily perceived as potential security risks. These factors are quite unfavorable for decentralization and community empowerment. They are also likely to reinforce structural bottlenecks in decision-making processes, i.e. tendencies of senior employees on all levels of the administration to retain as many competencies as possible without daring to take any decision. This leads to many paradoxes related to the fact that even simple decisions are often passed on and up to the ministerial level, thus discouraging experiment and innovation.

There are also constraints on the side of donors, development agencies and professional NGOs which depend almost exclusively on donor funds. Bottom-up community development is a motivational concept which needs considerable initial inputs of technical assistance and training. The expected positive long-term impacts on efficacy, sustainability, empowerment and social inclusion are often difficult to measure within the relatively short time spans of donor projects. It is much easier to implement more or less ready-made programs which demonstrate quick outputs. However, this approach creates also new dependencies and once donor funding stops and the development agency or the NGOs pull out, local community organizations are in most cases not able to sustain achievements and initiate new activities.

One major risk of urban development projects is that upgrading and legalization increase the value of land and may lead to future speculation which can again spur a dynamic of exclusion of the poor. However, it is expected that in Manshiet Nasser speculation will not happen on a wide scale. Despite its central location, it will never become too attractive an area due to its extremely high densities and difficult topography. It is also striking that many inhabitants who managed to become wealthy as contractors or through trade activities in the large trade and tourist areas El Muski and Khan El Khalili did not move out of Manshiet Nasser since they appreciate the social environment with relatives and kin living in close proximity. Most of them invested in their buildings, in the education of their children and in economic projects. The physical and social fabric may thus be a serious constraint to outside speculators.

Outlook and future concepts

The third and last project phase, which starts in January 2004, will entail a number of changes. KfW will provide additional funds for investments and German development cooperation will shift its engagement to three new focal areas: water, environment, private sector development and employment. Several activities and cooperation efforts have already been launched in the new focal areas. Currently, cooperation is being established with the Mubarak-Kohl Initiative to develop appropriate dual vocational training schemes targeted at the informal sector. First contacts have been made with the private Contractor in charge of garbage collection for Cairo West which includes Manshiet Nasser. The objective is to develop effective cooperation schemes between the community, the Zabaleen garbage collectors and the private Contractor. Finally, small initiatives have started to activate a local business association and to experiment with activities to support local businesses and promote youth employment.

The next phase will be a consolidation phase. It will see more emphasis on developing standard instruments out of existing experiences which can be used for replication. Structured and on-the-job training of the relevant agencies on district, governorate and ministerial levels will support the operationalization of these instruments. The project in Manshiet Nasser will continue to be relevant for demonstration in order to convince government agencies of the feasibility and benefits of the proposed mechanisms and solutions. More emphasis will be put on engaging other external actors. Experiences with participatory approaches will be applied to activities in the new focal areas. It is expected that more tasks can be outsourced as packages to NGOs, other development agencies and consultants. The project team will concentrate its inputs on facilitation, on-the-job training and further concept development to ensure integrated approaches and maximum stakeholder participation and to facilitate synergy effects.

Conclusion

Urban poverty and the manifold and interrelated problems of informal areas will continue to represent a major challenge for Egypt's development and stability. Although the short-living development discourse continuously produces new labels and shifts in attention, participatory urban development remains a major task with particular relevance for strategies of inclusion and poverty alleviation. As part of the Participatory Urban Management Program, the project in Manshiet Nasser has already created valuable experience in this respect. Much of this experience is relevant to poor informal areas in general and can contribute to design more effective policies and strategies of poverty alleviation and poverty reduction. The project addresses poverty and exclusion mainly through innovative solutions to problems related to service delivery, tenure security and empowerment strategies. Empowerment is by definition an element of inclusion. It has personal, relational and collective dimensions. Personal empowerment entails the development of a sense of self-confidence and capacity, i.e. power through greater confidence in one's ability to successfully undertake some form of action. Relational empowerment means to develop abilities to negotiate and shape the nature of relationships i.e. power to influence decisions and access resources. Collective empowerment requires that individuals work together to achieve more structural impacts, i.e. power to organize and achieve structural change.

The Manshiet Nasser project has conceptualized all community-based activities to serve two objectives simultaneously: the demonstration of innovative solutions as proposed in the Guide Plan as well as capacity-building and the promotion of collective action and organizational processes. It was thus able to capture untapped potentials for community participation, empowerment and social inclusion. Moreover, it succeeded to establish linkages and interactions with development agencies and representatives of local and national government through joint activities with the Participatory Urban Management Program.

The long-term impacts of this approach cannot be easily defined. Some elements of empowerment and inclusion, such as women's participation in project activities, are relatively easy to measure with quantitative and qualitative instruments of participatory process monitoring. However, social change and poverty alleviation will only unfold as long-term impacts. They are not easily quantifiable within the relatively short time spans of donor projects. Therefore, the question remains: do outcomes and impacts justify the comparatively high inputs required if development projects choose to follow bottom-up and process-oriented approaches? The challenge is to disseminate experiences by creating linkages among poor communities so that inputs do not have to be made with the same intensity in every new area. We may also question how we define impacts. Are we satisfied if x community members pay for services or participate in an awareness campaign or do we aim at building up capacities which enable community members to initiate action without creating new dependencies? And finally, we may also ask if impact is only achieved by visible structures and action or if it also entails changes in individuals' ambitions and lives, thus carrying on more structural processes at a deeper level of social change.

References

Assaad, Ragui/Rouchdy, Malak (1999), Poverty and Poverty Alleviation Strategies in Egypt, Cairo Papers in Social Science, Cairo, Vol. 22 (1).

Central Agency for Public Mobilization and Statistics (1996), 1996 Population Census.

Datt, Gaurav/Jolliffe, Dean/Sharma, Manohar (1997), A Profile of Poverty in Egypt: 1997, International Food Policy Research Institute, Cairo.

Denis, Eric (1999), Le Caire à l'orée du XXIe siècle: Une métropole stabilisée dans un contexte de déploiement de la croissance urbaine, in Lettre d'information de l'Observatoire Urbain du Caire Contemporain n. 48, CEDEJ, Cairo.

Denis, Eric/Bayat, Asef (1999), Urban Egypt: Towards a Post-Urbanization Era?, in Cairo Papers in Social Science, Cairo, Vol, 21 (4), p. 8-27.

El Baradei, M. (1995), Egyptian Children's Affordability to Education, UNICEF, Cairo.

El Laithy, Heba/Osman, M.O. (1996), Profile and Trend of Poverty and Economic Growth, Institute of National Planning, Cairo.

Fergany, Nader (1995), Summary of Research: Enrolment in Primary Education and Acquainting Basic Skills in Reading, Writing and Mathematics, UNICEF and al-Mishkat Center, Cairo.

Institute of National Planning (1998), Egypt Human Development Report 1997/98, Cairo.

Latouche, Serge (1993), In the Wake of the Affluent Society, An Exploration of Post-Development, London.

Ministry of Social Affairs (Cairo Directorate) (1998), Social Household Survey in Manshiet Nasser, Unpublished report in Arabic, Cairo.

Nassar, Heba (1999), Survey on Socio Economic Conditions of Work in Greater Cairo, Preliminary Report, Social Research Center, American University in Cairo, Cairo.

National Center for Social and Criminological Research (1998), Social Issues of the Population of Manshiet Nasser, In Arabic, Cairo.

Sims, David (2000), Residential Informality in Greater Cairo: Typologies, Representative Areas, Quantification, Valuation and Causal Factors, Institute for Liberty and Democracy, Lima, and Egyptian Center for Economic Studies, Unpublished, Cairo.

Singermann, Diane (1997), Avenues of Participation, Cairo.

Singermann, Diane/Hoodfar, Homa (1999), Between Marriage and the Market: Intimate Politics and Survival in Cairo, Cairo.

Zibani, Nadia (1994), Le travail des enfants en Égypte et ses rapports avec la scolarisation: esquisse d'évolution, Égypte-Monde Arabe.

Slum Upgradation in India - Steps Towards Inclusion

Neelima Risbud

Introduction

The growth of slums and squatter settlements in Indian cities is closely linked with the patterns of urbanization, migration and urban growth. The available estimates indicate rapid growth of slums on the whole, although growth rates and proportions of slum populations vary across different states and cities. Clearance strategies originally were initiated for the inner-city blighted areas in the mid-fifties and continued their focus on old parts of cities until the late sixties. Later, similar strategies were applied to squatter settlements. Acceptance of the Slum Improvement concept has grown since 1970's. The issue of tenure regularization was taken up much later in the 1980's, but there was never a common approach to upgradation or regularization of squatter settlements in India. Since the execution of slum improvement projects has been the responsibility of state and local governments, there has been wide variation between states and cities in terms of the tenure and improvement packages, investments, coverage, and sustenance of the programs.

Overview of urbanization and its impact on urban centers

Urbanization in India in the last few decades is marked by a continuous growth of the urban population with high urban growth rates, in comparison to rural population growth rates. Urban population growth has been more noticeable in the last four decades. In the three and a half decades since 1961, the urban population has increased three times. The decennial growth rate of the urban population has reduced from 46.14% in 1971-1981 to 36.4% in 1981-1991 and to 31.2% in 2001. According to provisional results of the Census of India, the population of India has exceeded one billion with 5,161 urban centers. The percentage of urban population to total population, however, is still low and constitutes 27.8% in 2001, whereas in the 1991 census it was 25.7%. Population density has increased from 117 persons per sq. km. in 1951 to 324 persons per sq. km.

in 2001. Apart from reduced growth rate, a point of equal concern is the decline in rural-urban migration. As much as 59.98% of urban growth between 1981-1991 was due to natural increase; rural urban migration accounted only for about 2262% and reclassification for about 17.4%. The rural urban migration assumes significance in light of the fact that the rural urban migration rate seems to affect the percentage of slum population across cities.[1] Researchers give various explanations like high retention capacity of rural areas, limited absorptive capacity of cities with their strained infrastructure, reduction in the top-heavy structure of urbanization, and balanced urban development for this phenomenon of reduced migration.[2]

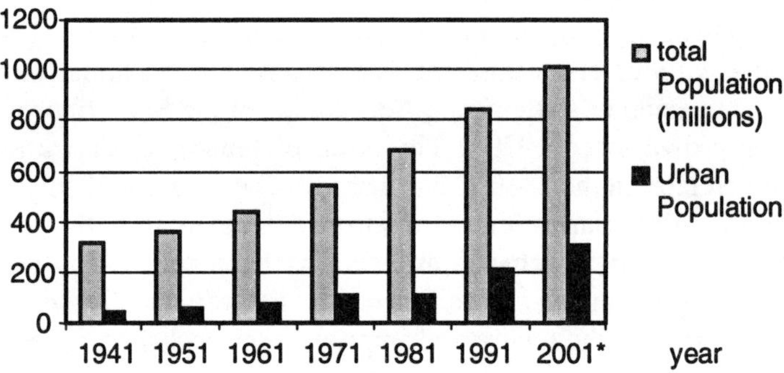

Figure 1: Trends of urban population growth in India

Urbanization levels in different states are found to be significantly related to their per capita incomes and shares of incomes generated in secondary and territory sectors and to economic growth rate.[3] In 2001, Tamilnadu, with 43.9% urbanization, is the most urbanized state, followed by Maharashtra with 42.4%, whereas the proportion of urban population is lowest (10.5%) in Bihar.[3] The urban growth has largely been accommo-

[1] Mitra, Arup (1993).

[2] Kundu (1993). Bose (1993). Racine (1996). Krishan/Singh (1996).

[3] Krishan/Singh (1996).

dated in bigger cities. Urban agglomerations and cities with populations of more than one million have increased from twenty-two in 1991 to thirty-five (including six mega cities) in 2001 with a share of 37.8% of urban population of the country. With a population of 16.4 million, Greater Mumbai has emerged as India's largest city.

Apart from contributing to large population concentrations, urbanization seems to act as a catalytic agent of economic growth. Informal employment is a major component of the urban economy in all the major sectors and increased over the period from 1981-1991, constituting more than 50% of urban employment. The large cities now form the hubs of the economic engine in terms of their contribution to the "New Economic policy" and to the operation of the manufacturing and financial sectors in a globalising economy. The impact of urban concentration has been briefly described in the India National Report for Habitat II (1996). Urban densities in general have increased from 2,998 persons/sq. km. in 1981 to 3,462 persons/sq. km. in 1991. This densification has led to drastic reduction of living space for most of the population.

Urban development and housing delivery for the poor

In the Indian federal framework, housing and urban development are encompassed by the state governments. Although local agencies formulate schemes, financial assistance and guidance are provided by the center, and the state government essentially decides the urban development strategy to be adopted. Liberalization of the economy and empowerment of local bodies through decentralization under the 74th Constitutional Amendment Act (1992) are likely to have far reaching impacts on urban development and housing of the poor. According to these amendments, urban planning, land use planning, provision of civic infrastructure, slum improvement, and urban poverty alleviation are all to be part of the local body's functional assignment. However, the Revenue Department of the State Government is responsible for management of urban and rural land as per the Land Revenue Code including acquisition and recording transactions.

A number of states enacted town-planning laws for preparation of the Master Plan for Cities for planned growth of urban centres. So far, about 900 Master Plans/Development Plans have been prepared under the State Town Planning Acts, Town Improvement Trust Acts, City Development Acts and other related acts. Implementation of the Master Plan is generally through city development authorities, urban local bodies, line departments at the local level, and other para-statal and specific-purpose agencies.

Most master plans were land-use plans with high space standards without any links to the state's investment planning. The effect of these high minimum standards was that the poor were driven to unauthorized and illegal/unauthorized housing due to poor affordability. [4]

Government interventions to improve housing conditions of the urban poor and especially squatters somehow remained independent of the Master Plans and still today are not fully recognized or integrated into the city development framework.

It was only after independence that government agencies started providing housing for the general public. Housing has been receiving low priority in terms of budget allocations in national Plans. Perhaps this is due to the fact that housing was often seen as a social welfare and not as a development activity.[5] However, concern for the housing needs of the urban poor can be seen throughout the national five-year plans. These are reflected as social housing schemes with different parameters but not as part of an urban development strategy. Direct intervention by the government through land acquisition has been the main tool to assemble land for the poor in the past in most cities. This option is becoming limited due to the increasing cost of compensation, to the short period within which compensation is to be paid, to the poor financial condition of housing agencies, and to the growing resistance to compulsory acquisition. Formal housing supply for the poor is also constrained by low budgetary supports to housing agencies, high cost of borrowings, and operational difficulties in identifying the poor. The urban poor's access to secure land tenure and institutional finance has also been negligible. This has resulted in the rapid growth of informal housing in the form of squatter settlements in all the cities. In a planned city like Delhi, 45% of the urban population lives on 20% of land in informal housing.[6] With reduced direct intervention of the State and with a visible gradual shift towards market-driven housing supply in recent years, the problem of accessing land for housing the urban poor is worsening.

On the other hand, sprawling residential dormitories and suburbs are being developed for middle and high income groups and for foreign investors around metropolitan and big cities, in which they find comfortable and efficient places to operate. They need luxury accommodations, and high specification work places and other service institutions. In response, city

---

4 Government of India, Planning Commission (1983).

5 Slingsby (1989).

6 Government of India, Ministry of Urban Affairs and Employment (1996).

services are improving at selected locations. As prime locations are preferred, classical urban renewal is gaining further momentum. Thus, the entry of foreign capital and professionals in real estate is making an impact on the physical form of cities. The state of living condition between the rich and the poor had polarized. The immense insecurity of perpetually belonging to the informal sector has forced these sections to rely on ethnic, caste or religious ties. They are forced to seek housing on land where real estate interests are minimal.[7]

The NIUA study (1997) indicates that although there has been significant improvement with regard to the availability of basic infrastructure in urban areas, the situation is still grim. There are severe deficiencies in the quantity, quality and regularity of available water.[8] There is a wide variation in the access to safe drinking water across the states and cities. Nearly 46% of urban households have water-sealed toilets, but only 28% of households are connected to public sewerage systems.[9]

Poor maintenance, poor recoveries, high subsidies, and inefficient management further hamper the delivery of basic services. Many settlements of urban poor are not eligible even for this, as they are not "declared slums." Kundu fears that, given the declining availability of government funds and considering that the private sector is unlikely to find this sector financially lucrative, the deterioration of the water supply situation in low-income settlements is eminent. The slums and particularly the informal settlements are the hardest hit, as they do not have any legitimate access to basic services. Deterioration of the availability of basic services as well as the polarization of living conditions between the rich and the poor have both taken place, which is also reflected in spatial segregation.

Urban poverty

The Planning Commission of the government of India decides annually on the poverty line for urban areas in the country. For this task, economic indicators are derived from the minimum income needed to ensure an intake of 2,100 calories. Poverty at the national level is estimated as the weighted average of the state poverty levels. According to official estimates, the level of urban poverty, expressed as a percentage of people living below the poverty line, has declined from 55% in 1973-1974 to 38%

---

7 Mahadeviya (1995).

8 Mehta (1996).

9 Mehta (1996).

in 1993-1994 and 23.6% in 1999-2000 with 67.1 million urban poor.[10] The percentage of urban population below the poverty line varies significantly, however, amongst various states (42.83% in Orissa and 4.63% in Himachal Pradesh). According to the Tenth Five Year plan's estimates for 2007, the percentage of urban poor is expected to decline to 15.1 %.

The National Commission on Urbanization (1988) stressed that poverty can not be characterized adequately in terms of income, expenditure or consumption pattern alone. Rather, it should include environment, access to services and social and psychological supports. It further noted that some of the visible forms in which urban poverty manifested itself were the "proliferation of slums and bustees, fast growth of informal sector, high rate of educational deprivation, and health contingencies."

Defining and assessing slums in various states and cities

Most cities refer to areas with poor living conditions as "slums" and do not distinguish settlements on the basis of illegality of tenure or poverty. As such, under the broad definition of "slum" as defined in the Slum Acts of various state governments, apparently physical substandard areas with varying tenure patterns are included. An area can be designated "slum" under the Slum Act when the competent authority is convinced that the area is a source of danger to health safety and convenience, or when buildings are found to be unfit for human habitation due to dilapidation, overcrowding or lack of ventilation, light or sanitation facilities. Designated slum areas include (i) freehold land (inner city blighted areas, urban villages), (ii) encroachments on public/private land (squatters) (iii) illegal land-subdivisions/unauthorized colonies (where land ownership may be legal or quasi legal but land subdivision is illegal), (iv) government/private leasehold land (resettlement colonies). Besides these, pavement dwellers, although small in percentage, are found in large mega-cities; however, not all such settlements are designated as slums. Squatters form the major and most rapidly growing component of slums.

The database is very weak and the authenticity of available estimates on slums is debatable because of the absence of any standard or uniform definition of slum between states and cities, which inevitably leads to the exclusion of many substandard settlements. Moreover, the estimates are not based on any empirical survey but on the data reported by various state governments and local bodies. Systematic assessment of slum populations

[10] Government of India, Planning Commission Tenth Five Year Plan (2002-2007)

at the national level began in the mid-seventies. According to NBO estimates in 1981, about 29.8 million, i.e. 18.75% of India's urban population, stayed in slums.

There are several inadequacies in data regarding the magnitude of slums, as census of slums were not regularly conducted. The estimates are also low because they include only declared slums, not those outside corporation boundaries. For the first time ever, the 2001 census has enumerated the urban population living in recognized slums or habitations meeting the identified criteria in towns with populations greater than 50,000. The population living in urban slums according to 2001 census was 40.6 million, which is 23% of 178.4 million living in 607 towns that reported having slums. The distribution of slum population estimates in different states varies considerably, Maharashtra having the highest slum population (10.64 million) of sixty-two towns.[11]

The slum population tends to concentrate in large cities. According to 2001 census, Mumbai has 5.8 million (49%), Delhi 1.9 million, Kolkata 1.5 million (33%), Chennai 1.1 million, (26%) and Banglore 0.3 million (8%) living in slums. All other cities have lesser percentages with the exception of cities like Nagpur, Patna and Ludhiana which had urban populations of 1.66 million, 1.09 million and 1.04 million in 1991, with the slum percentages at 31.9%, 63.5%, and 35.4%, respectively.

The environmental condition of slums is poor and deteriorating quickly due to the increasing pressure of population and the acute deficiency of sanitation and solid waste disposal facilities. Slum improvement programs and the suspension of major clearance operations in most cities over the last two decades have bolstered the perception of tenure security, leading to an improvement of the structural condition of dwellings in informal settlements. However, with the new economic policy involving deregulation and greater participation of the private sector, it is feared that in the future, the informal sector is likely to face a greater threat of eviction due to growing commercial interests in land on behalf of both the public and private sectors.

---

[11] Census (2001).

Overview of improvement and regularization policies for slums/squatter settlements

Initial policies towards slums in the 1960's were policies of slum clearance. Over the last four decades, policies towards squatters have shifted dramatically from the "clearance" and "improvement" approach to one favoring "regularization of tenure." The policy of upgrading has found favor with politicians in the last two decades due to the growing recognition of the political leverage that the urban poor enjoy as "Vote Banks," but the tenure issue, being more complex, has not received the same attention. The role of the central government is limited to allocating funding budgets, sponsoring improvements, promoting poverty alleviation schemes, and issuing guidelines for the schemes' implementation. These schemes are implemented by local governments, as state governments only oversee and disburse funds.

Bilateral and international aid agencies have stressed tenure regularization and its integration with improvement strategies in the context of time bound, targeted projects. Slums were improved in a few Indian cities through World Bank funding in the 1980's and DFID in the 1990's. Initiatives for regularization varied across different states and points of time as they had different objectives and met with varying degrees of success. As Spodek observed,

> *Squatter settlements follow different patterns from city to city and no unified government policy for them has evolved. Everywhere erratic, conflicting government policies exist, lacking clear sense of action. Unable to commit clearly to either policy – neither clearly forbidding squatter settlement and driving them out on one hand, nor facilitating their use of plot on the other. Its desire to provide at least a minimum level of necessities gets constrained by the knowledge of illegality of the settlement.*[12]

Unfortunately there has been little institutional learning from past experiences.

Tenure regularization for squatters in general has been undertaken as a welfare measure.[13] Most tenure regularization has been limited to state government-owned or municipal lands. States and cities have adopted varying strategies for granting *in-situ* tenure rights, but these rarely have been integrated into the city planning regulations. Slum improvement and

---

[12] Spodek (1983).

[13] Bhatnagar (1996).

tenure regularization have broadly been done through the following channels:

1) Central Government Policies for Slum Improvement and Poverty Alleviation.
2) Slum Improvement in selected cities through international and bilateral aid.
3) Slum Improvement/Tenure Regularization of Squatters through State Legislation
4) Slum Improvement & Tenure regularization through State Government Programs
5) Slum Improvement/Redevelopment projects with private sector participation.

Central government policies for slum improvement and poverty alleviation.

Clearance and resettlement of squatters

Although squatting on public and private land began to be noticed in cities like Mumbai, Delhi, Kolkata, and Chennai in the fifties, specific policy towards squatters was initiated in Delhi in 1950 for the eviction of squatters from public lands and for city beautification and the granting of tenure at the site of relocation. The scheme known as the Jhuggi Jhompri Removal Scheme (JJR) was formulated by the central government and included resettlement on flats/plots. With this began an era of eviction and resettlement of squatters in cities that continued for about a decade and a half, during which more than one million people were resettled on the periphery. The approach of eviction brought sharp reactions, primarily on "humanitarian grounds" for hardships of relocated families. The scheme neither conformed to the master plan in terms of land use, zoning regulation, plot sizes, and building bylaws, nor to the municipal regulations for water supply and sewage.[14] Delhi was a special case as the locus of the central government: under its jurisdiction the city experienced both the highest level of coercion and the highest level of funding in carrying

---

[14] Risbud (1989).

through its policies.[15] Eviction and relocation were given high political priority during 1975-1976. Similar relocation policies were taken up in other cities despite protests from slum dwellers. No unified governmental policy towards squatters existed.

The resettlement approach has undergone major changes and is now generally limited to settlements affected by major public projects or settlements on hazardous sites. In Delhi at present, 70,000 families are located on lands where priority public projects are to be taken up; 30,000 families are located on vulnerable/dangerous areas involving human safety; and 50,000 families are located on commercial sites, all of which are proposed for relocation. The Municipal Corporation has presented a comprehensive plan to the Supreme Court with targets of relocation of 30,000 slum dwellers every year, granting each family fifteen sq. m. of constructed space. Similarly, in Mumbai resettlement and rehabilitation (R&R) of 30,000 families affected by the World Bank funded Mumbai Urban Transport Project is proposed.

Environmental improvement of urban slums

Kolkata was the first major city to improve existing slums although, at the time, it was viewed as temporary stopgap. "Bustee Improvement" was seen as a political necessity and as a means of pacification: by providing facilities to these "breeding grounds of lawlessness," it tried to prevent the politically conscious West Bengal Urbanites from revolting against their poor living conditions.[16] Based on the Kolkata initiative, the scheme of environmental improvement of slums was formulated in 1972 as a result of the recognition that the policy of clearance and rehabilitation of slum dwellers had not been successful in the face of the growing problems. Widespread resentment from the people against large-scale demolition, inability of the government to increase substantially its investment in the housing sector, and the fast deterioration of environmental conditions in squatter areas led to the change in policy from clearance to improvement.

Financed by central grants, the scheme was extended to all cities in 1978 as part of the Minimum Needs Program.[17] Amenities to be provided under the scheme were community taps, community latrines, storm water drains, paving of lanes, and streetlights. These improvements were per-

---

[15] Spodek (1983).

[16] Borst (1990).

[17] Government of India, Planning Commission (1983).

ceived as temporary and minimum for slums not earmarked for clearance in the next ten years, thus lacking any long-term approach. Improvements were standardized with a limit on per capita ceiling costs. The task force set by the Planning Commission reviewed the scheme and identified several deficiencies in the implementation of the scheme as given below.

Lack of adequate administrative arrangements at the state or local level; inadequate budgets; absence of citywide data and projects; problems of maintaining improvements; and problems of coordination with concerned agencies like water supply, electricity departments, etc. were some of the common problems. Improvements were not based on felt needs and priorities but were instead standardized. The scheme lacked community participation and financial contributions by beneficiaries. Improvements were not linked to the security of tenure and shelter improvement. The progress of the scheme has been slow, firstly, because the new policy involved much more than engineering skill and, secondly, because the design skill for which professionals in the housing agencies were trained led to their unwillingness to get involved in activities which were considered lower than their status.[18] Nonetheless, 51% of urban slums have been improved under this scheme. Improvements by the government have given "perceived security of tenure" to slum dwellers and have encouraged their investment in shelter consolidation.

Housing policy initiatives

The Planning Commission (Government of India) set up a task force in 1983. It reviewed the entire range of policies and programs in the urban development sector, including those related to the shelter of urban poor and squatter settlements. It reviewed the government's efforts and identified several gaps and deficiencies in prevailing policies, approaches, legal provisions, institutional structures, and funding mechanisms. Slums and squatter settlements were recognized as products of poverty and social injustice; slum improvement instead of slum clearance was emphasized by firmly linking an improvement program with security of tenure. Social development programs and house improvement loans with certain cost recovery were introduced. Involvement of beneficiaries in shelter projects was stressed. It clearly stated that the poor performance of land policies had particularly affected the poor who were forced to illegally squat. It was noted that a drastic change in the orientation of public agencies from builder to land developer was necessary and further mentioned that in-

---

18 Slingsby (1989).

volvement of non-governmental organizations could help to achieve this change.

Subsequently, in 1988 the Indian government established the National Commission on Urbanization for comprehensive review of prevailing urban situation and policies. The commission recommended a bold, intensive and coordinated package for the urban poor relating to income and employment, basic services, shelter, public distribution, social security and the NGO sector. It recognized slums, squatter colonies and unauthorized colonies as part of the people's efforts to provide shelter for themselves and recommended regularization rather than removal. It noted with concern that none of the master plans drawn up for cities singled out the urban poor as the target group, nor did they respond to their needs. On the contrary, the plans worked against the poor. Site and services supply as an approach to improving supply of affordable land and slum improvement as a way of conserving existing shelter were once again advocated as major instruments of housing policy. Slum improvement aiming coverage widened to include slums on private lands, greater speed of implementation, improved quality in planning and implementation, increased resource allocation, and appropriate institutional structure was recommended while stressing the need for regularizing existing slums by providing secure tenure to occupants to eliminate fear of eviction. However, it cautioned against an "unqualified policy of tenure regularization in the long run, as it could provide an incentive for more encroachments and become a convenient tool in the hands of the professional colonisers (slum lords) to exploit the poor and reward the law breakers."[19] It was feared that haphazard and uncontrolled growth of cities could be a threat to the efficient functioning of cities and to the health of its residents.[20] The concerns for squatter settlements and urban poor expressed by the NCU provided the basis for various policy pronouncements and packages of the national government in the 1990's.

With the adoption of the "Global Shelter Strategy for 2000" by the United Nations in 1988, the process of consultation for formulating National Housing Policy began. The policy was finally tabled in parliament in 1992 and approved in 1994. The policy was based on the principle of an "Enabling Approach of State." It marked a significant shift by recognizing the importance of secure land tenure in dealing with the informal sector. The National Housing Policy gave a definite direction towards informal settlements by recommending that "central and state governments would

---

19 National Commission on Urbanization (1988).

20 op.cit. p. 224.

take steps to avoid forcible relocation.... encourage in situ upgrading with conferment of occupancy rights wherever feasible." As a follow up of to the National Housing Policy, state-wise action plans have also been prepared, but not much has been done in the area of slum upgradation and tenure regularization.

Inspite of such official acceptance, even where the government owns most of the land and it is possible to grant tenure, tenure policy has not been implemented. The paradox is that, on one hand, the government accepts the importance of granting tenure, but on the other hand is unwilling or unable to implement these at the local level. Governments, for a variety of reasons, avoid granting legal land tenure: firstly, because conditions of land supply greatly differ between different cities, secondly, because the political context and the perceived political benefits of granting tenure regularization at a point of time vary, and, lastly, because the administrative will and institutional mechanism to effect actual implementation of policy differ greatly between cities. Moreover, in many instances, the granting of legal tenure has tempted beneficiaries to sell their plots for windfall gains. This has cautioned the administration that this may escalate the illegal process and eventually may get out of hand.

The National Housing & Habitat Policy of 1998 recommends slum improvement/reconstruction programs through land sharing, release of additional F.A.R. and use of transferable development rights. While the granting of homestead rights to rural landless and SC/St communities is recommended, there is absolutely no mention of regularizing land tenure for squatters in the urban context. The policy, however, stipulates that land/shelter rights provided to the poor/slum dweller would be non- transferable. The Draft National Slum Policy was developed by the Ministry of Urban Affairs and Employment in 1999. The main objective of the slum policy was "to strengthen the legal and policy framework to facilitate the slum development and improvement on a sustainable basis."[21]

The 1990s marked an era of integrated slum improvement with increasing emphasis on poverty alleviation.

Urban Basic Services for the poor (UBSP)

A convergence of various social services with environmental improvement at slum level was first initiated under the Urban Basic Services Scheme (UBS) as a pilot project in 1986. A scheme was taken up with

---

[21] Government of India (1999).

joint funding from the central government, state government and UNICEF in the form of grants for slums in cities selected for implementation. The program focused on towns with a population of 100,000 and above. Apart from focusing on women and children, the scheme aimed at organizing and promoting leadership within slum communities. The emphasis was on a participatory approach more than on the program components.

In 1990, the government revised the scheme as Urban Basic Services for the Poor (UBSP) and integrated it with other urban poverty alleviation programs like Environmental Improvement of Urban Slums (EIUS), Nehru Rojgar Yojna (NRY) and Low Cost Sanitation (LCS). The scheme aimed at coordination and convergence of physical services, income generating supports and social services for urban poor, especially those living in slums, to enhance the reach and effectiveness. The program was to be implemented with the effective participation of organized communities, especially women, in order to install them in roles of decision-making and community management. Field studies show that sometimes UBSP funds were not adequate to meet the expressed needs of water and sanitation[22], and in other cases, UBSP funds remained unspent for lack of proper coordination, monitoring, planned activities, and personnel.[23] It appears that in an effort to deal with too many activities, insufficient funds were thinly spread. Monitoring was not strong, and the required level of sustainable improvement and community organization was not forthcoming. The tenure issue, which could have made a substantial difference in motivating and empowering the community, was not considered. Similarly, linkages of these schemes to city planning proposals are missing.

Low Cost Sanitation (LCS) and liberation of scavengers

The scheme sponsored by the Ministry of Urban Affairs in 1993-1994 was originally meant to liberate scavengers from the demeaning practice of handling human excreta by converting dry latrines into pour flush latrines. It also involved the construction of new latrines. Funding to the state government is channelled through HUDCO, which also monitors the progress. Funding is provided on a sliding loan/grant scale depending on the income of the beneficiaries. Beneficiary contributions vary from 5% to 25%. The performance has been poor in terms of achieving targets. Identification of beneficiaries, lack of tenure, small plot sizes, complexity of the funding mechanism, poor recovery of loans, and lack of awareness and

---

[22] Mehta (1992).

[23] Wishwakarma and Gupta (1994).

training are some of the problems faced by implementing agencies. Further, a major national sanitation program to supply all state capitals and metro cities with 100% sanitation coverage is being conceived and as of 2002 has been launched on a pilot basis in ten metro cities.

National Slum Development Program (NSDP)

Having considered the dismal performance of slum improvement schemes in almost every state, the central government significantly revised the improvement package in 1997 by introducing grants under Special Central Assistance to States for National Slum Development Program. The magnitude of the urban slum population was to be the basis for allocation of funds to states. The scheme attempted to converge schemes implemented by different departments. The components of the package included

1) Physical infrastructure such as water supply, storm water drains, community baths, paving of lanes, sewers, community latrines, street lights, etc.;
2) Construction of community center for community activities;
3) Community primary health care center;
4) Social amenities such as pre-school education, non-formal education, adult education, maternity, etc.

The scheme has a component of shelter upgradation or construction of new houses for EWS. A minimum 10% allocation is to be used for the shelter component. On two points the scheme departs from earlier approaches. Firstly, the states have the flexibility to design situation-specific projects, and, secondly, the funding has a loan component besides subsidy. The scheme is to be implemented by grassroot-level neighbourhood committees and community development societies set up for SJSRY and UBSP. The scheme offers promising possibilities if used; however, lack of a trained staff for the formulation of the project is one of the serious problems in making use of the scheme. Also there is apprehension about the recovery of the loan component. Although shelter improvement forms an essential component, there is no mention of tenure regularization.

Valmiki Ambedkar Malin Basti Awas Yojna

On Independence Day in 2001, the Prime Minister announced the unique scheme of Valmiki Ambedkar Malin Basti Awas Yojna for the urban poor. The scheme is to be implemented on a fifty percent loan and fifty percent subsidy basis. Rs. 20,000 million have been allocated for this project every year. This scheme proposes to provide 400,000 houses for urban poor and slum dwellers. The beneficiaries would be those below poverty line who do not possess houses in urban areas.

Urban poverty alleviation programs

Other important schemes that received priorities in the 1990's focused on the eradication of urban and rural poverty. These programs have been designed to provide the poor with access to various developmental inputs like skills, credit and employment along with access to shelter and basic services. Nehru Rozgar Yojna was one of the first Indian Urban employment programs introduced in 1989 that was target-group oriented. It had three sub-components, namely Scheme for Urban Wage Employment (SUWE), Scheme for Employment through Housing and Shelter Upgradation (SHASU) and Scheme for Urban Micro Enterprise (SUME). For the first time, housing and shelter upgradation was undertaken to generate employment.

Implementation of the scheme has suffered from difficulties of coordination of inadequate follow-up and monitoring, delays caused by complicated procedure, lack of commitment and corruption. There is no unified policy statement to address the convergence effect. The Ninth Plan approach paper has attempted to introduce the convergence of urban development programs at settlement level. These programs are often considered as vote-catching programs and therefore tend to be politically oriented producing marginal results.[24] It provides some degree of relief but no real structural change, as the relation of the poor to the productivity of the urban economy has not been addressed.[25]

The central ministry of urban development was renamed Ministry of Urban Affairs and Employment. In 1997, the ministry launched a rationalized poverty alleviation scheme named Swarna Jayanti Shahari Rozgar Yojna (SJSRY) to mark the fiftieth anniversary of independence, therein replacing the three existing schemes of Nehru Rojgar Yojna (NRY), Urban Basic Services for the Poor (UBSP) and Prime Minister's Integrated Poverty Alleviation Program (PMIUPEP). The new scheme was operative in all towns in India that, according to 1991 census, had populations of 50,000 to 1,000,000. The SJSRY seeks to provide gainful employment to

---

[24] Kruse (1996).

[25] Government of India, Ministry of Urban Affairs and Employment (1998),

the urban poor living below the urban poverty line and the unemployed or underemployed by establishing self employment ventures or by providing wage employment. The scheme was to be funded on a 75:25 basis between the center and state. The scheme was to have two components – i) The Urban Self Employment Program (USEP) and ii) The Urban Wage Employment Program (UWEP). The program aimed at community empowerment by establishing and promoting community organizations like Neighborhood Groups (NHGs), Neighborhood Committes (NHCs) and Community Development Societies (CDSs). The CDSs were to identify viable projects, set up thrift and credit societies and act as a focal point for identification of beneficiaries, providing support, linking up local resource generation with institutional finance, and monitoring of recovery. Non-economic parameters were also to be applied in identifying the urban poor.[26]

Slum improvement projects funded by international and bilateral aid

World Bank funded projects

The Bombay Urban Development Project (BUDP) of granting tenure was taken up as a part of a slum upgrading program funded by the World Bank in 1985. Leasehold tenures were granted to cooperatives of slum dwellers for periods of thirty years. The program was extended to other cities of Maharashtra in a two-pronged attack of regularization of squatters and supply of serviced land to manage the problem of slums. In line with the IDA's philosophy, secure, long-term legal tenure was to be granted along with provision of basic services with recoveries for 100,000 slum households. The price, to be repaid over twenty years, was based on the zonal location of the slum and the plot size and use. Leasehold rights were to be granted to cooperative societies of slum dwellers covering corporation and government land and 10% private land. Individual members of the society were entitled to home improvement loans, which could be advanced against the mortgage of individual leasehold rights. The scheme, however, did not benefit slums on private and central government land. Until 1993, only 22,000 households were covered under the program, after which it seems to have been virtually abandoned.

---

[26] Government of India, Ministry of Urban Affairs and Employment (1997).

Similarly, in another state of Tamilnadu, land tenure was regularized along with improvement inputs under the World Bank-assisted Tamilnadu Urban Development Program. Leasehold tenure was granted and converted to freehold upon receiving the cost of development. The program was implemented for more than a decade and was stopped with the discontinuation of international aid in the 1990's.

DFID-funded projects

Since 1986, UK Overseas Development Administration (DFID) has been one of the main international funding agencies in India involved in urban poverty alleviation through integrated slum improvement projects. Cities identified as project partners were Hyderabad (1989-1996), Visakhapatnam (1988-1996), Vijayawada (1989-1998), Indore, Kolkata, Cuttack and Cochin. The main aim of the program was to integrate the slum communities into economic and social networks, as well as into the physical fabric of the cities. This integration is achieved through a problem-solving approach toward slum improvement and community development with clearly stated objectives: improvement of health of the families living in slums; improvement of education and literacy levels; development of opportunities for employment and income generation; and improvement of housing and environmental conditions. The development of the communities is seen as fundamental to achieving these objectives and to sustaining the program. These programs have not attempted any tenure regularisation while upgrading slums.

In recent DFID urban projects, the focus has shifted to expanding institutional capacity and local bodies' financial management systems to enhance sustainability. In the state government of Andhra Pradesh, an alternative state-wide program has been initiated to improve services in thirty-two class I towns. The project is commencing with 94 million pounds over seven years. The overall purpose of the program is to ensure that the poor in these towns benefit from improved access to more appropriate and sustainable services.[27]

---

[27] Barret (2001).

Slum improvement/ tenure regularization of squatters through state legislation

The social objectives of urban land policy of the Government of India included the following goals: i) to achieve optimum social use of urban land ii) to make land available to in adequate quantity, at the right time for reasonable prices to both public authorities and the individuals iii) to encourage cooperative community effort and bonafide individual builders in the field of land development iv) to prevent concentration of land ownership in few private hands and safeguard specially the interest of poor and underprivileged sections of urban society.[28] As far as access to land for housing is concerned, the urban poor are left in practice with no option for meeting their basic need of shelter but to squat on public or private land. The Constitution confers on individuals the right to property; however, the operation of this provision restricts property rights in public interest. Since land and urban development are state subjects, the role of the national government is advisory and the power to enact laws relating to land is vested within the state governments.

The State Slum Clearance Acts

The first Slum Legislation was enacted in Delhi in 1956. Subsequently, other states followed. The legislation primarily addressed inner-city slums with dilapidated buildings. It also protected poor tenants from eviction by owners. The Slum Clearance and the Improvement Boards were set up, and the scheme of slum clearance envisaged the rehousing of inner city slum families in tenements on subsidized rents and also improvement of the slum areas by amendments made in 1964. The act also encompassed unauthorized hutments (squatters). The definition of "slum" under the act is quite loose, and a liberal application of the law may cover substantial parts of cities as "slums." On the other hand, "declared slums" may not include newer squatter settlements and settlements outside the municipal boundary which in turn may result in an underestimation of slum population. It is for this reason that no firm estimates of the country's for slum population exist.[29]

The act empowered the competent authority to serve notice to the owner and required the owners to execute the improvement work or else

[28] Government of India, Ministry of Health (1964)

[29] Government of India, Planning Commission (1983).

carry out improvement and recover the cost from the owners. It provided for the clearance and redevelopment of structurally dangerous buildings and protection to tenants against eviction. Over the last forty years, the act has been ineffective in improving the Old City, where extensive illegal conversions and rebuilding continue with total disregard to environmental considerations.

The Calcutta Thika Tenancy (Acquisition and Regulation) Act of 1981/1994 provides tenure regularisation to bustee dwellers on private land and incorporates provision against their eviction. Under the Premises Tenancy Act, these bustee dwellers are ensured the rights to water supply and electric connection. In other towns of West Bengal, refugee colonies were given occupation certificates, and later in 1987 the government gave freehold titles to all registered refugees. Services were extended as a part of the Calcutta Urban Development Project (CUDP) in the early seventies, and later DFID funded the Calcutta Slum Improvement Project (CSIP).

The State of Maharashtra provides security against eviction for slum dwellers of designated slums under the Maharashtra Slum Areas Act of 1971, and similar provisions have been provided in slum acts of other states.

Tenure regularization through legislation in Madhya Pradesh

In some states, legislative provisions made operational by political initiatives and administrative orders have been used to grant tenure to squatters. In Madhya Pradesh, land tenure for all the squatters on public land was regularized for cities with populationa greater than 0.1 million through a unique act commonly known as the Patta Act of 1984. Under the act, persons occupying government land of not more than fifty sq. yds. before the cut-off date were given non-transferable leasehold rights of thirty years.[30]

Slum improvement / tenure regularization through state government programs

In a few cities, tenure has been granted as part of a special program of the state government. Through an administrative order of the state government, house sites in Andhra Pradesh were given to landless families

---

[30] Government of Madhya Pradesh,(1984) "*Patta Act of 1984.*"

under the A.P. Land Revenue Code.[31] Those occupying government lands for more than five years are allotted plots up to a maximum of seventy-five sq. m. on freehold basis. Private land hosting designated slums is acquired under the A.P. Slum Improvement (Acquisition of Land) Act. Possession Certificates for tenements are given in cities like Hyderabad. *Pattas* are for residential use and are non-transferable. Andhra Pradesh State Housing Corporation Ltd. also gives loans for house construction. Available land allotments are handled by the Collectorate. The Municipal Corporation, through negotiations, has successfully attempted land sharing with the landowner, where acquisition was not possible. Granting of tenure is accompanied by physical as well as social and economic improvements. Convergence of development programs with participatory approaches has been attempted by local agencies.

The state government of Maharashtra in 2000 launched a scheme for provision of housing called *Lok Awas Yojna* geared toward the urban poor living in squatter settlements designated as "slum" in sixty-one cities of the state. Initially, the plan is proposed to regularise the tenure for settlements on government-owned lands for a nominal price. The lease is to be executed in favor of the female member of the household. Those having lived in slums since January 1, 1995 were considered eligible. The lessee will be required to pay service charges, administrative charges and ground rent. Financial support to back the construction of houses is also envisaged in the form of grants from the NSDP scheme and as loans. The houses are to be constructed with the participation of the beneficiaries under the overall supervision of District Housing Committee, managed by the the District Collector. Building materials are to be made available at reasonable rates by setting up building centers. If the land occupied by slum residents is not required for public purpose, eligible slum dwellers who are occupying lands owned by the state, municipal corporations or other state parastatal agencies, the inhabitants should be rehabilitated at the *in situ* site on the same land with leasehold rights for thirty years. Many other states have taken similar initiatives.

---

[31] Government of Andhra Pradesh (1995).

Slum improvement / redevelopment projects with private sector participation

Slum Redevelopment in Mumbai

The Slum Redevelopment Scheme (SRS) and Slum Rehabilitation Scheme (SRD) were introduced in Mumbai with the involvement of the private sector in the nineties. Private builders, given the additional incentive of extra floor area ratio, are expected to provide built-up tenements of 225 sq. ft. for slum dwellers at the same location and are allowed to sell the surplus floor space in the open market. All slum dwellers included in the 1995 electoral rolls and pavement dwellers were covered by the scheme. The tenements are given free of cost to slum dwellers. For every ten sq. ft. of rehabilitation floor space constructed in Island City, builders were offered a free sale component of 7.5 sq. ft. Incentives were given to construct transit accommodation on vacant public lands. The scheme was proposed to cover 2,335 slum pockets and 902,015 huts. A Slum Rehabilitation Authority was constituted for approving these schemes.

Ahmedabad Pariwartan Program

After implementing the "slum-networking" concept in Indore and Baroda, a similar scheme was considered for Ahmedabad under the Public-Private Partnership Program. The program was launched in 1995 with the partnership of Ahmedabad Municipal Corporation, the corporate private sector (Arvind Mills), and NGOs SAATH and Gujrat Mahila Housing Sewa Trust (MHT). The project aimed at improving the physical infrastructure with individual water supply and sewerage connection along with community mobilization for education and health care and involvement of the community at all stages of program implementation. Cost sharing was on an equitable basis between AMC, the private sector and the slum dwellers, each paying one-third of the capital cost of on-site services. However, the program does not include granting of legal land tenure, but rather only a written assurance by AMC not to evict beneficiaries for the next ten years if they join the scheme. Considering that seventy percent of slums in Ahmedabad are on private land, replicability/coverage and sustainability of this approach is limited.

Other emerging interventions - judicial intervention

Two events in 1980 brought into sharp focus the issue of rights of slum dwellers and the question of forced eviction. The first one is the Mumbai Slum Dweller's Case in the Supreme Court against forced eviction by the Municipal Corporation by Peoples' Union of Civic Liberties (PUCL). In the above case, the Supreme Court upheld that the fundamental constitutional right to life was closely linked with the right to livelihood. It granted stay order upon the eviction of pavement dwellers unless the government could provide an alternative.

Outbreaks of epidemics like the plague of 1994 and dengue in 1996 created major health crises and bought into sharp focus the poor and quickly-deteriorating sanitary conditions of the Indian cities. It was realized that many cities are sitting on "volcanos of epidemics." Indian cities abound with slums which long have been seen as eyesores, but they are moreover health hazards, not only to the slums' unfortunate inhabitants but also to the city as a whole.[32] The crisis created by epidemics invited the intervention of the highest court when the Supreme Court ordered civic agencies in March 1996 to have Delhi cleaned and scavenged every day and directed the union government to make it a greener and cleaner place in which to live. In a misguided attempt to make the capital spotlessly clean, the Supreme Court removed 400,000 squatter huts in Delhi. The court also ordered the appointment of seventeen magistrates to monitor the "Clean Delhi" drive to take positive action against offenders.[33] In another petition, the Delhi high court considered squatters as "trespassers on public land." The high court directed Delhi administration that, pending further orders, alternative plots for rehabilitation should be allotted to eligible squatters only on a license basis with no right to transfer or part with possession. Any transfer of possession would amount to an automatic cancellation of the license without notice.

In a similar instance, a petition was filed in high court by a Cooperative Housing Society of Nagpur alleging that the state government and its officials – as well as the the local bodies – had allowed the public land to be encroached, and that the local authorities had notified such lands as "slum," thereby depriving the petitioners who had been lawfully pursuing their demands for land allotment. The high court noted that, as in Nagpur and other towns, slumlords grabbed public land and disposed of it through hapless victims. The court directed the collector and the local authorities to

[32] Steinberg/Singh (1996).

[33] Times of India, (1996).

remove encroachments on public land vesting in the state and other local bodies. After this, the collector, in a joint operation, took steps to remove encroachments. At this stage, the matter was referred to the Supreme Court, which decided that encroachments be removed from public lands required for public projects.

The judiciary seems to consider squatters a blot on civilized society, as ingrates who want everything for free. Increased incidence of resale in resettlement colonies has further contributed to their loss of sympathy. This has made evictions more possible than ever. In the case of evictions, residents of Mumbai, Baroda and Surat have approached the Human Rights Commission. Different courts have taken varying stances on the issue of slums. In some cases, harsh steps have been ordered, while in others a very humane approach has been advocated.[34] Authorities have expressed helplessness to stop further growth of slums in the city, as this requires policing powers. There have been similar petitions in the high courts and Supreme Court on the issue of the regularization of unauthorized colonies without provision of services and against commercial use of residential properties, illegal encroachments on public land and illegal additions to residential flats. Courts have taken serious views and have ordered local bodies to take punitive action.

Political intervention

The political dimension is emerging as one of the strongest implicit factors affecting slum improvement and regularization and resettlement policies, as slums have been firmly integrated into the electoral politics of the metropolis.[35] Slum dwellers have suffered the most from political manipulations. Before every election, politicians of different hues and affiliations encourage, aid, abet, and assist the creation of slums over fresh lands while doling out generous promises of regularization and extension of civic amenities.[36] In a study of Bhopal, Risbud found that housing benefits are increasingly used as a tool by politicians to make slum dwellers vote in a particular block.[37] Joop De Wit observed for Chennai, "Slums can be viewed as massive and rather easily accessible 'Vote Banks' where slum

---

[34] Takru, Rajiv (1997).

[35] Singh, Gurbir, Das,P.K. (1996).

[36] Venkateswarlu (1997).

[37] Risbud (1987).

dwellers may barter their votes for any improvements."[38] Desai's findings in Mumbai are similar; she noted, "Political patronage is a critical variable in determining the rate of servicing. The basis of strength for slum leaders is the number of voters in their settlement...There exists some extent of positive relationship between number of voters and extent of political patronage."[39] The general complaint in slums is that politicians can be easily approached to get things done before elections, visit slums and make promises, while after elections no one can find them. Describing the passive role that slum communities play, Desai wrotc that many slum dwellers did not know much about policies or show any genuine enthusiasm for participation. A major problem of slum activities is that of continuity.[40] Short-term political objectives and frequent change of government have prevented adoption and implementation of long-term comprehensive policies for squatter settlements in most cities. As Schenk quotes a Councillor in Bangalore, "Slums are not improved for political reasons: poor men have to remain poor and be kept dependent."[41] The presence of the government in the state capital makes decision making quite centralized. The situation is further complicated when the ruling political party at the center, state and local levels are different and cooperation is not forthcoming (e.g. Delhi). There is great competition among politicians to woo the electorate by waving off outstanding recoveries. The question of granting land tenure through legislation is subject to political processes prevalent in the local and state governments.

Interestingly, there is stronger political support for regularising illegal land subdivisions and unauthorised colonies (e.g. Delhi, Rajasthan, Maharashtra, and Karnataka), whereas such support is limited to preventing evictions or getting some improvements for squatter settlements.

Role of the NGOs

The last two decades saw the emergence of NGOs in the shelter sector. NGO interventions on behalf of the poor had taken two main directions. The first stand was strongly leftist and activist. It opposed the powerful cliques in society on behalf of the poor who were organized to fight

---

38 De Wit (1989).

39 Desai (1995).

40 Desai (1995).

41 Schenk (1996).

evictions. These were basically ideologically driven.[42] The works of Youth for Voluntary Action in India (YUVA) and Unnayan's National Campaign for Housing Rights (NCHR) are examples. Unnayan, the Kolkata-based NGO, got involved in campaigning in 1982-1983 when there were major evictions in Kolkata. The second category of NGOs sometimes got involved in the rehabilitation projects for people displaced by flood or proposed for resettlement by government. Ahmedabad Study Action Group (ASAG) in Ahmedabad, Don Bosco Social Service Society (DBSSS) in Chennai, Seminary Shramadan Sangh (SSS) in South Karnataka district, and SPARC in Mumbai are some of the examples. Many NGOs got involved in the provision of health, education, income generation, and credit facilities. While being less paternalistic and more participatory than government, this approach also created dependency among the poor. Essentially led by middle class activists, this stand was independent of the government but not averse to building collaborative arrangements with it.[43] NGOs, although successful in small isolated efforts, proved to be too small in scale for the daunting task at hand. One factor that contributed to the weakness of NGOs was their inability to cooperate with each other, and an unwillingness to forge institutional linkages with the government also greatly reduced their impact.[44]

The National Housing Policy recommended the involvement of NGOs in housing activities in the planning and implementation of strategies, but international aid agencies are promoting their involvement in aid projects. Thus, NGO activities have become donor-driven and hence are not sustainable. NGO involvement is at present, however, at a small scale, and invariably they are asked to support government programs. They lack technical and managerial capacities to increase their activities. Availability of funds, ambiguous policies, lack of formal representations and channels of communication with government departments, multiple authorities that they have to deal with, and lack of information about government programs limits their efforts.

---

[42] UNDP (1996).

[43] UNDP (1996).

[44] Sanyal (1995).

Conclusions

- Housing was often seen as a social welfare and not a development activity in India during last five decades. Although the need for the socialization of land was recognized for achieving equity in the land market, the role of the government has gradually changed from provider of subsidized built houses in 1976 to facilitator of housing in the 1990's.
- Zoning and building regulations as stipulated by Master Plans are rigid and unaffordable for the majority of the urban poor. Policies to improve and regularize informal housing have been formulated and implemented outside the framework of Master Plans; therefore, informal settlements have never been integrated into the city.
- Policies towards squatters have changed from clearance and resettlement in the 1970's to improvement and regularization in the 1980's and improvement/resettlement/reconstruction of squatters with emphasis on poverty alleviation programs in the 1990's. International donor agencies like the World Bank played an important role during the eighties in influencing government policy in regularization of squatters.
- The recognition of informal housing and concerns for urban poor is reflected in various policy pronouncements at national, state and local levels. There is also greater emphasis on the convergence of policies for the poor with participatory processes.
- Provision of a basic minimum infrastructure to slums is the most dominant policy. A few states have implemented programs and projects for granting non-transferable leasehold rights and occupancy rights to squatters, but the coverage varies from city to city.
- There is greater a realization than before that the top-down approach of policy formulation has not worked. The change in role is accompanied by a decentralization of responsibility from central to local governments. The restructuring of institutions responsible for slum improvements will have to be done in the light of the 74th Amendment Act that gives more authority and responsibility to local bodies. At the local level, however, poor planning delivery mechanisms, inappropriate institutional structures and lack of coordination and managerial capacities adversely affect policy impact.
- In response to writs filed by squatters against evictions and sometimes to public interest litigations filed by land owners or higher income residents of adjoining locality against continued occupation of land by

squatters, intervention by courts has increased. Different political parties are increasingly using policies for squatters as political strategy.

- With the government's withdrawal from housing delivery, land supplies for the poor are shrinking. Squatting is likely to remain the dominant option for the poor in the future, fending for themselves in the informal land market. "Cities without slums" seems a distant dream, as there is no policy to forestall the growth of future slums.

References

Afzulpurkar Committee Report (1995), Reconstruction and Rehabilitation of Squatters in Greater Mumbai.

Banerjee, Banashree (2002), Security of Tenure in Indian Cities, in Alain Durand-Lasserve and Lauren Royston, eds., Holding Their Ground: Secure Land Tenure for the Urban Poor in Developing Countries, London.

Bapat, Meera (1983), Slum Areas Legislation: Its relevance for Slum Improvement and Upgradation, Paper prepared for Task Force of Planning Commission on Urban Development, New Delhi.

Barret, Alison J. (2001), Learning from Slum Improvement Projects in the move Towards Cities Without Slums, in Shelter, Vol. 4, No. 3, New Delhi.

Bhatnagar, K.K. (1996), Extension of Security of Tenure to Urban Slum Population in India: Status and Trends, Shelter, January, New Delhi.

Borst, Frank Jan (1990), Slum Improvement in the Major Cities of India: a Tentative Evaluation of Some Distinctive Types, paper presented at the 11th European Conference in Modern South Asian Studies, July 2-5, Amsterdam.

Bose, Ashish (1993), Urbanization in India-1951-2001, in Bidyut Mohanty, ed., Urbanization in Developing Countries: Basic Services and Community Participation, New Delhi.

Census of India (Provisional) (2001), Slum Population in India, Office of the Registrar General, India.

Center for NGOs (1993), Sustaining Slum Improvement, Proceeding of workshop, September 21, New Delhi.

CMDA (n.y.), Evaluation of the Bustee Improvement Program: Design and Organisation, Kolkata.

Desai, Vandana (1995), Community Participation and Slum Housing: A Study of Mumbai, New Delhi.

Government of India, Ministry of Health (1964), Report of the Committee on Urban Land Policy, Delhi,

Government of India, Planning Commission (1983), Task Forces on Housing and Urban Development: Shelter for the Urban Poor and Slum Improvement, New Delhi, Vol. IV.

Government of India (1988), Report of National Commission on Urbanization, Part-I, Delhi.

Government of India, Ministry of Urban Development (1992), National Housing Policy, New Delhi.

Government of India, Ministry of Urban Affairs and Employment (1996), India National Report for Habitat II, New Delhi.

Government of India, Ministry of Urban Affairs and Employment (1997), The Swarna Jayanti Shahari Rozgar Yojna, Guidelines, New Delhi.

Government of India, Ministry of Urban Affairs and Employment (1998), Report of the Task force on Urban Sector Reforms.

Government of India, Ministry of Urban Affairs and Employment (1999), National Slum Policy (draft), New Delhi.

Government of India, Planning Commission (2001), Report of the Steering Committee on Urban Development, Urban Housing and Urban Poverty for the Tenth Five Year Plan (2002-2007).

Government of Madhya Pradesh (1984), The Madhya Pradesh Nagariya Kshetron ke Bhoomihin Vyakti(Pattadhriti Adhikaron ka Pradan kiya Jana), Bhopal.

Government of Madhya Pradesh (1998), The Madhya Pradesh Nagariya Kshetron ke Bhoomihin Vyakti (Pattadhriti Adhikaron ka Pradan kiya Jana) Sanshodhan Adhiniyam, Gazette Notification, August 31, Bhopal.

Government of Andhra Pradesh (1995), Order no. 508, Revenue Department, Hyderabad.

Krishan, Gopal/Singh, Nina (1996), Urbanization: Emerging Scenario and New Challenges, in Kulwant Singh and Florian Steinberg, eds., Urban India in Crisis, New Delhi.

Kruse, Beate (1996), Employment Generation Programs in the Urban Context of India: The Nehru Rozgar Yojna, Paper presented at the Symposium on Urban Poverty Alleviation in Asia: Challenges and Perspectives, Kaiserslautern, Germany.

Kundu, Amitabh (1993), Urban Growth in the Context of Changing Policy Perspective on Provision of Basic Amenities in India.

Mahadevia, Darshini (1995), Emerging Process of Residential Segregation in Metropolitan Cities: Case Study of Mumbai and Chennai, Doctoral Thesis, Center for Regional Development, School of Social Sciences, Jawaharlal Nehru University, New Delhi.

Maitra, M.S. (1979), Calcutta Slums: Public Intervention and Prospects, in Nagarlok, April-June, Vol. XI, No.2, p.34-60.

Mehta, Dinesh (1996), New Economic Policies and Urban Housing, in Kulwant Singh and Florian Steinberg, eds., Urban India in Crisis, New Delhi.

Mitra, Arup (1993) "Status of Basic Services in Indian Cities," New Delhi.

Panwalkar, V.G. and Pratima (1988), Slum Upgradation: A policy Alternative to Management of Spontaneous Settlements: Mumbai Experience, IHSP Research Report No.22, HSMI, New Delhi.

Patel, Sheela/d'Cruz, Celine/Burra, Sunder (2002), Beyond Evictions in a Global City: People Managed Resettlement in Mumbai in Environment and Urbanization, April, Vol. 14, No. 1.

Racine, Jean-Luc (1996), Trends of Urbanization and migration in India: an alternative view of urban-rural relationship, Paper presented at symposium on Migration and Urbanization in Asian Countries, Darmstadt, Germany.

Risbud, Neelima (1986), Socio Physical Evolution of Popular Settlements and Government Supports: Case Study of Bhopal, IHSP Research Report No.3, New Delhi.

Risbud, Neelima (1989), Relocation Programs of Rental Housing in Delhi, in Rental Housing, proceedings of an Expert Group Meeting, UNCHS.

Risbud, Neelima (2002), Policies for Tenure Security in Delhi, in Alain Durand-Lasserve and Lauren Royston, eds., Holding Their Ground-Secure Land Tenure for the Urban Poor in Developing Countries, London.

Sanyal, Bishwapriya (1995), NGOs Also to be Blamed, in Housing by People in Asia, September, p. 13-14.

Schenk, Hans (1996), Slum Improvement as an Exponent of Physical Poverty Alleviation: the Functioning of the Karnataka State Slum Clearance Board in Bangalore, paper presented at the Workshop on Urban Poverty Alleviation in South Asia: Challenges and Perspectives, University of Kaiserslautern, Germany.

Singh Gurbir, Das P.K. (1996), Building Castles in the Air-Housing Scheme for Mumbai's' Slum Dwellers, in Economic and Political Weekly, 3Feb, 1996.

Slingsby, Michael A. (1989), Development of Post War and Post Independence Housing Policies, In: Michael Dewit and Hans Schenk, eds., Shelter for the Poor, Delhi.

Spodek, Howard (1983), Squatter Settlements of Urban India, in Economic and Political Weekly, September 3-10, Mumbai.

Steinberg, Florian/Singh, Kulwant, eds. (1996), Urban India in Crisis, New Delhi.

Takru, Rajiv (1997), Issues of Slum Development in India, Base-cum-Issue paper presented at National Seminar on Future Cities-Urban Vision: 2021, October 6-7, New Delhi.

Times of India(1996), 8 November, Delhi.

Venkateswarlu, U. (1997), Urban Vision 2021: An Agenda for Shaping the Urban Future,National Seminar on Future Cities:Urban Vision:2021, Ministry of Urban Affairs and Employment, 6-7 October New Delhi.

UNDP (1996) UNDP, ESCAP, (1996) "Living in Asian Cities, The impending Crisis - Causes, Consequences and alternatives for the future," Report of the Second Asian Pacific Urban Forum, New York.

UNCHS (Habitat) & Government of India (2001) Ahmedabad Parivartan Programme, Good Urban governance campaign-India Launch, New Delhi.

Verma, Gita Dewan (2000), Indore's Habitat Improvement Project: Success or Failure? Presented at Habitat International 24.

Wishwakarma, R.K./Gupta, Rakesh (1994), Organisational Effectiveness of Urban Basic Services Program in Selected Slum Areas of Delhi, Study sponsored by WHO, Center for Urban Studies, Indian Institute of Public Administration, New Delhi.

De Wit, Joop (1985), Slum Dwellers, Slum Leaders and the Government Apparatus: Relationships between actors in Slum Upgrading in Madras, Urban Research Working Papers, Institute of Cultural Anthropology/Sociology of Development, Free University, Amsterdam, pp.23-30 and 50-63.

Neighbourhood Management and the Future of Urban Areas

Anne Power

Introduction: What is neighbourhood management?

This paper is about low-income neighbourhoods, their organisation and management. It is not a study in deprivation, although all the areas we discuss are within the 10% most deprived areas in the country.[1] It is about problem-solving, about the reforms in delivery underway in Britain, about long run attempts to tackle deprivation, about the central role of local government and housing organisations in changing conditions on the ground. It addresses environmental and social problems within neighbourhoods as part of a wider understanding of social exclusion, sustainable development and the need for greater care of our urban communities. Although its perspective is shaped by British examples, many of the issues are relevant to other countries.[2]

Firstly, we set out the ideas behind neighbourhood management, why it is necessary and how it is organised. Clarity over the meaning of the term, neighbourhood management, is fundamental. *Management* involves the organisation, supervision and delivery of goods and services, the maintenance and enforcement of reasonable standards of repair, maintenance, supervision and provision of acceptable environmental conditions within agreed lines of control and accountability. Implicit within management responsibility lie the ability to make decisions and authority over identified and dedicated budgets to match the tasks necessary for making things work. Neighbourhoods require management just like any other structure, particularly if many residents rent their homes and ownership of property is held outside the neighbourhood – for example, by a local council.

A *manager* is the person where "the buck stops." There is no one else to blame for failure within the agreed management remit. The performance of services outside the manager's direct control is one of the most problematic aspects of successful management. Therefore the co-operation and

---

1 Neighbourhood Renewal Unit (2003), ODPM.

2 Power (1993).

support of as many local services as possible is essential to success in neighbourhood management. The art of management involves delivering all elements *within* the manager's control *as well* **as** negotiating and ensuring the successful delivery of elements outside the manager's direct control. A manager makes things happen *and* keeps things working. Lack of management causes a breakdown in control, delivery and enforcement of acceptable standards. The management of neighbourhoods shares these core management characteristics with other types of organisations – businesses, service bodies such as schools or hospitals, and specific programmes such as regeneration.

A *neighbourhood* is a delineated area within physical boundaries where people identify their home and where they live out and organise their private lives. However different residents and organisations will not always agree on the actual boundaries, as neighbourhoods are fluid, reaching out as well as in. However, the boundaries of urban neighbourhoods are often clear, if unwritten. There are both physical and psychological barriers between neighbourhoods such as a road or the tenure of the housing, or the social composition of residents. Some neighbourhoods, particularly near urban cores, with good transport links, are **mixed** socially and in property values. But most neighbourhoods are recognised either as "better off" or "poorer." More mixed neighbourhoods are often "going up" or "down," rarely static.

Neighbourhoods share many characteristics with an onion. The inner core is tightly drawn. In this core the home, immediate neighbours and security are paramount. Around this core, are the neighbourhood environment, shops and schools. The outermost layers can reach into adjacent neighbourhoods, the city centre or city rim for jobs, friends, relatives and wider services such as leisure.

A recognisable urban neighbourhood for social and management purposes is rarely more than 5000 households (the size of a large ward) and often much smaller with around 1000-2000 households, up to 6000 people. According to Peter Hall, it should be possible to walk across a neighbourhood in fifteen minutes or less – about three-quarters of a mile.[3] There is no absolute size of urban neighbourhoods. But neighbourhoods are complex, ill-defined areas that require clear definition and boundaries if their management is to be effective.

There is a strong social component to neighbourhoods. People connect with their neighbours in many, often unspoken ways – security, cleanliness, the environment, social behaviour, networks and conditions, access

---

3 Hall (1999).

to basic services such as schools, doctors, transport and shops. Neighbourhoods provide important supports, particularly to families with children and more elderly residents. They can therefore also undermine that support if conditions are not maintained. The quality of a neighbourhood's physical and social environment determines its value and status, the competition to access homes within it, the quality of services provided and how much people are willing and able to pay to live within it. Who lives in any area is a powerful determinant of both neighbourhood quality and property values. Therefore it is a circular process, with conditions influencing behaviour and behaviour influencing conditions. Poorer neighbourhoods invariably experience poorer conditions and lower property values. The quality of services tends to reflect this, but also helps determine it.

We would define *neighbourhood management* as the local organisation, delivery and co-ordination of core civic and community services within a small, recognisable, built-up area of under 5000 homes. In the most disadvantaged neighbourhoods where there are many environmental and service issues to tackle, the "manageable" size will rarely be above 2000 properties for the direct delivery of core services. Neighbourhood management requires a neighbourhood to have a logical identity, clear boundaries and manageable size for a single organisational structure and team.

Box 1 shows the core services neighbourhood management can offer and the prerequisites for its success.

Approach to the study

This paper investigates and explains some of the forms of neighbourhood management that are being tried in England today. Scottish, Welsh and Irish experiments could be highly relevant but are not covered. We show what benefits neighbourhood management can bring, with what costs; and what structures are needed to deliver it. Working examples of neighbourhood management are often linked to local housing management in areas with significant social and private renting and we therefore include housing management in the discussion where relevant. Our study uncovered clear organisational characteristics, involving an agreed approach to a specific neighbourhood and its management. We therefore highlight the most significant elements of good practice in the area-based management of conditions and services.

- *security, control of nuisance and general supervision;*
- *environmental maintenance and repair of damage to public areas;*
- *street cleaning, refuse collection and rubbish removal;*
- *community liaison, contact, consultation and support;*
- *co-ordination of specific services coming into the neighbourhood - co-ordination of inputs to maximise benefits and minimise waste and overlap - this includes housing, repairs, health, education, policing, leisure, regeneration;*
- *links with local businesses;*
- *links with wider and central services that are required for the successful functioning of a neighbourhood e.g. adult education, job centre, library;*
- *the development of local initiatives, special projects and new ideas;*
- *co-ordination with and support for local voluntary groups.*
- *a defined area of operation;*
- *a manager of sufficient seniority to control and co-ordinate major service inputs;*
- *a small locally based and locally accountable staff team to implement management decisions;*
- *a defined budget to fund the team and agreed services; and to allow flexible local management decisions;*
- *a local base through which services can be organised and local residents can be contacted and make contact;*
- *a high priority to basic services, in order to make a visible impact on conditions, thus gaining the confidence and support of other services such as doctors and schools;*
- *an entrepreneurial approach to problem solving and to involving partner services in the neighbourhood effort;*
- *clear lines of communication with local authority policy makers and other decision making and service bodies;*
- *Mainstream core funding;* ***not*** *short term, project-based funding.*

Box 1: Core services of neighbourhood management

The structures we outline are based on actual examples and illustrate the potential for neighbourhood management as well as underlining its complexity. They encompass services that extend far beyond traditional housing management and have, as a major component close resident liaison.

We have based our discussion of neighbourhood management on what is already happening rather than what is theoretically possible. We use working models, most of which are based within the framework of social housing, in order to examine what is actually being delivered on the ground. This paper also draws on the work of the Neighbourhood Renewal Unit within the Office of the Deputy Prime Minister. Since March 2000, government has supported thirty pilot areas in developing neighbourhood management in deprived areas. These experiments will now be extended to a further twenty areas. We also include reference to town centre management as this approach has informed the development of neighbourhood management.[4] The report also makes frequent reference to neighbourhood warden services: we include this in our model as these have great relevance and in practise overlap with neighbourhood management. They are extremely popular and far more wide spread than neighbourhood management. In practise, there are around 450 warden schemes, around 250 of which are government sponsored. Our main focus is on neighbourhood and town centre management, organised by local authorities, housing associations or dedicated management companies. As a result we discuss policing and security as part of the neighbourhood focus rather than as separate issues.

One major limitation of neighbourhood management is that there is no strategy for implementing it beyond a series of experiments. This study of live experiments provides an "implementation focused" understanding of what is going on at the neighbourhood level. We can offer an "insider" view of the organisational and financial pre-requisites for neighbourhood management, since our direct sources of information are ground level accounts of how it works. It does not focus on the strategic framework proposed by the Social Exclusion Unit in 2000, and further developed by the Neighbourhood Renewal Unit since then.

The neighbourhood management approach can be applied to the delivery of all neighbourhood services, and not just housing, for in practise all the experiments we studied are addressing local problems on a much broader front than simply housing.

In 1999, when neighbourhood management became one of the government-supported approaches to overcoming social exclusion and to neighbourhood renewal, we investigated 7 already existing models. We collected detailed information through visits to seven areas, meeting with the most senior person at neighbourhood level (chief executive/ neighbourhood manager/ project leader/ board chairman/ area manager) of the case study organisations; also meeting with housing officers, caretakers, repairs personnel, wardens, police officers, health officials, community workers and community representatives. Follow up contact was made with

---

[4] Power/Bergin (1999).

the lead officer in each of the areas to check facts and add extra information.

We have also conducted some secondary research, through our review of all relevant documentation published by the case study organisations and our examination of the local authorities' Annual Statements of Accounts. In 2001-2003, we worked with the Neighbourhood Renewal Unit on further developments in neighbourhood management, collecting up-to-date information on the thirty or so experiments they are supporting. Chart A gives basic information about the areas we originally investigated, showing their organisation and remit.

The paper explains why neighbourhood management is necessary and how it is organised based on current experience. It outlines the basic components of neighbourhood management drawing on experience to date. We investigate the pattern of services provided, tracing the common patterns of provision, outlining the elements of good practice in neighbourhood management. We explore the services provided by other agencies, for example the police and the health authority and the extent of co-ordination by the neighbourhood organisation, usually housing-led. We detail the role of residents in the different models. We estimate the costs and benefits of neighbourhood management more generally, including warden services, and we set out ways in which it can be funded through mainstream budgets and responsibilities, based on our examination of actual budgets and funding streams. We then draw out the lessons for the future development of neighbourhood management.

Chart A: Information about the seven examples of neighbourhood management

ISSUE	**Community Housing Trust, Hackney**	**Regeneration Company, Tower Hamlets**	**Community - based Housing Association, Waltham Forest**	**Tenant Management Organisation, Birmingham**	**Council Estate, Haringey**	**Mixed Tenure new build and refurbishment housing area, Manchester**	**Town Centre Management Company, West Midlands**
Type of area	4 ex - council estates	7 ex-council estates	4 new build estates	council estate	council estate	multi-landlord estate	shopping centre
Size of area - no. of	1044	4539	862 (rising to 1500)	716	1063	648	city centre area
Location	inner city	inner city	outer city	inner city	outer city	inner city	core city
Property Type	balcony flats	mixed high density, mainly flats	new terraced houses (replacing high rise)	dense high & medium rise (some towers demolished)	dense high & medium rise	new houses, converted tower block	busy shopping area
Organisation	local housing company	local housing company	community based housing association	tenant management organisation	council initiative	council and RSL partnership	independent company
Founding partners	Hackney Council and housing association partner	Tower Hamlets Council with RSL support	government, council, housing association, residents	council residents, PEP	council, residents	council & housing associations	council and private retail partners
Status	Semi - autonomous	Full ownership	Semi-autonomous	Local authority sponsored	Local authority sponsored and funded but some local autonomy	Partnership of local authority and local housing associations	Legally autonomous
Government role	Regulator and funder	Regulator and funder	Regulator and funder	Local authority funded/ regulated	Regulator and funder	Regulator and funder	Council sponsored
Funding	Government and private	Government and private	Government and private	Local authority	Local authority	Government and private	Council funded
Remit							
• Housing	✓	✓	✓	✓	✓	✓	-
• Security	✓	✓	✓	✓	✓	✓	✓
• Environment	✓	✓	✓	✓	✓	✓	✓
• resident involvement	✓	✓	✓	✓	✓	✓	user liaison owner involvement
• wider initiatives/ special projects	✓	✓	✓	✓	✓	✓	✓
• other services		✓	✓	✓	✓		

Why do we need neighbourhood management?

There are many factors at play in the drive for a tighter control over neighbourhood conditions and a more locally focused delivery vehicle for services. Modern society is increasingly mobile, urbanised, international. This makes neighbourhoods more transient. We live in increasingly fragmented and complex households within segmented and often highly polarised neighbourhoods. We rely more and more on remote and mechanical forms of communication and as part of this technological change, we have abolished many front-line manual and low skill jobs, reducing informal control and basic services. We live at far lower population densities as households have shrunk in size but multiplied in number, creating more spread out, "thin" neighbourhoods; but lower densities generate less informal street activity and less informal guarding. The spread of car transport to cope with lower density and higher mobility reduces social interchange, affecting simple neighbourhood activities such as taking children to school. There is more fear of strangers, more insecurity and fewer levers of control, as people have spread outwards, families have fragmented, and cars have increasingly displaced pedestrians and cyclists.

The consequences of these changes hit much harder in poorer neighbourhoods for many reasons – above average population turnover, less resources, weaker social and service organisation, less access to influence and information, greater social dislocations through the concentration of problems.[5] All these factors make problems of disorder more intense and create the need for neighbourhood management. Problems become concentrated and compound each other in ways that have been well documented in the Social Exclusion Unit's report *Bringing Britain Together.*[6] They do not need elaboration here but one result of these changes is a continuing, long run exodus of families from inner urban neighbourhoods.

Neighbourhood management is central to sustaining urban conditions, thereby stemming the demand for "thinned out" housing in green fields. If we do not change the way we manage urban neighbourhoods, we could experience in Europe the intense ghetto collapse of US inner cities. Thus there is a general need to manage urban neighbourhoods differently, to improve environments, increase security, attract back and hold onto more mixed income groups and more families. Urban management can help compensate for the breakdown in more informal controls resulting from radical social change. Our study explores the role of neighbourhood man-

---

[5] Mumford/Power (2003).

[6] Social Exclusion Unit (1998).

agement, including a senior neighbourhood manager based at a local level, assessing its impact on the ability of front line staff to affect conditions.

There is a particular and urgent need to install neighbourhood management in unpopular, difficult and disadvantaged areas. Without any special inputs, declining neighbourhoods can enter an accelerating spiral, leading to eventual collapse in conditions. They simply do not have the organisational resources to hold up under intense social pressure if conditions begin to get out of control. This is already happening in many city areas. The process is fully documented in earlier studies[7].

Although better off neighbourhoods can benefit from and often need neighbourhood management, they face less acute problems for three main reasons. Firstly, most households have the resources to maintain their property and pay for the additional services that make for greater security and better general conditions. Housekeeping, childcare, maintenance, gardening, are but a few examples. Secondly, some residents are professionally and politically connected in ways that ensure delivery of core services. For example, police and cleansing often respond faster and service firms operate to higher standards in better off areas.[8] Thirdly, more people have the resources to buy their way out of problems - private schools, trips and leisure activities. Better off people also have more freedom to move out altogether? However, neighbourhood management is applicable to most urban areas and is actually needed in inner urban and central areas, regardless of income. The core ideas apply to many rural areas too. The government has recognised this in the recent round of neighbourhood management pathfinders,[9] which specifically set out to apply the concept in more scattered and more rural communities.

Neighbourhood management cannot operate in a vacuum. It requires leadership, political clout, dedicated funds and above all the creation of a neighbourhood level vehicle in every neighbourhood where it is needed. So far it has usually been created in response to extreme problems and has not been adopted more widely. This is because it requires the combination of many elements which are not within the direct control of a single body. In other words, the very complexity and fragility of modern urban systems make urban management more difficult to deliver and more urgent because without it conditions run out of control – a classic chicken-and-egg situation. However, as the neighbourhood management pathfinders (of which there are now fifty sponsored by the government's Neighbourhood Re-

---

[7] Power (1997). Power/Tunstall (1995). Power/Tunstall (1997).

[8] Burrows (1998).

[9] Neighbourhood Renewal Unit (2003), Press release, Guidance of Neighbourhood Management.

newal Unit) chalk up some clear and visible successes, the government and local authorities may decide to establish a clearer and more general framework.

Progress is slow because it requires considerable organisational energy to break away from centralised structures and controls. Neighbourhood management cuts across traditional hierarchies and forces middle managers into a much more exposed position nearer the front line. It also forces a radical restructuring of the central organisation with a loss of some second and third tier central jobs, which are moved out to the front-line, pushing erstwhile bureaucrats into a much more delivery-focused set of tasks. Although overall it does not reduce the number of jobs, long-term funding and staff must be diverted from existing patterns.[10] There is inevitable resistance to such change and real obstacles in the path of people who try to achieve neighbourhood level gains. Therefore neighbourhood management will require a new delivery framework and considerable commitment to make it happen on a broader front.

Although many local authority decentralisation initiatives have been launched over the last fifteen years, they invariably provide little more than an arm of central control. They are too generalised, too tied into central procedures, too lacking in local powers, covering too large areas, to make a noticeable difference on the ground, even though they offer better information and a loose form of co-ordination and consultation. The rationale for decentralisation is to reduce the scale of central systems whereas in practise they often add a layer of bureaucracy. We came across four main variants; one-stop shops, area offices, call centre services and area co-ordination, none of which attempts to perform the actual neighbourhood management task we have identified - hands on management and organisation of core services, conditions and standards. Something more is needed. Neighbourhood management offers a local identifiable organisation through which local residents can secure reasonable services and conditions – it offers a method for large urban local authorities to manage and respond to the areas that currently barely turn out to vote (in some cases only 11% of the electorate); it offers government a mechanism for delivering neighbourhood renewal; it offers universal services such as education, health, police, a local framework for support and co-ordination; it offers a structure for housing management which is invariably a core requirement in neighbourhoods of predominately rented housing; it creates a clear organisational and co-ordinating vehicle for core services, such as security, cleansing, environmental maintenance; it can prevent urban decay and help otherwise collapsing areas become viable.

---

[10] Birmingham City Council (2002).

The following Chart B summarises the rationale for neighbourhood management as we have explained it in this section.

Chart B: Rationale for neighbourhood management

Urban Neighbourhoods

Wider problems	**specific problems**
• mobility	• polarisation
• thinning out	• lack of resources
• loss of front-line services	• poor services
• reliance on technology	• poor conditions
• insecurity	• rapid turnover
• poor quality environments	• acute decline
• family exodus and family breakdown	• breakdown of controls
general needs	**specific need**
• accessibility	• enhanced inputs
• increased security	• special supports
• better environments	• hands-on contact
• enforcement of basic conditions	• intensive management
• core neighbourhood services	• small area structure and organisation
• more compact living	• strong consultation and involvement
• more attractive neighbourhoods	

Neighbourhood Management Framework
- a local base
- a dedicated manager
- direct organisation and control
- a staff team to deliver basic services
- links to residents
- links to other services

Delivery Vehicle
- a base for action
- a conduit for special projects
- co-ordination of multiple service inputs
- power to enforce basic conditions
- integration of service providers and users

Direct Service Links
- environmental maintenance
- security, crime prevention and reporting
- housing management
- repair and building maintenance
- caretaking and neighbourhood warden services
- social care, schools, shops etc
- resident priorities, initiatives, facilities

The evidence from experiments in neighbourhood management, including the fifty government-sponsored pathfinders, show how directly the **housing service** is already involved. This is because of the historic role of local authorities in providing rented housing, its concentration in large urban estates (originally 40% of the urban stock, now down to about 25 to 30%), its strong welfare role and its steeply declining condition and popularity. The combination of public ownership, concentrated poverty and weak, urban management structures have created extremely serious problems. Social landlords, as the owners of property usually concentrated in low-income areas, have a direct responsibility for neighbourhood conditions. If they are council landlords, then under the extreme pressures they encounter, they launch bold experiments based on the neighbourhood management concept and the rationale we have outlined. Most experiments in neighbourhood management derive from these housing management requirements. The United Kingdom shares this experience with other European countries.[11] Almost all the new neighbourhood management experiments are housing-based, and three quarters have been created directly by local authorities.

Town and city centre problems have generated similar impetus for change. Town centres are the hub for many neighbourhoods and central to urban vitality. But town centres have often gone into acute decline following the expansion of large out of town shopping centres and inner city decay, leading to a drop in use, declining security, worse services, a rise in littering, vandal damage, crime and disrepair. Businesses and local authorities have found common cause in developing a dedicated town centre management structure, with many of the same ingredients as neighbourhood management, and for similar reasons. Most major cities but also many smaller towns and cities have a dedicated town centre management company.

There is another highly relevant neighbourhood level activity with a direct bearing on neighbourhood management – the rapid rise in popularity of *neighbourhood warden schemes*. These are often housing led or linked, focusing on security, guarding, crime prevention, basic environmental conditions and resident support. The police also play a critical role in supporting wardens and schemes can sometimes be organised by bodies such the police, or other local authority departments, such as regeneration departments or by registered social landlords for particular schemes. They can be seen as a low cost version of neighbourhood management but to be effective in difficult neighbourhoods they do require a dedicated manager and they do have a distinctive role and contribution. In many neighbourhood management schemes, there are wardens services.

---

[11] Power (1997).

What should neighbourhood managers manage?

The boundaries of neighbourhood management activity can be tightly or loosely drawn. The first layer of activity is the most visible and immediate failure in *conditions* – cleanliness, order, security and maintenance. These basic conditions should logically be a first target of improvement. The most efficient delivery structure may be wider than a single neighbourhood but a neighbourhood manager will have the task of making them work for the benefits of the neighbourhood, acting as client, honest broker and conduit for delivery – the central role of all effective managers.

The second layer relates to *major welfare, public and social services*, including education, health, employment, income support. Each of these services is nationally funded, inspected and in some cases, organised. But they are invariably delivered within neighbourhoods, affect all local residents and have great potential for impact on conditions and opportunity. Each has its own professional and management structure and cannot be directly run through neighbourhood management, for example, a local school, or elderly care. However, there is scope for collaborative effort, local links and special partnerships. A neighbourhood manager can have a major impact on how they work together and how much they benefit the neighbourhood.

A third layer covers the multiple *functions of local authorities* beyond the basics and mainline services we have already mentioned. These include all publicly provided amenities, social services and special responsibilities such as those imposed by the Crime and Disorder Act. These impact on neighbourhoods directly and some specifically need a neighbourhood delivery structure to work properly. Crime and anti-social behaviour are the obvious ones.

The fourth layer includes the *special programmes and regeneration initiatives* that are often directed at specific neighbourhoods. All the neighbourhoods we examined had more than one special initiative and several sources of special funds. Special programmes, which offer a lever to establish longer-term neighbourhood management, are a common and obvious starting point as they offer immediate funding and the need for locally co-ordinated supervision. Most initiatives we visited began in this way. However, they only became effective neighbourhood management initiatives when they became part of a core, mainstream revenue funded locally-based service. Therefore the two main challenges for neighbourhood management are: creating a "launch pad" with at least minimal pump-priming funds over several years; and devising a long-term, affordable funding stream within the main public structures.

Chart C sets out the layers of responsibility, showing how many publicly funded activities need to be devolved down to neighbourhood level.

The value of all public support is around £10,000 per household.[12] Public bodies must take responsibility for seeing that it is well managed. Only the public realm can broker and orchestrate resources and conditions on such a broad front. Therefore central and local government will be the inevitable drivers and creators of neighbourhood management - our models illustrate this and government programmes targeting the most deprived neighbourhoods underline this inevitable conclusion.[13] There are limits to the scope of neighbourhood management. For example, education, health, police services, each have an independent professional remit, with separate lines of accountability. They can have a neighbourhood focus and can benefit from neighbourhood management but essentially they retain their organisational integrity. However, they greatly benefit from better, more controlled neighbourhood conditions.

The size of areas managed by the neighbourhood manager ranges from 1,000 to 4,000 households. The size depends on the geographic distribution of properties, the configuration of housing estates and road patterns. The recurrence of managed neighbourhoods of 700-2,000 households and their efficiency compared to many earlier decentralisation experiments covering larger areas suggest that size of area needs to be examined carefully. There may be efficiency losses in larger areas. One of the most successful, long run neighbourhood management models is Broadwater Farm in Haringey with 1,000 units. Others are the Bloomsbury Tenant Management Organisation in Birmingham and the Monsell Estate in Manchester, both with under 1,000.

---

[12] Glennerster, eds. (1998).

[13] National Strategy for Neighbourhood Renewal (2000).

Chart C: Layers of responsibility for neighbourhood services & tasks from local to national

FIRST LAYER:	Enviromental
Basic conditions	Street cleaning
	Refuse collection
	Nuisance control
	Repair and maintenance of public spaces
	Parks and playgrounds
	Security
	Sometimes provided through housing
	A direct police responsibility
	Warden, concierge and super-care-taking services
	Sometimes privately organised
	Housing
	Rent account
	Access, allocation, advice
	Investment
	Repair and maintenance
	Tenancy liaison, enforcement
SECOND LAYER:	School/Education
Major public welfare services	Policing
	Social Services
	Elderly/community care
	Warden services
	Childcare/nurseries/Family centers
	Protection and enforcement
	Mental health
	Health
	Social Security/Income Support
	Job centers/Employment
	Higher & Further Education
THIRD LAYER:	Leisure & Amenities
Local authority wider functions	Libraries
	Youth service
	Sports facilities
	Community centers
	Parks
	Special Responsibilities
	Social Services
	Crime prevention
	Partnerships
	Business liaison
	Security
	General well-being of area
	Promotion
	Neighborhood/community development
FOURTH LAYER:	Regeneration Programs e.g. SRB
Special programs	Service initiatives
	Additional funding e.g. National Lottery
	Targeted area initiatives e.g. Sure Start, New Deal for Communities, Neighborhood renewal

However, for many purposes – secondary schools, libraries and so on – the viable catchment area is far bigger and the permeability of neighbourhoods is a crucial component in realising the potential of neighbourhood management. In spite of this, larger areas have to be subdivided for many purposes, particularly resident involvement. In all areas, neighbourhood managers have responsibility for building links with residents, involving them in priorities and organising consultation over local services, investment and proposed changes. These local links are a key role for the neighbourhood manager.

There are many routes to putting "someone in charge" of the resources heading for each area. Most organisations manage at a level far removed from real neighbourhoods. Therefore political will, commitment to neighbourhood management, matched by financial incentives and scope for experiment will determine how neighbourhood services develop. Arm's length companies, public-private partnerships, private companies, charities and trusts all have the potential to deliver neighbourhood management alongside local authorities, as Chart A shows. Neighbourhood management can also be delivered directly by the local authority, although this model eventually requires a clear long-term, ring-fenced neighbourhood-level vehicle too, to guarantee its stability and dedication to neighbourhood tasks. Our discussion below of Broadwater Farm illustrates this. More often an arm's length structure is created with the local authority as the lead organisation.

There is no escaping public responsibility for neighbourhood management. Residents contribute through council tax and income tax to the provision of basic services. It is possible to levy limited additional charges for specific additional services. Concierges and warden services are often funded this way. Housing revenue budgets can support neighbourhood management for socially rented housing areas because so many of their responsibilities overlap with neighbourhood management. The more autonomous local organisations such as housing companies can identify revenue resources within their overall budgets, as our examples show (see Chart A). Town centre companies are supported by retailers. So far private housing areas have been the most difficult to secure funding for, except in new mixed used, condominium-style developments where a management company is set up, such as the Greenwich Millennium Village. This provides a valuable model for the future.

There are several reasons why housing organisations may play a leading role: they have to manage their assets and as part of this, neighbourhood conditions; they have a vested interest in tackling local problems; they assume responsibility (and credit) for progress. It makes sense for the government to promote arms length housing management vehicles as part of the drive for neighbourhood management in order to generate the regeneration and revenue resources that give impetus to change; and to give organisational momentum to neighbourhood management. Many major urban local authorities are already planning and adopting this approach. If the arms-length companies are sufficiently independent of the local authority, they have the power to access private investment funds along the continental lines of publicly or privately sponsored housing companies.[14]

Our definition of neighbourhood management – direct responsibility and control of some specific services, co-ordination of and liaison with other services, and responsibility for neighbourhood improvements – must be combined with the four layers of responsibility for services set out in Chart C to establish the manager's role in a neighbourhood management framework. Chart D sets out the different roles in relation to the local delivery vehicle and to the local authority.

Chart D: Role of neighbourhood manager

Senior Neighborhood Manager

Answerable to local delivery organization	**Accountable to local authority for delivery**
company	specific neighborhood responsibilities
trust	fixed boundaries
partnership	clear span of control
management board	visible staff inputs
committee	budget responsibility

1. Dedicated **budget** and spending power with local delivery team
2. Direct **delivery** of core services
3. Coordination of wider service inputs
4. Direct responsibility for consulting and **involving** residents
5. Usually includes or is closely linked to **housing management** but involves many other services - neighborhood environmental and social onditions are a main focus
6. Answerable to **council chief executive**
7. **Links with wider service**
   - this acknowledges professional and funding separation between services
   - policing, health, social services, education operate within their own professional hierarchies
   - these can be focused on neighborhoods

---

[14] Power (1993).

How neighbourhood management works in practise

In this section we set out the essential components of neighbourhood management that we uncovered through visits and through evidence from the Neighbourhood Renewal Unit.[15] Chart E shows these.

Chart E: The essential components of neighbourhood management

How neighborhood management works

Neighborhood manager

seniority
budget
control over neighborhood conditions
coordination of services
community involvement
Hands-on responsibility

Neighborhood office

organizational base
delivery of core services
information and access point for local and external liaison

Neighborhood team

dedicated to specific area
enhancing security
tackling basic conditions
building community support and involvement
providing/organizing local staff to cover basic services
small core, multiple links
developing special initiatives

What neighborhood management can deliver

Core Services

housing management (where renting from social landlords)
repair
super-care-taking and environmental services
warden, concierge and security services
nuisance control

Cooperation with other public services

police
health
education

training and jobs
community provision

Community representation

local agreements
local boards
arms length models

• community based housing association
• local housing company
• tenant management organization
•community trust

Retail management

security
enviroment
insurance
customer liaison
public transport links

[15] Pathfinders (2003).

The role of neighbourhood manager

A senior manager is essential to ensure successful delivery of services on the ground. He / she needs to have the seniority and capacity to ensure joined up delivery across all local inputs. The manager needs to be able to co-ordinate housing services, deal directly with the police, link with health, education, social and other services and respond to the needs of residents. Schools, shops, bus links and transport make a vital contribution to neighbourhood success and their interests also need to be encompassed.

In all of the case studies we visited and in the Neighbourhood Management Pathfinder programme there is a neighbourhood manager or company chief executive on the ground, managing some core services and helping to co-ordinate other local authority, statutory and community services. Almost all include basic housing management alongside their wider remit. Each manager has considerable experience. Each manager attracts a principle-level salary or higher within the organisation. All have responsibility for their budget spending. All have direct support from the local authority chief executive, or in the case of independent companies, the chief executive has delegated financial control, monitored by the Housing Corporation and Audit Commission, and works closely with the local authority.

Neighbourhood office

A neighbourhood office provides the local base within which neighbourhood management is organised. The neighbourhood office is also often the organisational hub of housing management services. This works very well. In neighbourhood initiatives which are housing-led or housing-based there is a layer of responsibility above the direct housing service with a broader remit to work with residents, support and address community needs, create a secure, attractive, well maintained environment and develop initiatives to support community development, expand the resources and enhance the viability of the area. The neighbourhood office in each of the cases that we examined closely provides a functional base, with a practical focus, essential services are often provided directly through it. Cleaning, security and environmental care are the most common, but youth activities and direct resident priorities run alongside housing management as central to progress. Some neighbourhood offices manage repairs, cleaning, caretaking, environmental improvements and tenancy matters directly.

Housing management

Evidence from the Neighbourhood Renewal Unit is not available on how housing and neighbourhood management fit together. The neighbourhoods that we visited delivered most or all housing services locally. The main exception to this pattern was the allocation of council housing, although in low demand and difficult to manage areas, "community lettings" and resident involvement in recruiting new applicants is being increasingly encouraged. Choice-based lettings, whereby vacancies are advertised and people needing a home can choose to apply, are also beginning to show positive results.[16]

Some key housing functions impact on neighbourhood conditions directly and are needed in almost all urban areas. Box 2 sets out these functions:

- *reinvestment and regeneration*
- *repairs and maintenance*
- *caretaking*
- *environmental care*
- *warden and concierge service*
- *enhanced security*
- *empty property and derelict land*
- *tenancy conditions and enforcement*

Box 2: Housing management functions

- *nuisance*
- *anti-social behaviour*
- *abandoned buildings and spaces*
- *roads, traffic and parking*
- *arson and fire hazards*
- *sub-legal activities*
- *drugs*
- *support for community self-help*
- *poor quality shops*
- *racial harassment*
- *youth needs*
- *gang fights*
- *family needs*
- *extended family conflicts*
- *local community facilities*
- *mixed tenure management and leaseholder problems (often a result of the right-to-buy for council tenants)*

Box 3: Housing related issues

[16] ODPM (2002), Choice-based lettings pilots.

Many of the targets for neighbourhood management, some of which affect all tenures, most often land in housing manager's laps. Some examples are shown in Box 3:

Box 2 underlines the need for a wider neighbourhood management role, even where the main focus is on housing. The advantage of the neighbourhood management structure, particularly where it encompasses housing management, is that signs of social and environmental decay can be tackled quickly and directly.

Many services are involved and below we discuss the ones we believe are most important.

Super-caretakers, wardens and concierges

The responsibilities, expectations, training and involvement of caretakers in many different non-manual and manual tasks – community liaison as well as basic conditions – defines their role as "super-caretaking," rather than basic caretaking. Caretakers are identified closely with the local community and spend all their time on the ground. Caretaking historically has been funded from rents for housing estates and everywhere on the continent it is still considered essential to the viability of rented housing. The idea of concierges and super-caretaking derived from this source. The functions of caretakers and wardens vary but they typically have security, cleaning, repairs, environmental care, youth and community liaison roles. Caretakers or wardens are a popular feature of neighbourhood management experiments. A MORI survey of residents in Hackney found that on the question of dedicated new services, the top request was for resident caretakers (49%), followed by a locally-based estate manager (36%) and a local estate office (35%).

Warden, concierge and caretaking services offer local employment possibilities to people of the local neighbourhood. Some managers argue against residents holding caretaking, warden or concierge jobs because of fear of intimidation or corruption. Others regret its passing or advocate it strongly. In any case concierges and caretakers can be locally-based and cover areas other than their own home. Close supervision, training and senior management are essential to their success in tackling poor conditions.

We group caretakers, wardens and concierges together because their role is similar even though they are often deployed in different ways. While concierges are suitable for high-rise properties, the use of wardens works best in low rise/low-density areas and in areas of high crime. Wardens often perform functions similar to super-caretakers.

Concierges operating within dense flatted building can bring about a significant reduction in vandalism, an increased sense of security and higher occupancy levels, which further reduce overheads and increase income. According to staff, concierge surveillance has strengthened the hand of neighbourhood offices in dealing with difficult tenants. Reduced vandalism and crime, higher occupancy, lower turnover and lower repair costs all create savings. The value of a concierge in high-rise apartment blocks is widely accepted in neighbourhoods where they have been properly introduced.[17] It is an expensive service and is usually used to control large blocks of flats or dense flatted estates. Concierges are invariably organised and funded through housing management, but housing managers commonly argue that they pay their way through major savings.

Wardens take on multiple tasks in the areas we studied: security patrols, brokering neighbourhood disputes, informing the office and police about disruptive behaviour and criminal incidents. Other tasks, such as fixing minor repairs, tenant liaison, visits to vulnerable tenants, running youth activities, are also taken on by wardens. A warden scheme is usually less than half the cost of the high-rise concierge services. Warden schemes in terraced and low-rise areas offer a solution in places of high crime and low demand where a neighbourhood presence is desirable. Wardens are often funded by housing management even though half of their tasks relate to wider environmental and social issues. But they can also be supported through general funding or as a supplement to the police.[18]

Concierges, wardens and super-caretakers offer a human link in insecure environments.

Policing

Partnership with the Police is central to neighbourhood offices in disadvantaged areas. All the areas we looked at did at one time and often still do face high levels of crime. A major unresolved policing problem in some of the worst areas is witness intimidation and difficulty in obtaining evidence to combat crime. This drives law-abiding residents away. A dedicated neighbourhood police unit is the optimum local service and sometimes essential to winning over the co-operation of residents. One major problem with special policing initiatives is that they tend to be withdrawn

---

[17] Bradford City Council (2002).

[18] See Neighbourhood Warden Team in ODPM website for details of the many schemes.

as soon as more normal conditions prevail. Dedicated police are often called away to other emergencies. This often results in a return of crime and the need for another bout of anti-crime activity. Sustained, visible, ground level policing, linked to warden-style services, can transform conditions. The police generally support the creation of local offices as it makes their job more manageable. Very often local housing officers set up close liaison with police. For all these reasons, neighbourhood management now invariably involves strong police links and inputs.

The addition of wardens, concierges and super-caretakers have all been important factors in the reduction of crime in each of the areas we visited. An estate level supervised service in all the areas we visited has resulted in lower crime rates and less fear of crime. In other words, ancillary security and custodial services, such as concierges and wardens, add to and enhance the police role and resources. Warden-type services are only effective with police backing.

Repairs

Repairs are often thought of as the most distinctly housing-related of all the functions, yet failure to repair and maintain property to a high standard has significant repercussions on neighbourhood conditions more generally. In fact, maintenance and repairs matter for pavements, street lighting, gates, fences, bollards, open spaces, empty buildings as well as for homes. It is the service that often most clearly signals neighbourhood conditions. In older low income owner-occupied areas it is a major unfounded problem.

Community Representation and Provision

Neighbourhood management specifically targets community needs and community involvement. A community base within the neighbourhood management structure helps to facilitate participation and leadership from the community. The business plans of the independent non-profit companies responsible for neighbourhood management need to include social provision and support.

The extent of community involvement is partly dependent on the area's history of community activism and the profile of residents. Some areas have much stronger traditions of involvement and an accumulated experience of running things jointly or with residents in the driving seat. Where an area has a poor history of community relations, a great deal needs to be invested in this work to get it off the ground, particularly if the area is rundown and depopulating.[19]

Community Development Trusts provide an important model. Through them, a local community asset, such as a community centre, can be run and managed through a local community based charity or trust. In some cases the ownership is vested in the trust. There is now significant experience of community representation, leadership and ownership, providing models for neighbourhoods everywhere.[20]

Chart F sets out the main forms of community representation and ownership found in each case study.

Chart F: Forms of Community Involvement and Ownership

1. Consultative/Public Liaison Structure
2. Negotiated Agreement
   - Estate Agreement with multiple landlords
3. Representative or company board and community provision
4. Resident Control
   • Tenant Management Organization
   • Community Based Housing Association
5. Community Trust
   • assets and organization owned by elected community representatives

All the neighbourhood management organisations we visited provide community development support, training for residents, pump priming for local initiatives and constant effort to involve local people in decisions. This effort is necessary, partly because of the social pressures poorer neighbourhoods are under, partly in recognition of the major contribution resident involvement makes to successful management of conditions. It would be difficult to overstate the role of community representation and involvement in the progress of the areas we visited and in the Neighbourhood Management Pathfinders.

Health and social services

Joint working between the neighbourhood and the health authority can lead to exciting stand-alone community health projects. Many health issues

[19] Poplar HARCA (1999).

[20] For general concepts and outlines, see Development Trusts Association.

affect low-income areas: diet, smoking, disability, depression, asthma, isolation of the elderly and vulnerable, drug and alcohol abuse. Crime and its side effects have health implications. Adopting a more "public health" approach with an emphasis on prevention can help tremendously. The Sure Start programme, supporting vulnerable mothers and young children in high poverty areas, is a good example of a health-related preventative programme. It operates in a number of areas that are the target of regeneration and neighbourhood management. Group practices and healthy living centres are also emerging under the umbrella of neighbourhood management.[21] This approach crosses the divide between health and social services, which is increasingly the way thinking and delivery should go.

Education

The emphasis on area conditions and housing problems has limited the links between neighbourhood management and schools. Yet, there is considerable scope for greater joint working between the schools and the neighbourhood office. Most neighbourhood management areas are trying to do more with the help of and in support of the schools, with the aim of integrating schools far more into the communities they serve – creating schools that are used for many different purposes.

Training and Employment

Landlords are obviously constrained in what they can do to bring people who are hard to employ into jobs. In spite of this, there is a focus on employing local people where possible in the housing and neighbourhood services, and linking residents to the wider job market. The employment of residents channels some extra money into the neighbourhoods while at the same time giving the organisations greater credibility and visibility in the eyes of residents. Some cost-free measures (such as residents' membership on interview panels) for the appointment of local staff also help to build good will and a neighbourhood identity when outsiders are being recruited for jobs. There is great scope to do more on this.

---

[21] Broadwater Farm Estate, Haringey, and Waltham Forest Housing Action Trust (1999).

Town Centre and Shopping Area Management

Some of the ideas for neighbourhood management have been borrowed from the much more commercially driven successes of town centre management. Government restrictions on out of town shopping have encouraged a focus on town centres and the recognition of the need for careful management of conditions to encourage this. In a similar way, the growing restrictions on green field house building should drive the recovery of declining urban neighbourhoods, driving the impetus for stronger neighbourhood management. The experience of town centre management shows that it can reduce insurance costs and therefore the overheads on goods.

The emergence of the town centre manager role over the last ten years – co-ordinating the basic services: cleaning, security, environmental care – has increased customer satisfaction and therefore expanded trade. The main requirements are: a competent manager; a clear service contract; agreement with traders of funding, services and standards; a dedicated budget; a contribution to costs from traders and the local authority; a significant input of dedicated staff. Town centre management can reduce crime and vandal damage, keep public areas clean, attractive and in good repair, improve customer relations, upgrade the quality of services provided and help promote the image of an area. It also cuts insurance costs and this can be critical in funding the service.[22]

Securing the future of shops and facilities in neighbourhoods is central to recovery, vitality, a broader mix of activity and population – all of which are central to survival. Many neighbourhood shopping areas are in acute decline. Shops have a need for security, cleanliness and intensive refuse collection. These basic services help attract trade and sustain businesses. Bus links, attractive secure environments and a good mix of traders affect the viability of shops. There often needs to be a critical mix of services and a clear maintenance agreement for a shopping parade or centre to work. But getting shopkeepers to co-operate as well as compete is often difficult. A reduction in insurance costs is a major selling point. Where there is a shopping parade or high street in a neighbourhood, it is a key function of neighbourhood management to make it work.

---

[22] Government Office for the North West (2000).

Costs and benefits of neighbourhood management

In this section we outline the benefits of a neighbourhood-based service. We compare the costs of local housing management, including the neighbourhood management role, with the cost of the centrally run locally authority housing service, drawing on Birmingham City Council figures to update the work we did in 1999.

Most areas of neighbourhood management have a poor reputation, severe social problems and serious disrepair. Broadwater Farm estate, Haringey, where severe riots and a breakdown in police-community relations occurred, is one of the longest running and most thoroughgoing experiments in neighbourhood management. We carried out a more detailed study of Broadwater Farm and present some key findings, to indicate how neighbourhood management can be funded within a housing budget and mainstream local authority budget.

The strongest assets of the Broadwater Farm model include:

- a local base with a cohesive staff team covering basic services, ongoing maintenance and environmental care
- well-organised resident input into decisions and development, far beyond accepted consultation e.g. resident representation on job recruitment panels
- a neighbourhood manager with a broad remit to include community relations, direct services and wider co-ordination
- a training approach to caretaking leading to outstanding cleanliness, maintenance and tenant liaison
- close liaison with the police, health, education and social services
- a clear role for black and other minority ethnic community representation
- direct work with young people and support for youth initiatives
- a clear security role – combining super-caretakers, concierges, active residents involvement and a dedicated police unit
- support for other agencies and activities – a health centre, a sports centre, churches, employment and training services for the elderly.

The main ingredients of the model are replicated in most of the other neighbourhood management examples we found. The following chart summarises the costs and benefits of this important model.

Chart G: Broadwater Farm – Estimate of costs and benefits of five main components of service including neighbourhood management function

Costs	% total local cost	Benefits
a) Neighborhood officer £ 35, 798 p.a. £ 33.68 per unit £ 0.65 p.u.p.wk.	3%	(I) Seniority and clout in Council (II) motivation and energy to deliver (III) clear coordination & cooperation (IV) high level, local supervision (V) high performance on basics (VI) strong tenant support
b) Housing Management £ 176,041 p.a. £ 166 p.u.p.a. £ 3.18 p.u.p.wk.	15%	(I) occupancy - 98% - above national average - previous high void rate (II) rent collection – 99.5% (III) rent arrears halved (from 1990) - still high at £ 588 per household (IV) tenant satisfaction above national average (survey findings)
c) Super-caretaking £ 164,800 p.a. £ 155 p.u.p.a. £ 2.98 p.u.p.wk.	16%	(I) clean, graffiti free environment (II) no visible vandalism (III) clean lifts, corridors, stairs, entrance (IV) personal contact with tenants (V) daily liaison with senior staff (VI) close collaboration with repairs staff (VII) enhanced security, supervision (VIII) watch-out for vulnerable tenants (IX) regular contact with police
d) Concierge system (estimate for whole estate, currently half) £ 400,000 p.a. £ 376 p.u.p.a £ 7.24 p.u.p.wk.	33%	(I) saving of £ 100 per unit in reduced repair costs (II) elimination of vandal damage (III) much improved block condition (IV) increased sense of security/reduces fear (V) informal and formal surveillance (VI) close liaison with office over difficult tenants (VII) friendly, positive contact with residents
e) Repairs Unit £ 431,271 p.a. £ 406 p.u.p.a. £ 7.80 p.u.p.wk.	36%	(I) fast response to emergencies, e.g. floods (II) mutual reinforcement with caretakers (III) collaboration with housing office (IV) familiarity with estates residents (V) costs one fifth below borough average (VI) high tenant satisfaction - Borough survey - higher than other estates (VII) extremely well maintained estate
f) Community support	Own budget	(I) large council funded community center (II) strong community involvement in decisions and priorities
g) Links with other services	Part of a)	(I) police
Total:		£ 1500 with concierges per unit per annum £ 1125 without
Source:		Haring Council, 1999
Note:		This funding framework is broadly in place in 200

The cost to the authority for warden services allowing for savings elsewhere is probably negative, which is why at least 200 local authorities have established warden services without additional funding from central government and why many independent, non-profit housing associations have also set up schemes. However, up front direct costs have to be met. It may be possible to charge people for the extra service and security - less than £1 per week for the cheapest security service, £2-£5 per week for warden services, £4-£8 per week for more intensive concierge services. Although more costly than warden services, but the potential savings of concierge schemes are much greater. Both services enhance conditions as the uncosted benefits show. Chart H sets out the overall costs and benefits.

Imaginative new ways have to be found of funding this basic security and environmental maintenance if we are to keep city neighbourhoods and housing estates working. Private development companies in and near city centres who are responsible for new mixed developments are now generally providing local services through management companies, in order to protect property values and entice higher income residents in. They offer some clues of what is necessary to maintain the viability of estates. Innovative experiments in mixed-tenure and private areas, particularly in declining inner city areas, are now common. So most of the new mixed-tenure, mixed-use regeneration schemes that public-private partnerships are now developing will need to adopt this neighbourhood based approach.[23]

Funding problems arise in privately owned areas needing intensive management or in more scattered rural areas. It is not obvious who, other than the local authority, can organise, manage and pump-prime neighbourhood management. Slimmer central management structures and greater focus on front line delivery makes neighbourhood management surprisingly cost-effective, as well as motivating. The efficiency and service gains seem to justify the investment. Chart I sets out the costs and benefits of neighbourhood management.

---

[23] Greenwich Millennium Village (2003).

Chart H: Warden-concierge costs and savings – per annum, based on examples we visited

(a) Concierge/warden costs	Estimated costs per dwelling/per annum
Wardens	£ 50 - 200
Concierges	£ 200 - 400

(b) Concierge/warden savings	Estimated savings per dwelling/per annum
Savings on repairs due to reduced vandalism, quicker relets, etc.	£ 100
Additional rent income of 5% from lower voids, lower arrears, quicker re-lets, reduced turnover/transfers	£ 150
Reduced property insurance charges due to lower claims, enhanced security, clearer supervision, etc.	£ 100
Costed savings	£ 380
In addition, reduction in demolition creates significant savings per dwelling saved	£ 17,000 - 35,000

(c) Uncosted benefits of warden/concierge schemes

High visibility resulting from uniforms and local liaison responsibilities

Reduced crime, greated security do not affect both repairt costs and insurance for landlords other owners (e.g. shops) and residents

Clear police liaison and reporting, control over anti-social and criminal behavior

Resident liaison, information exchange, support for vulnerable household.

Clear records, more careful monitoring of costs, etc.

Clear lines of reporting because of proximity to problem

Close supervision of ground level staff

Higher standards of cleanliness and maintenance

Safer, more welcoming environment

Improved appearance and marketability of blocks

Innovative approach to local problems, e.g. wardens using bikes; wardens helping with young people

Note: Costs and saving are derived from actual services.

Chart I: Costs and benefits of neighbourhood management based on the models

Costs/Inputs	Benefits/Outcomes
ESSENTIAL	
• senior manager locally based	• Better environmental conditions
• cleaning, wear & tear repair, security services	• General improvement in repair, cleaning & other basic services
• close rapport with residents/users	• More patrolling, super vision & control over conditions
• discreet local budget under control of local manager	• More social contact & liaison
• strongl y linked into & supported by local authority and police	• More reporting, more local information, better informed action
• proactive police liaison	• More co -ordination between local actors e.g. housing & police
• focus on basic conditions	• More resident inputs & liaison
• open co -ordination with other services, e.g. schools, doctors	• New projects & initiatives
• political backing & central support/reorientation	• Greater sense of pride & commitment to area
• links with investors, enterprises (s hops), community bodies (churches, playgroups)	• More occupied property, stronger income base
• increase ground -level staff – caretaking/cleaning/basic repair (i.e. warden / super -caretaker). An area of 1000 properties requires 4 - 6 ground level staff & 1 neighbourhood manager	• More interest from senior politicians & city officials/more visitors creating virtuous circle (until lots of neighbourhoods do it!)
• housing revenue for rented housing areas to provide local staff – 20 per 1000 properties	• Knock -on development of local jobs
• initial up -front investment (e.g. office, equipment etc.)	• Skill development among residents - greater access to training - new roles, demands, responsibilities
Summary:	**Summary:**
• Costs are comparable to the centrally organised service	• Direct benefits stem from the local framework & local delivery with face to face contact as a key
• Staff are highly visible on the ground.	• Staff / property ratio is comparable to the centrally based service Human contact & manual tasks are combined
• Costs of repairs, lettings, vandalism are lower	

Birmingham City Council offers a current example of the costs and benefits of neighbourhood management.24 As a result of the failure to secure tenant support for the transfer of the whole council housing stock (80,000 properties) the city has backed proposed to created Community-Based Housing Organisations (CBHO) in all the areas of the city where the tenants favour this approach. Each CBHO will have the potential to manage neighbourhood conditions within a local housing management framework. It includes funding (from the housing revenue account) for super-caretakers or wardens, local repairs and a neighbourhood manager.

So far forty community-based groups within the city have declared an interest in pursuing this option. This is over and above the council's planned and much publicised devolution plans to much larger constituency areas covering around 90,000 people.

Birmingham, the second largest city in the UK, with a population of just under one million, is running a live experiment, citywide, in the potential for neighbourhood management. Historically, it was the pioneer of civic responsibility for neighbourhood conditions – sewers, lights, pavements. Today it wants to demonstrate the untapped capacity of our big cities for neighbourhood renewal. It is breaking new ground in attempting to secure urban neighbourhoods for future generations.

Previous proposals encouraged large-scale demolition whereas current proposals attempt to secure their repair, upgrading, security and better environments. The acid test for Birmingham will be whether it "lets go" of the central bureaucracy and supports the 40 communities and willing staff across the city in tackling often appalling local conditions directly.

Box 4: Cost-sharing: the example of Birmingham

Box 4 offers a worked example which can be funded from currently available mainstream resources.

Birmingham is not the only council to go down this route and Wolverhampton Council has now developed a city-wide neighbourhood management strategy. Leeds, Kirklees, Derby and several other cities are going towards full arms-length management of all city neighbourhoods with majority social housing.

[24] Birmingham Housing Commission Report (2003). Birmingham City Council (2003).

Lessons and ways forward

Lessons of neighbourhood management

There are limits to what neighbourhood management can do. Firstly, it is hard to measure the direct impact of neighbourhood management on jobs, health, education, crime without much more detailed research. But it is clear that successful neighbourhood management is beginning to impact on these, particularly crime (through greater security measures) and jobs (through local recruitment, training and more jobs on the ground). Secondly, neighbourhood management costs around £70 per household per year. There is no dedicated mainstream fund outside housing revenue budgets to pay for it, although many services could contribute. Thirdly, it is impossible to launch something as complicated and sensitive as neighbourhood management in one go. It needs to grow with the capacity of local authorities and other bodies to organise it. There is a logic, underlined by the Social Exclusion Unit's reports, to focusing on the most difficult urban areas first. But even these, with 2000-3000 such areas, will take time. Fourthly, in most cases, initiatives are coupled with other targeted spending programmes. This additional investment provides a strong incentive to break out of the traditional management structure. Fifthly, many other types of neighbourhood, including more rural areas, would like to benefit.

The most encouraging elements of our evidence are that: neighbourhood management has become permanent and mainstream funded in all cases we used in our initial study; investment money has come through additional one-off start-up programmes; it costs about the same to provide neighbourhood management as to organise services centrally and it can help all services work better because it improves both conditions and co-ordination; its impact is verified by all the parties we spoke to and by the evidence we gathered on our visits and by the findings of the Neighbourhood Renewal Unit.

Such measures as resident satisfaction and involvement, support from schools, doctors, police, reduced empty property, vandalism and nuisance, high staff morale operating within core cost limits, all suggest that neighbourhood management is a critical piece in the jigsaw of solutions needed to tackle distressed, declining and highly built-up neighbourhoods. If such neighbourhoods were better managed, they would retain and attract more people in work. If they did that, there would be more resources to fund better management.

Neighbourhood management is doable but it needs vision, energy and dedicated resources. It must have a strong local focus but a broad remit within the area to give it vitality and scope for radical change. It has major knock-on impacts on the environment, security, jobs on the ground, and service innovation. It could make cities and inner neighbourhoods much more attractive. It can be applied and work almost anywhere.

Acknowledgements

Thanks are due to Emmet Bergin, who conducted the original research, to the Neighbourhood Renewal Unit for providing up to date information on the pathfinders, and to Alice Coulter for constant editorial and research support.

References

Birmingham Housing Commission Report (2003).

Birmingham City Council (2002), Housing Commission Report.

Birmingham City Council (2003).

Bradford City Council (2002).

Broadwater Farm Estate, Haringey, and Waltham Forest Housing Action Trust (1999), Supplementary Report on Neighbourhood Management.

Burrows, Roger (1998), Unpopular Places?: Area disadvantage and the geography of misery in England, Bristol.

Development Trusts Association. Accessed at http://www.dta.org.uk/index2.html.

Glennerster, Howard, et al., eds. (1998), The State of Welfare: The Economics of Social Spending, Oxford.

Government Office for the North West (2000), Report on Town Centre Management.

Greenwich Millennium Village (2003).

Hall, Peter (1999), Evidence on Urban Neighbourhoods, Presented to the Urban Task Force.

Mumford, Katherine/Power, Anne (2003), East Enders: Family and community in East London, Bristol.

National Strategy for Neighbourhood Renewal (2000), Action Team Reports (1998-2000) SEU.

Neighbourhood Renewal Unit (2003), Press release, Guidance of Neighbourhood Management.

Neighbourhood Renewal Unit, ODPM (2003).

Office of the Deputy Prime Minister (ODPM) (n.y.), Creating sustainable communities: Neighbourhood Wardens. Accessed at

http://www.odpm.gov.uk/stellent/groups/odpm_urbanpolicy/documents/page/odpm_urbpol_608201.hcsp.

Office of the Deputy Prime Minister (2002), Choice-based lettings pilots.

Pathfinders (2003), Evaluation Framework, press releases, ODPM, Unpublished.

Poplar HARCA (1999), Supplementary Report on Neighbourhood Management.

Power, Anne (1993), Hovels to High Rise, London.

Power, Anne (1997), Estates on the Edge, London.

Power, Anne/Bergin, Emmet (1999), Supplementary Report on Neighbourhood Management, Coventry City Council.

Power, Anne/Tunstall, Rebecca (1995), Swimming Against the Tide, York.

Power, Anne/Tunstall, Rebecca (1997), Dangerous Disorder: Riots and Violent Disturbances in 13 Areas of Britain, 1991-92, York.

Social Exclusion Unit (1998), Bringing Britain Together: A national Strategy for Neighbourhood Renewal.

The Regeneration of Fatima Mansions: Lessons from Dublin

Mary P. Corcoran

> *"Where we live makes a big difference in the quality of our lives, and how the places in which we live function has a big impact on the quality of our society."*[1]

In the 1990's, Ireland entered an unprecedented period of economic growth characterised by falling unemployment rising income levels and property prices, a dramatic increase in the numbers of the cars on the road, and greater levels of consumer spending. There is considerable evidence however, that the benefits of economic growth are unevenly distributed across the population.[2] Socio-economic inequalities in Ireland were deepening rather than attenuating at the turn of the twenty-first century. The global re-organisation of production that has contributed to the country's economic boom has concomitant social costs. While there has been growth in the technology and service sectors of the economy, the relatively high incomes, good skills and steady work that epitomised traditional manufacturing industries, are in decline. Spatial and regional cleavages are proliferating. These divisions are brought into sharp relief in the city of Dublin, which is highly spatially segregated in relation to social class and property ownership.[3]

---

1 Drieir (2001).

2 O'Hearn (1998), p. 117-146.

3 It is not yet possible to obtain disaggregated data on unemployment levels from the 2002 Census. While the numbers are likely to have declined since 1996, the district electoral divisions (DED) with the highest levels of long term unemployment are likely to be the areas where the risk of social exclusion remains highest. These areas are principally concentrated in the north inner-city and in outer suburban districts that have a high concentration of local authority housing. Research based on household level data demonstrate that many local authority estates tend to have above average concentrations of households experiencing multiple deprivation, (National Institute of Regional and Spatial Analysis, 2001). Furthermore, the 1999-2000 Household Budget Survey reported a widening gap between high income and low income groups in the state in the preceding five years. The ratio between the average weekly income of households in thc lowest income decile compared to those in the highest decile was approximately 13 to 1 compared with 11 to 1 in 1994-1995.

In recent years, Dublin has become one of the most fashionable of European capitals. The city's image as the symbolic homeland of literary and popular cultural icons combined with its reputation for charm and friendliness have been feted in the international press. Once a dreary provincial backwater on the periphery of Europe, Dublin has entered the twenty-first century as a magnet city for the global tourist. The built environment of the city has changed inexorably, driven in large part by tax incentives made available to developers, investors and owner-occupiers under urban renewal schemes. Meanwhile, many inner-city communities reliant on social housing continue to face the challenges associated with de-industrialisation in their neighborhoods and the proliferation of locally organized drug economy and cultures.

The purpose of this paper is threefold: firstly, I will briefly examine Dublin's socio-spatial configuration, particularly in light of the accelerated economic growth that has occurred since the mid 1990's. Secondly, I will summarise the characteristics of the housing market in the city of Dublin, with a particular focus on the social housing sector. Finally, I will present a case study of a single social housing complex, in the city – Fatima Mansions – which, having fallen into a state of structural crisis, is now the target of a major urban regeneration project. The re-imagining of the Fatima Mansions that is ongoing – in terms of its physical structure and layout, social structure and composition, economic potential and cultural creativity – is the outcome of a hard won partnership between local champions, community groups and activists, municipal authorities and central government representatives.

The decline of the inner city and the ex-urbanisation of Dublin

Despite the establishment of a network of towns in the eighteenth century, the proportion of the Irish population that is urban based has historically remained relatively low in comparison with other European countries.[4] Nevertheless, the most recent census data available indicate that in 2002, just under sixty percent of the population was located in urban areas, that is settlements of 1,500 people or more. In the 1990's, Dublin consolidated its dominant position within the Irish urban system. The population of Dublin City is just below 500,000, while the population of the Dublin region has a population in excess of 1.1 million.[5] Dublin City has a thriv-

[4] McKeown (1986), p. 326-343.
[5] Central Statistics Office (2002).

ing central business district that co-exists with pockets of neighborhood dereliction which have recently become targets of a range of integrated development plans. Like many British and North American cities, Dublin suffered from poor planning in the 1960's and the 1970's. Much of the fabric of the city centre was bulldozed out of existence, to create the semblance at least of a 'corporate city in-the-making.' Considerable profits were derived by key individuals from property development in the city centre, and land speculation in the city's sprawling suburbs. At the same time, the city council vigorously pursued a policy of relocating inner-city residents to new social housing schemes on the city's perimeter. The social fabric of the city and its capacity to form sustainable communities was systematically undermined. The erosion of inner-city communities through job loss and the disappearance of homes, was paralleled by the growth of new ex-urbanised communities on the fringes of Dublin City, where population growth continues to increase at a dramatic rate.

Rapid suburban development contributed to the decline of the inner-city residential area partly because, in the 1970's, most private and state investment, not only in housing but also in retail, was channelled into suburban areas.[6] The drive toward suburban homeownership also produced a *residualisation effect* in the social housing sector. In 1994, 62 percent of all households living in public housing in Ireland's five main cities were poor, as compared to 48 percent in 1987.[7] Today, the boundaries of Dublin continue to expand in a relentless process of ex-urbanisation such that private housing, shopping, entertainment and employment are increasingly located on the city's outskirts. This growth on the edge of the city "is impelled by suburban values...and the economic logic of an informational economy and consumerist society."[8] These suburban outposts are linked through a series of ring roads and motorways largely financed by European Union structural funding.

Urban renewal

Beginning in the mid 1970's, community activists and environmentalists in Dublin began to express a growing disquiet about ex-urbanisation and its effect on the city core and inner-city communities. Responding to public pressure, the city government in 1975, changed its public housing policy of building blocks of flats in favour of building houses on sites

---

[6] McKeown (1986), p. 368.

[7] Breathnach (2000).

[8] McGuigan (1996), p. 100.

within the inner-city. Fiscal rectitude, however, dictated that the number of these houses would be relatively small. Inner city regeneration was given a further boost in 1982, when a political deal negotiated between the government and a community activist who held the balance of power in the newly elected parliament, guaranteed Exchequer funding to revitalise a designated area in the north inner-city. These two episodes marked the beginning of a re-orientation of urban policy in the city of Dublin, although the short-term impact was piecemeal and limited. It was not until the mid-1980s that state sponsored urban renewal began in earnest and private capital began to flow into urban areas. This inward capital flow was predicated on a core economic logic. Reinvestment occurred precisely at the point when generous tax incentives were made available by the Exchequer to reduce risk exposure on the part of potential developers on the one hand, and to create a market of largely gentrifying consumers, on the other.

Explanations of the revitalisation of the inner city must take account of the key role played by producers – builders, developers, landlords, mortgage lenders and government agencies – in that process. In the 1960's and 1970's, developers set their sights on sites on Dublin's perimeter where extensive spatial expansion was both possible and cheap. The alternative--urban renewal and the regeneration of the built inner-city environment--would have been too costly for private capital to undertake. Eventually though, the depreciation of capital invested in residential inner-city neighborhoods produced the objective economic conditions that makes capital revaluation a rational market response.[9] In the Irish case, the market needed a push in this direction. The impetus was provided by the Urban Renewal Act (1986) which made available a generous package of tax-based incentives to developers, investors and owner-occupiers. The urban renewal scheme was designed to promote *private investment in the built environment* of designated inner-city areas either through refurbishment of existing buildings or through new developments. More than ten thousand new apartments have been built in the inner-city since the inception of the urban renewal scheme.

There is considerable evidence that the urban renewal schemes have opened up inner city space for the urban gentry and the visiting tourist, while at the same time, offering little to better the quality of life of the indigenous population. The back to the city living trend has reversed a pattern of population decline in the inner-city wards of Dublin, which was consistent since the 1920's. While urban renewal in selected areas and an influx of apartment dwellers has reversed the physical decline and in-

9 Smith (1979), p. 538-48.

creased the population, existing class divisions have, in recent years, been exacerbated.[10] The economic restructuring of Dublin has proceeded in tandem with the increased social and cultural segregation of the city's population. A number of surveys profiling the beneficiaries of tax designation and urban renewal schemes, reveal that the typical apartment resident is young, highly educated, in employment and has the expectation to move out of their current dwelling and to the suburbs within two years.[11] This profile is in stark contrast to that of the indigenous inner-city community which has higher than average proportions of population under fifteen years and over 65 years, a high incidence (over 30 percent) of lone parenthood, and high levels of unemployment.[12] A major review of the urban renewal schemes published by the Department of Environment ten years after their inception concluded that "in those designated areas which have adjacent indigenous inner-city communities, the local communities believe that urban renewal as defined by the incentive schemes, has not addressed issues which are central to the regeneration and sustainable redevelopment of those areas such as unemployment, the lack of public amenities, education, training and youth development."[13] The government approved a new urban renewal scheme which became operative on August 1, 1998, and which was based on the recommendations set out in the consultants review. The second round of the urban renewal schemes were re-oriented to provide for a more planned, integrated and focused approach to urban renewal designations. As a result, Dublin City Council adapted an integrated area planning approach to urban regeneration. Within this strategy the rehabilitation of old housing stock and the development of new stock have become major priorities.

Housing and the housing market

Until recent years, housing has not been central to policy debate or academic research on poverty issues in Ireland.[14] In the 1980's Irish housing was characterised by falling demand and falling production. While 5,500 social housing units were completed in the state in 1981, this had

---

[10] Connolly (1997), p. 14.

[11] *Ibid*, p. 26.

[12] *Ibid*, p. 27.

[13] KPMG (1996.

[14] The National Economic and Social Council which advises the government on social and economic policy is currently undertaking a major review of housing policy in Ireland with a view to making strategic recommendations.

dropped to 800 in 1989.[15] The fall in completion rate was accompanied by a decline in the number of people seeking social housing. More recently, the rapid growth in the economy since the mid-1990's, the rising rate of family formation and the increase in net immigration has brought considerable pressure to bear on the housing market. Private house prices doubled between 1994 and 1998, and doubled again by 2002. The social sector share of the housing market fell as a result of low output and the sales of existing units. In 2002 social housing output represented 10% of all housing built. This figure was 7% in 1992, and 21% in 1982. The total number of households in need of social housing in 2002 stood at 48,413.[16] To provide an appropriate level of social rented housing stock to meet current and anticipated need, it will be necessary to significantly increase the proportion of social housing that is being built each year.

The model of social housing provision in Ireland has been distinguished by three key characteristics: (1) it is based on subventions which are sourced from central government (2) policy implementation occurs through local authorities and (3) there has been a tendency to use standardised (and consequently stigmatising) housing designs.[17] Housing policy developed in urban areas only after the 1930's, and primarily in the form of slum clearance programs. Even at this early stage in the State's development the practice of providing either direct or indirect subsidies to those purchasing houses had been established. The state support of private housing persists to the present day and has been a key factor in Ireland's internationally high eighty percent rate of home ownership. Given the centrality of the principle of home ownership in Irish society, social housing has generally been viewed by home-owners and tenants alike, as an inferior option. If private ownership is for the upwardly mobile, then social housing tenancy is for those who are going nowhere.[18]

In addition to the supports put in place for private house building (for example, mortgage interest relief, regular re-zoning of agricultural land, first time buyer's grant) there has been a long tradition of sales of local authority housing to tenants, which continues to the present day. As a result, local authorities – particularly in Dublin – have relinquished a considerable amount of housing stock, thus limiting the overall growth of the local authority rental sector.[19] Rental purchase and shared ownership

---

15 Paris (2003).

16 Irish Council for Social Housing (2002).

17 Fraser (1996).

18 The author was one of the investigators on a national study of quality of life in Irish social housing estates carried out in the late 1990's. Fahey, ed. (1999).

19 Fahey (1998).

schemes promoted by Dublin City Council have reduced the pool of housing available for people in need, and have had the effect of narrowing even further the range of households likely to obtain local authority housing. Tenants and housing officials readily agree that the "flight from the flats" of many who formed the backbone of inner-city communities is at least partly attributable to the incentives available in the private and local authority housing sector to purchase one's own home.

In light of the current levels of housing need, and mindful of limitations on resources since the downturn in the economy in 2001-2002, Dublin City Council has had to look creatively at its housing provision and how that might be better managed and delivered in the future. A number of regeneration projects currently underway in the city of Dublin are exploring new and better ways of providing for the housing needs of communities in deprived neighborhoods. It is to an examination of one such case study that we will now turn.

Fatima Mansions- A case study

Fatima Mansions was built between 1949 and 1951 by Dublin City Council (formerly Dublin Corporation), in the south west of Dublin's inner-city. The development originally consisted of fifteen blocks of four storey flat units, with an average of 27 units per block. The complex is configured inwardly which has had the effect of cutting Fatima Mansions off, both physically and symbolically, from the surrounding neighborhood of Rialto. Residents and ex-residents of the complex who recalled the early decades of the estate were generally very positive in their evaluations. Most of the men worked locally in manufacturing and service sector jobs. The community was tightly knit and relations with neighbours were governed by a norm of reciprocity. One old-timer recalled the estate in the early days:

> *I was like a child when I came to Fatima first. I thought it would never get dark until I switched on the light. I thought I was in heaven with a living room, a kitchen, three bedrooms and a bathroom. We had been living in one room before then, with a tin hut out the back, and a zinc bath for the children. It was great in Fatima while the good people lasted, until the bad type moved in. Like everywhere else the bad apple in the barrel, you know what I mean. We had lovely neighbours back then. Our block was something. If you ran short of anything, you just*

had to hint. You didn't even have to ask, and it would be on your doorstep. You would do the same for people.[20]

While there is no doubt that the flats were a vast improvement on the tenements that had preceded them, they were essentially a "bricks and mortar" solution to the problems faced by the Dublin working class. Little thought was given to the provision of recreational facilities or to the highly salient issues of housing density and housing allocation policy.[21] In the 1970's, a confluence of factors propelled the estate into a spiral of decline. The closure, and in some cases, relocation of local industry, adversely affected job opportunities in the area. This factor alone would have pushed an estate such as Fatima from relative stability into transition. Local government policy initiatives, which promoted home ownership, rewarded tenants who left Fatima Mansions. Weaker tenants frequently replaced those who had moved on to purchase a local authority house elsewhere, undermining the social fabric which had been the basis of a strong community. Dublin City Council services to the state declined during the 1970s, with the removal, for example, of the uniformed officials who had informally "policed" the estate. It became more difficult for both the remaining tenants and Dublin City Council to exercise moral authority on the estate. A spiral of decline was set in motion. The estate became vulnerable to problems of social disorder – vandalism, joyriding and later, drugs. Fatima Mansions earned the reputation of being an undesirable place to live. As one resident put it:

Flats were built in order to maintain social distinctions. Fatima were luxurious flats when they were built because they were third or fourth up the pecking order in the Corporation's housing. But you always had somewhere that was bottom of the heap. Fatima was a definite step up in the world. Keogh Square's was where you went if you didn't pay your rent or you were evicted or whatever. In the fullness of time, Keogh Square got knocked down because it wasn't fit for human habitation. Once they got knocked down, the flats built in the 1940s and 1950's, became bottom of the pile.

The situation in Fatima grew steadily worse throughout the late 1970's. A survey conducted in 1980 demonstrated the extent of people's dissatisfaction with the estate. At that time, two thirds of residents expressed dissatisfaction with the maintenance of their flats and sixty per cent expressed dissatisfaction with block maintenance. Lack of cleanliness

---

[20] *Unless otherwise stated all information on Fatima Mansions was collected by the author while conducting a research project there in the late 1990's. See Corcoran (1998).*

[21] Tobin (1990).

and unhygienic conditions were key complaints. Nearly three quarters of residents wanted to move out of the complex, and two thirds felt fearful living in the estate. One third of residents surveyed had experienced a break in. The presence of stolen cars in the estate was identified as a constant worry, particularly to those with children.[22] There was no question on drugs in the survey instrument used, but the drugs problem was serious enough in 1981 for a "pushers out" campaign to evolve. Under the auspices of the Fatima Development Group a campaign to improve the quality of life on the estate was initiated. A survey conducted in 1986 by a Barnardos project leader employed on the estate found that the priority issue people wanted tackled was the physical environment.[23] The campaign for change eventually resulted in a refurbishment and modernisation program carried out by Dublin City Council in the late 1980s. A report conducted in 1997, however, found that the refurbishment program was widely perceived to have failed, because it had not been preceded by an adequate consultation process with the local population.

In 1997, Fatima Groups United (FGU), Fatima Task Force (FTF) and Dublin City Council joined forces to initiate a research project entitled "Making Fatima a better place to live." FGU is the representative body of residents and groups that operate and deliver services to the residents of Fatima Mansions. FGU is the driving force behind the estate's regeneration agenda and remains the key agent in the process of social change today. It acts both as a *catalyst* of change by conceiving and implementing initiatives and as a *stimulant* in that the actions of FGU often provoke or require responses from statutory bodies. Key individuals in Fatima Groups United were born and raised in the area. Although they work as professionals and service providers, they have important street credibility on the estate because they simultaneously occupy *insider/outsider* status. FGUs key objectives are to address and prevent poverty by:

- Bringing together the various community groups in Fatima that are involved in social and community development. To improve and develop the capacity of these groups to plan, manage and operate both existing services and new services and programs
- Leading the regeneration of Fatima through working pro-actively to develop Fatima in the areas identified by the residents: education, housing, youth and child care services, treatment, health and employment

---

[22] Beggan (1981).

[23] Tobin (1990).

- Drawing in statutory agencies to engage cooperatively to further the positive development of Fatima as a better place to live.[24]

The Fatima Task Force was established in 1995 to develop a partnership model for dealing with the problems on the estate. FTF consisted of representatives from Dublin City Council, local political representatives, community police officers, health board officials, Community drugs team, Rialto Youth project and FGU. Both groups supported an integrated approach to addressing the problems affecting the area including drugs, unemployment, education, youth and the deteriorating living conditions within the complex. Both FGU and FTF had come to the conclusion that Fatima Mansions was no longer manageable as an estate and significant changes needed to be made so that people could live in safety and with dignity. Central to the commissioned research was the belief that *the needs of the community must be identified by the community* in relation to the future of Fatima. A research consultant was retained to work with the community and representatives of Dublin City Council to assess the needs of the community and to identify the way forward toward the regeneration of Fatima into a viable and sustainable community. The adapted research protocol placed a special emphasis on the residents' "definition of the situation," and was conducted in a spirit of partnership with Dublin City Council, FGU and the tenant population.[25]

Demographic profile

The most typical household type in Fatima Mansions is the lone parent family, a group that has a higher than average risk of poverty. The rise in the number of lone parent households is one of the most distinctive features of the estate since the earlier survey that was conducted in 1980. Then, ninety per cent of households conformed to the traditional nuclear family unit comprising of two parents and children. That figure has fallen dramatically to 21 percent in 1998. Lone parents and their children make

---

[24] Fatima Groups United (2002).

[25] The research involved the conduct of interviews with all residents of Fatima Mansions in 1998. Twelve local residents were hired to help structure the questionnaire and to carry out interviews with the resident population. The interviewers underway a short training program on interviewing techniques. The use of local interviewers produced a very high response rate—239 completed interviews out of 300 households (80%). The survey data was supplemented by information gathered through focus groups, participant observation on the estate and in-depth family interviews. For further details see Corcoran (1998).

up 38% of the population, considerably higher than the national average of lone-parent families as just over ten per cent of all family units. Furthermore, half of the estate population is in the highly dependent 0-15 year age group. The 26-45 age group – the cohort most likely to be exerting social control on the estate – makes up just thirty percent of the population. These statistics resonate with residents' overall perception that there are too many children – often unsupervised – on the estate. Research has demonstrated that a low rate of children to adults makes for good social control whereas a high ratio of children to adults – as is the case in Fatima Mansions – makes it difficult to maintain control.[26]

A very low level of educational attainment was recorded for the survey population. Less than five percent had attained a third level qualification, and less than ten percent had been educated to Leaving Certification level (completion of senior cycle school). The largest group, comprising 44 percent of the population, are early school leavers having left school without any formal qualifications. High levels of early school leaving led to high rates of unemployment. The employment level on the estate is extremely low at just under ten percent. About a third of respondents are engaged on full-time home duties. The next largest group, at thirty percent, are either seeking their first job or unemployed. Assuming that the questionnaire respondent was the head of household, it is possible to make some comparisons with the survey conducted in 1980. Then, when the status of the breadwinner in each household was examined, the figure of those in employment was 58 percent. This of course was in the context of a two-parent family, in which the vast majority of the women worked in the home. Only five percent of mothers were employed at that time. The decline in two-parent families on the estate and the concomitant increase in number of lone-parent families has significantly impacted on the employment rate. This probably reflects the fact that in the absence of qualifications, adequate training, accessible child care, and appropriate financial incentives, most lone parents remain full-time in the home to take care of their children.

One third of respondents stated that they had to cope with a chronic illness in the household. The most frequently cited illness was asthma. A range of other disorders including arthritis, breathing problems, bronchitis, tuberculosis, kidney and bowel troubles and epilepsy were also cited.

---

[26] Page (1993), p. 16.

A community that endures and an enduring community

By the late 1990's, daily life in Fatima had become a feat of endurance. The most common motif employed by residents to characterise their daily lives was that of imprisonment. Trapped in an environment over which they had little or no control, they expressed feelings of hopelessness and despair. Their lives were dominated by two factors in particular: firstly, the breakdown of social order on the estate which facilitated a drug economy and culture that continues to the present day, second, the inadequate upkeep and maintenance of the public areas of the estate. Both factors are of course inter-related, as the degraded environment, with dimly lit stairwells and boarded up flats, provided a safe haven for those seeking to buy and sell drugs without fear of apprehension. Even Dublin City Council officials had come to recognize the indefensibility of the public space on the estate. The weakness of a moral authority structure means that public spaces, in particular, had become the virtual fiefdom not only of those involved in the drug economy and culture, but also of children and youth who literally run wild. This problem of anti-social behaviour is a long standing one, and remains unresolved.

Residents had internalised the belief that they were perceived as "second- class" citizens by the statutory authorities, and that the quality of service provided to them reflected their overall status in society. Hence, they tended to be highly critical and mistrustful of the local authority. By the end of the 1990's, Fatima Mansions had become a blight on the city's landscape. It is not surprising, therefore, that people felt ashamed of where they lived and did not feel comfortable about asking a friend to visit. Although difficult to quantify, it is generally accepted that residents of areas with "bad reputations" suffer from "address effects" – "an intangible but pervasive form of discrimination based on their place of residence."[27] This serves the dual effect of reinforcing their social exclusion and inhibiting the prospect of economic regeneration through inward investment. It is impossible to escape being labelled by virtue of being in residence.

Among the population, high levels of distrust were recorded in regard to Dublin City Council, politicians and the Gardai (national police force). Residents felt strongly that in policing the estate a distinction ought to be made between reactive policing (apprehending drug users, moving on "undesirables") and pro-active policing (protecting citizens). This lack of trust in the statutory authorities who are charged with delivering services to residents on the estates, has a corrosive effect in that "police pessimism, pessimism about the police and tenant feelings of ambiguity about strang-

---

[27] OECD (1998), p. 57.

ers, conspire to erode any residual faith in the effectiveness of community or official responses to crime."[28]

Alongside the simmering despair at the level of degradation into which the estate had fallen by the end of the 1990's, there was also a strong sense of an enduring social fabric and cohesive social networks. A high proportion of people in Fatima have lived there for more than twenty years, and in some families, tenancy has passed down through a second and third generation. Social ties with neighbours and extended families are extremely strong. Significant numbers believe there is a good community spirit in Fatima, although this is most prevalent at block rather than estate level. A majority expressed an interest in getting involved in lobbying to bring about change on the estate. Although people speak about the horrors of daily life and child rearing in Fatima, they, nevertheless, display remarkable resilience and a sense of humour in the face of these difficulties. There is a very real discrepancy between the total social breakdown which residents have had to live with on a daily basis- the physical degradation of the environment, the difficulty in securing adequate maintenance, the constant presence of drug dealers and users, the stigma attached to living in the complex—and their frequent reference to the great neighbours they have or have had, and the supportiveness of extended family networks. In 1998, a substantial majority of residents (58%) felt that there was still a sense of community on the estate, and that that was something valuable and worth trying to save. The overwhelming majority of residents saw the way forward as total demolition and a re-design of the flat complex.

In summary, Fatima Mansions suffered a crisis of transition in the 1970's and early 1980's. In the 1990's, the estate moved into a situation of "structural crisis:" the complex was beset by high rates of poverty and unemployment, low levels of educational attainment, and increased criminality and drug related activity. The problems on the estate clearly resulted from the spatial, social and economic inequalities that characterise the city of Dublin. A structural crisis on this scale demands a structural solution. Thus, it became clear to Fatima Groups United (FGU), to Dublin City Council and to the residents themselves that Fatima Mansions must be targeted as a priority area for regeneration.

[28] Newman (1972), p. 49.

Steps toward regeneration

For some time, FGU had been the most active agency at work on the estate. Since its inception FGU has sponsored a range of initiatives in research, policy, local development, education and training courses, community consultation and participatory courses. In particular, since 1998, FGU has undertaken a series of innovative actions and programs to drive forward and help shape the regeneration process. This has involved a visionary and courageous approach to a set of very real challenges set against the backdrop of extreme deprivation and the failure of previous public policy interventions.

The findings of the report "Making Fatima a Better Place to Live" were presented to the Fatima Task Force and were widely disseminated and debated throughout the Fatima Mansions community. Drawing on the recommendation in the report, that greater community awareness and participation could be fostered by implementing a block-level representative scheme, FGU set in motion a further consultative initiative aimed at community capacity building at block level in the estate.

Recognizing that it is often difficult to motivate people in marginalized communities to go onto committees, FGU introduced a different model for electing residents onto its management committee in 2002. Traditionally, as with most community representative structures, notices would be sent to residents informing them of the annual general meeting, and depending on a range of factors including the weather, attendance would vary on the day. The new system for electing representatives onto the residents panel involved a number of elements:

- A communication strategy to both encourage residents to go forward for election and to participate in the process.
- Clear procedures and guidelines were drawn up for the election process including eligibility requirements and rules governing the process

The idea underlying this strategy was to promote and encourage participation of residents in local democracy and in their community. Furthermore, by creating awareness of the electoral process it may encourage more participation in national and local government elections.[29] In the recent election for block representatives to FGU, 46% of the residents voted. Six out of a total of eleven candidates were elected to represent the community voice in the ongoing regeneration process.[30]

---

[29] FGU Annual Report (2002), p. 9.

[30] Inside Fatima (2003).

In 2000, FGU approached the local health board to carry out an audit on the health and well-being of Fatima Mansion's resident population. This work was carried out in 2000-2001. A link was established with the ARK, a children's arts resource centre based in the city of Dublin, in order to develop and devise a participatory arts program for children and adults on the estate. An oral history project was initiated under the auspices of FGU in 1998. Project members have worked with a historian to present oral history workshops and devise presentations and slide shows based on the photographic and archival records compiled. These kinds of projects are crucial for restoring a sense of identity and re-kindling a sense of belonging in communities that have become fragmented through deprivation and decline.

Along with this range of initiatives, a process of negotiation on the future of the estate between FGU and Dublin City Council was initiated but ended inconclusively. FGU then established an ad hoc regeneration team that produced an innovative and colourful manifesto, titled *Eleven Acres: Ten Steps*. The document was the outcome of a creative thinking exercise which involved the entire community in Fatima in articulating their visions and needs regarding the place where they live. *Eleven Acres: Ten Steps* comprised a brief from the community of Fatima Mansions to the planners, developers and service providers tasked with the regeneration of the housing estate. It set out the community's vision for its future, and invited Dublin City Council to enter into a dialogue on how the area ought to be regenerated. Crucially, the impetus for a plan for the regeneration came from the community, who placed themselves firmly in the driving seat of the proposed regeneration. *Eleven Acres: Ten Steps* was launched at the end of 2000 by a high profile television and radio presenter. The community took the opportunity to demonstrate their talents and entertainment skills to a media used to covering only "bad news" stories about Fatima Mansions.

In Februrary 2001, Dublin City Council published its own plan for the regeneration, Regeneration/Next generation. This plan commits to key principles of urban regeneration including the creation of sustainable housing and sustainable communities. According to Dublin City Council's master plan for the estate, the regeneration is driven by the need to rehouse 700 residents in high quality, low rise, low density homes. It is envisioned that this housing together with the community facilities that will come on stream will occupy nine acres of the site. The remaining two acres plus additional land acquired by Dublin City Council, will provide additional high quality private housing plus community and commercial facilities. This model of public/private provision on a single site is in accordance with guidelines that require the optimal use of city land and the promotion of mixed residential areas and better integration.[31] Research in Britain has demonstrated that compared with large deprived estates, socially balanced neighborhoods are likely to be less stigmatised by outsiders.[32]

The publication of Dublin City Council's regeneration plan was followed by extensive consultation over a three-month period with residents of Fatima Mansions and people living in the adjoining neighborhood. Following consultation and further negotiation under the auspices of the newly established, Fatima Regeneration Board, consensus was reached among the stakeholders. An overall physical plan was agreed and is now in its final stages of implementation. Fatima Regeneration Board draws together residents, the community sector, local government representatives and state services. It is chaired by an independent – a highly respected, retired High Court judge. The regeneration plan will cost in the region of Euro 125m. and involves the demolition of all the existing blocks of flats and their replacement with 230 social housing units consisting of two-storey, three-storey and four-storey homes in the form of duplexes and some traditional type houses. All existing Dublin City Council tenants in Fatima Mansions will be accommodated on the re-developed site. A further 300 private apartments will be constructed on a portion of the site. Dublin City Council hopes to purchase land alongside the estate to develop light industrial and other commercial enterprises to provide jobs locally. Crucially, the plan maintains a dual commitment to both the physical and social needs of the area. Over the course of the next five years, the plan aims:

- To deliver new standards in quality of public housing and community facilities
- To undertake innovative actions aimed at breaking the cycle of poverty on the estate
- To foster effective social integration and measures that promote and safeguard community participation in developing and sustaining the new Fatima, which will triple in size.

While the physical regeneration plan is well underway, the social regeneration agenda has yet to be finalised. At present, there are five working groups loosely grouped under the regeneration board. Each group will tackle a specific issue: anti-social behaviour, health and well-being, education and training, arts and culture, and economic development. A strategy has yet to be drawn up for the prioritising and goal setting in relation to the

31 Dublin City Council (2001), p. 14.

32 Goodchild/Cole (2001), Vol. 19, p. 118.

community needs. Unlike the physical regeneration, no funds have been set aside to implement a social regeneration plan. As a first step toward formulating medium to long-term objectives, a social audit has been undertaken of existing services and projected future needs in Fatima Mansions and the surrounding neighborhoods.

Conclusion

The Fatima Mansions urban regeneration project examined here raise many pertinent questions about the process of urban regeneration in Dublin. In particular, there are several key lessons that can be derived from those experiences:

- The necessity to adapt a partnership approach to planning and to consult with the local community and stakeholders
- The necessity to develop projects that are sustainable in the long-term
- The necessity to include a principle of equity so that the benefits of urban renewal are more widely distributed across the urban population
- The necessity to counteract tendencies toward social polarisation in the city.

Dublin has long suffered from an absence of a coherent urban policy. In recent years, however, the city council has begun to take a more proactive role in developing urban initiatives that will go some way toward addressing the lessons learned from the earlier urban renewal experiences. The integrated area plans (IAPs) which address the economic and social regeneration of designated areas, while protecting and enhancing the built environment and green space, have adapted an integrated and partnership approach toward urban redevelopment. There is also evidence of the emergence of a culture of resistance to development which is perceived as non-contiguous with the current scale and scope of the city. Community voices, in particular, are not prepared to accede to development which does not have a partnership element built into the design, planning and implementation process. Furthermore, there is a growing awareness on all sides that unfettered development which does not take account of the vernacular of the city, and the needs of those without means, can only lead to a Dublin which is more placeless and more polarised. If Dublin is to look for models of urban development it is to European cities rather than American cities that it must orient itself.

References

Beggan, M. (1981), Draft Report of Survey of Fatima Mansions, Dublin City Council, Dublin.

Breathnach, Proinnsias (2000), Social Polarisation and Exclusion in Urban Ireland, Paper presented to American Conference for Irish Studies, University of Limerick, July 1.

Central Statistics Office (2002), Preliminary Findings of the 2002 Census, Dublin.

Connolly, David (1997), Developing Dublin's Inner City-Who Benefits? Unpublished thesis, Master of Science in Policy Studies, Trinity College Dublin/ Institute of Public Administration, Dublin.

Corcoran, Mary P. (1998), Making Fatima a better place to live, Fatima Groups United: Dublin

Dublin City Council (2001), Regeneration/Next generation: looking forward to a new future for Fatima, Dublin.

Drieir, Peter/Mollendkopf, John/Swanstrom, Todd (2001), Place Matters: metropolitics for the twenty-first century, Kansas.

FGU (2002), Annual Report.

Fraser, Murray (1996), John Bull's other homes: state housing and British policy in Ireland, 1883-1922, Liverpol.

Fahey, Tony (1998), "Housing and Social Exclusion" in Seán Healy and Brigid Reynolds, eds. (1998), Social Policy in Ireland: principles, practices and problems, Dublin.

Fahey, Tony, ed. (1999), Social Housing in Ireland: A Study of Success, Failure and Lessons Learned, Dublin.

Fatima Groups United (2002), Annual Report, FGU, Dublin.

Goodchild, Barry/Cole, Ian (2001), "Social balance and mixed neighborhoods in Britain since 1979: a review of discourse and practice in social housing" in Environment and Planning D, Society and Space, Vol. 19, p. 103-121.

Inside Fatima (2003), FGU Newsletter, July.

Irish Council for Social Housing (2002), Annual Report, Dublin.

KPMG (1996), Report on the Urban Renewal Schemes Department of the Environment, Dublin.

McKeown, Kieran (1986), "Urbanisation in the Republic of Ireland: A Conflict Approach" in Patrick Clancy et al., eds. (1987), Ireland: A Sociological Profile, Institute of Public Administration, Dublin.

McGuigan, Jim (1996), Culture and the Public Sphere, London.

Newman, Oscar (1972), Defensible Space, London.

OECD (1998). Integrating Distressed Estates. Paris: Organisation for Economic Cooperation and Development.

O'Hearn, Denis (1998), Inside the Celtic Tiger, London.

Page, David (1993), Building for Communities, Joseph Rowntree Foundation, London.

Paris, Chris (2003), Charting the direction: future prospects for social housing ICHS Paper presented at the Biennial National Housing Conference, September 30-October 2.

Smith, Neil (1979), "Toward a Theory of Gentrification." Journal of the American Planning Association, Vol. 45, p. 538-48.

Tobin, Pat (1990), Ways ahead: a case study of community development in an inner-city area of Dublin, Dublin.

Socially Integrative City Strategies in Germany - Experience and Prospects

Heidede Becker / Rolf-Peter Löhr

This article is about the implementation of the joint program of the German federal government and the *Länder*. The program is called "Districts with Special Development Needs – the Socially Integrative City." ("Soziale Stadt") – Experiences and Prospects. Like similar policies in other European countries, the program responds to overall changes to the urban fabric.

Fundamental socioeconomic change has aggravated social inequality German cities and towns as well. More and more neighborhoods are becoming the focus of negative trends. For almost twenty years evidence has been mounting that traditional urban development support is not able to solve the complex problems in disadvantaged urban districts. The joint federal *Land* program Soziale Stadt (The Socially Integrative City) was launched in 1999 as an addition to conventional urban development aid. The Socially Integrative City program is based on an administrative agreement between the federal government and Germany's *Länder*.

After consultation with *Land* authorities, the Federal Ministry of Transport, Building and Housing (BMVBW) delegated several aspects of the initial program implementation phase, ending in February 2003, to the German Institute of Urban Affairs (Difu). The agency handled information, consulting and communication services. This activity was not financed by the program Socially Integrative City. The funds came from the Federal Office of Building and Regional Planning Agency (BBR) Experimental Housing and Urban Development (ExWoSt) scheme. Difu assistance comprises four core elements: erecting a nationwide Socially Integrative City network; establishing onsite program support (PvO) in sixteen model districts, one chosen by each *Land*; conducting good-practice analyses; and preparing a Socially Integrative City evaluation.

In late 2002 the BBR, at the behest of the BMVBW, awarded a contract to provide an expertise Interim Evaluation of the Federal *Land* Socially Integrative City Program to the Urban Research Institute (IfS). Findings will be available by the middle of 2004. They will furnish input for further implementation of the program. Results of Difu support are a fundamental source for the interim assessment.

Currently there are 331 "urban districts with special development needs" in 229 cities and towns. The districts aided in 1999, 2000 and 2001 had a total of about 1.74 million residents. Western German *Länder* accounted for 1.34 million and the territory of the former East Germany 0.4 million. However, there is considerable evidence that many more urban districts have comparable development requirements but have not yet been targeted by the program.

Figure 1: Elements of the program

National 'Socially Integrative City' network 300 program areas 1999 – 2002			Onsite Program Support	Program evaluation preparation
Central and decentralized events **Kickoff event** 5 July 1999, Berlin **Starter conference** 1/2 March 2000, Berlin **Impetus congresses** 26/27 October 2000, Leipzig; 5/6 November 2001, Essen **Congress: Socially Integrative City – An Initial Appraisal** 7/8 May 2002 **Regional feedback exchanges** **Local starter and topic-based conferences in pilot areas**	**Reports** **Information on the Socially Integrative City** topical information, 1-13 published to date **Working Papers on the Socially Integrative City Program** project findings, documentation, materials; volumes 1-10 published to date **Instruction book to the Congress Socially Integrative City – cooperation, security, future** **Strategies for the social city. Report of the program company**	**Internet Forum** **Program information service** including dates and material on specific events, regional information, publications, project data-base, online versions of reports, contact with Difu project group **Public discussion forum**	**16 pilot areas** Singen – Langenrain (BW) Nürnberg – Galgenhof/Steinbühl (BY) Berlin-Kreuzberg – Kottbusser Tor (B) Cottbus – Sachsendorf-Madlow (BB) Bremen-Gröpelingen (HB) Hamburg-Altona – Lurup (HH) Kassel – Nordstadt (HE) Schwerin – Neu Zippendorf (MV) Hannover – Vahrenheide-Ost (ND) Gelsenkirchen – Bismarck/ Schalke Nord (NW) Ludwigshafen – Westend (RP) Neunkirchen – Innenstadt (SL) Leipzig – Leipziger Osten (S) Halle – Silberhöhe (SA) Flensburg – Neustadt (SH) Leinefelde – Südstadt (TH) **Support and documentation** **Activation and support**	**Two country wide inquiries** with the partner for the program Socially Integrative City in the cities and municipalities **Good practice analyses** Projects and measures Integrated Action Plan Resource pooling Management and organization

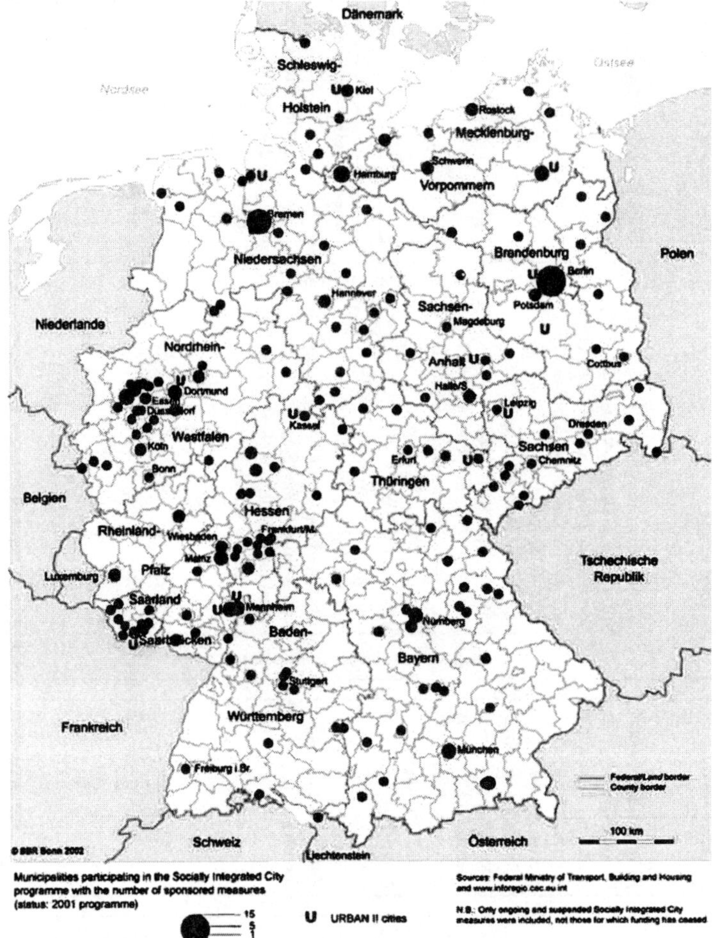

Figure 2: Federal/Länder Socially Integrative City Program and URBAN II cities

Areas with "special development needs" – Socially Integrated City program districts

A prerequisite for allocating urban planning funds – also applicable to the Socially Integrated City program – is the well-founded identification of geographical units as program districts, according to ARGEBAU (Planning Panel of the Housing Committee) guidelines (4.2, Paragraph 2). "Delimiting the district is the task of borough and town councils. Before they can do that they need a detailed picture of the envisioned improvements in the entire municipality. They must analyse all major aspects of life. Assisted areas must prove that their deficits place them distinctly below the average." ARGEBAU recommends that such "district selection is to follow transparent local government procedures and be decided by the appropriate representative body."

The "special" development need justifying admission to the Socially Integrative City program presupposes a citywide comparison. Candidates must demonstrate that they have an urgent need for support exceeding that of other districts, that their development should thus be given higher priority and that they should be favoured with available resources. The selection procedure should therefore be transparent and plausible to merit adoption as municipal policy.

When delimiting their program districts, the integrative aspirations of the program have eventually determined their size- they dictated to accept larger territories. Decisions have taken into account important infrastructure. Schools, cultural institutions and convenient shopping centres with their catchment areas were considered. Other criteria included spatially overlapping problems. Socially Integrative City districts are on an average 12 times as large as subdivisions in traditional urban renewal.

Problems and potentials as selection criteria

Which problems and capabilities, gauged by which indicators, identify districts as having special needs? Both surveys reveal a broad spectrum of oft-lamented problems compounding one another in the program districts. Unsurprisingly, the most frequent complaints were about structural and urban planning shortcomings such as backlogs in modernization, drops in investment or even urban decay and living environment misgivings. Respondents also mentioned deficits in the social and cultural infrastructure, links to local supply networks, and public spaces. They also pointed out the lack of socio-structural facilities and functions. The poll evidenced insufficient work opportunities but ample cases of conflict with other inhabitants.

The populations in the Socially Integrated City program areas suffer much more from unemployment and require much more social assistance than the average of all districts in the municipality. These are the central criteria for selecting the areas. Some districts offer almost no jobs whatsoever. Program districts in Schleswig-Holstein, Sachsen-Anhalt, Niedersachsen and Saar*Land* have the highest average unemployment rate. Comparing the respective districts with the city as a whole demonstrates their special development needs.[1] Over half the selected districts (53%) have unemployment figures of fifteen percent or more, only nineteen percent of the cities' remaining districts have such high jobless rates. Unemployment in the Socially Integrated City districts tended to cluster between fifteen and twenty percent.

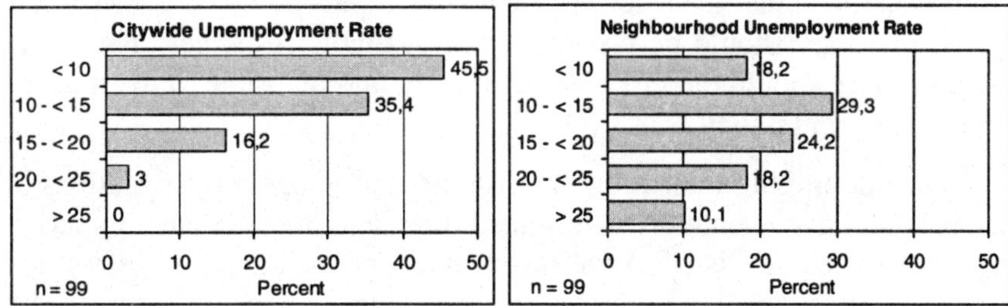

Figure 3: Unemployment Rate in City and District
(n = 99) second survey (Difu 2002)

It is striking that program districts in the former West Germany rely much more heavily on social welfare than eastern districts do. Districts in Niedersachsen, Baden-Württemberg and Schleswig-Holstein top the list. The program districts also had a far higher proportion of social welfare recipients when compared to the city as a whole. 46 percent of all city districts have a social welfare recipient level of under five percent. Only seventeen percent of the disadvantaged areas have a figure this low. The picture is reversed when we consider rates over ten percent. Only five percent of the rest of the city exhibit such high figures. Ten percent or more of the population in over half the program districts (58%) were on welfare.

As a general rule, the combination of high unemployment and excessive dependence on welfare is the main reason for selecting a district. In some cases drops in population, a negative image, social conflicts, despair and lack of perspective, isolation and uncertainty can furnish further grounds.

Around a third of all program districts (72) record many vacant properties. Clearly and not unexpectedly, the former East Germany suffers more from this than western *Länder* (83% and 21% respectively of all districts). More than a fifth of eastern program districts have a vacant property rate of over twenty percent. In some places the figure is as high as

[1] When comparing indicator values between districts and the entire city, only those program areas were included that provided data on both.

forty percent. However, this is also a major problem in the former West Germany. Two thirds of the program districts with the highest number of vacant properties are found there.

District selection in the former West Germany is clearly also influenced by above-average proportions of immigrant households (in places over 50%).

Structures and urban planning also featured most strongly in responses about district potential and resources. Examples were renovation and modernization possibilities, development and redesign options for green spaces and vacant lots. However, around half the districts applauded the willingness of the population to participate and the opportunities for expanding the local economy and sociocultural infrastructure.

Classifying and weighing districts' significance for the whole city

1999, 2000 and 2001 Socially Integrated City districts were remarkably heterogeneous. Their main common denominator was a concentration of problems exceeding those of the rest of the city. Two distinct types of "districts with special development needs" have long since been identified. One type is the densely populated neighborhood with old buildings usually from the early days of the German Empire and the industrial age. It may feature a large number of juxtaposed small settlements. The other type is the primarily prefabricated housing estates from the 1960's to 1980's (called *Großtafel* in the west and *Plattenbau* in the east).

The survey results confirm this typology. Neighborhoods consisting of only old buildings (20%) and mixed-age neighborhoods (21%) constitute two fifths of all program districts. However, 55 percent of the districts are new estates. In the former East Germany this figure is even higher, at 68 percent. The preponderance of large postwar housing estates in the program proves the special significance of housing companies as integrated urban development advocates and providers.

Experiences in pilot districts and discussions and publications have demonstrated that the Socially Integrated City program districts have special citywide significance in two particular respects. Firstly, they relieve burdens by providing living space for people who would otherwise have worse accommodation or none at all. Secondly, they can stimulate new developments and take on a model function.[2] Many different groups emphasize the great integration function of the program districts, particularly for people with numerous different cultures, ways of life and modes of behaviour.

The "testbed" function of the Socially Integrated City districts and the special expectations of (and demands on) their development was clearly expressed at the Socially Integrated City – Unity, Security, Future congress where a provisional appraisal of the program took place. German chancellor Gerhard Schröder regards them as "laboratories assessing new formulae for social integration" which must be supported in their "difficult task of integration, so vital to the community". Klaus Selle called the Socially Integrated City districts "proving grounds for the urban policy of the future."[3]

Program implementation – successes, snags and suggestions for improvement

Performance and assessments of program implementation apply to the Socially Integrative City's two central fields of intervention. The first is the implementational, instrumental and strategic aspect concerning the integrative influence of the action plans, procedures used in developing and updating them and their actual implementation. It concerns the effects of resource pooling, the clout of organizational, cooperative and managerial structures, the impact of activating and participatory strategies and the degree of commitment displayed by local players and. Last but not least, it concerns the suitability of the selected districts based on "special development needs." The second field of intervention has to do with substantive Socially Integrative City issues, improvement of situations and outlooks in the district. This involves the material and physical environment in the neighborhoods, improvement of individual opportunities and the quality of communal living and embodiments of local opinion as well as psychological changes, which result from concrete upgrades and enhancements and from aggressive public relations and image projection.

---

[2] Beer/Musch (2002), p. 164 f.

[3] Deutsches Institut für Urbanistik, ed. (2002), p. 15 and p. 98.

Integrated Action Plans

The German federal government and the *Länder* assign fundamental and strategic significance to the integrated action plans when implementing “Districts with Special Development Needs – the Socially Integrative City.” This is clearly spelled out in the administrative agreement on urban development support (1999 to 2002) concluded between German federal and *Land* governments:

> *"The problems of urban districts with special development needs are to be tackled with an integrative concept amounting to a holistic improvement strategy in a comprehensive array of targeted social and environmental infrastructure policies. ... The local authorities are to produce a long-term, integrative, district-based urban development policy action plan to support measures. The action plan (preparation and implementation model and cost and financing overview) is intended to offer targeted, integrative solutions for complex problems, feature all steps required to achieve the goals – including those of developers, builders and funding providers – and present spending estimates and means of financing."*

This stipulation makes the fundability of a district contingent on the elaboration of an integrated urban development action plan for the neighborhood. One important function of the plan – or at least of the policy decision to draft such a plan – is giving the *Land* a basis for awarding Socially Integrative City grants. The updating of the plans specified in the government accords facilitates annual review of appropriations and spending by *Land* award bodies.

At the outset of implementation, municipal government exhibited a sceptical-to-negative attitude towards the control and coordination tool known as an “integrated action plan.” This scepticism has since given way to widespread approval. Assessments of integrated action plans and their implementation are clearly positive in two thirds of all program districts. Government respondents see this tool as the “necessary basis for implementing the program.” Currently 84 percent of the districts have integrated action plans in place or in the making.

Integrated action plans induce various positive programing effects. One indication of this tendency is the fact that the “new packaged services” are primarily rendered when an integrated action plan is in effect. The drafting and updating of integrated action plans are important communications platforms. They instigate dialogue between the players and lay foundations for trustbuilding and planning reliability. Wherever integrated action plans have been adopted, cooperation between agencies has improved, according to municipal respondents. Integrated action plans have gained sharper contours both in practice and in expert discussion, but they are still at the development stage.

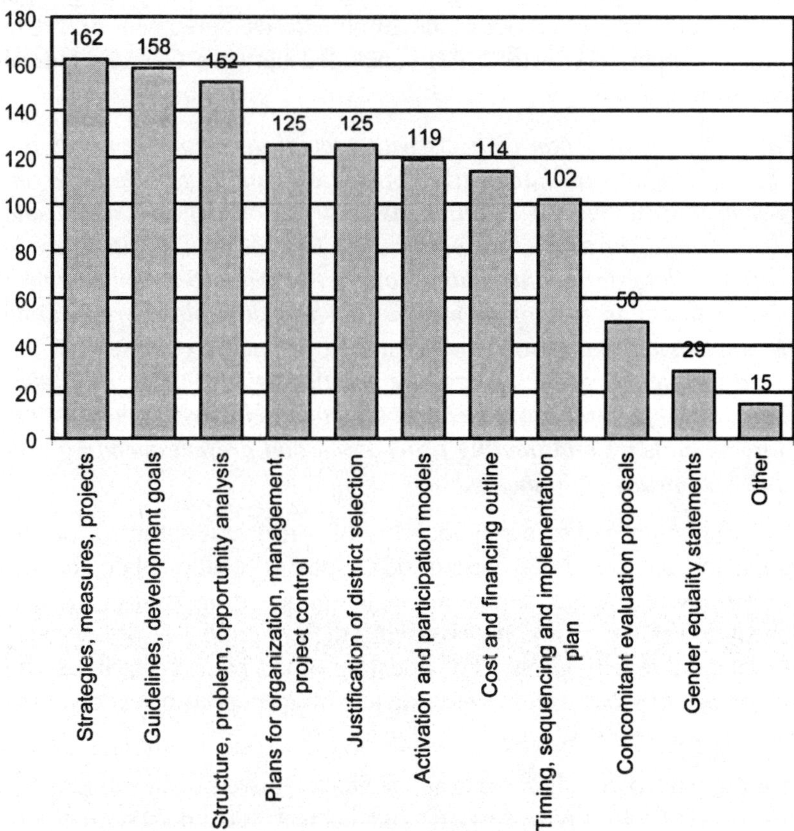

Figure 4: Components of Integrated Action Plans
(n = 222, multiple answers, second survey – Difu 2002)

A grave deficit is that integrated action plans remain separate from the development policy of the city as a whole so that one can hardly speak of systematic integration of district policy in citywide development approaches. Success in implementing the Socially Integrative City program will partly depend on how well district-based measures, projects, procedures and strategies can be yoked to the whole city's development policy and their citywide impact taken into consideration instead of being filtered out of the equation, as was attempted in City Renewal East.

Cooperation and resource pooling

Resource pooling in line with the Socially Integrative City program is a strategic approach to district-oriented application of miscellaneous resources. The program is designed to pool resources from various departments and private enterprises and channel the money, know-how and commitment needed from these sources into the areas concerned to implement both investment and non-investment measures. The BMVBW allocated DM 100 million to the program in 1999 and again in 2000. In 2001 and 2002 the figure was DM 150 million, or about 76.7 million. From the inauguration of the program until the end of 2002 approximately 770 million, including matching funds from the *Länder* and municipalities, has been invested in the scheme. The 2003 federal budget dedicates 80 million to Socially Integrative City.[4]

Resource pooling means neither unconsidered additive use of various support programs for one district, nor the lumping of several programs into a consolidated budget. Instead it describes coordinated action of different sponsors and coordinated application of financial and human resources from various policy areas on the basis of integrated action plans. Implementing the strategic goal of resource pooling requires harmonization of conceptualization at the federal, *Land* and municipal levels and with project-related work on site. It involves marrying investment and non-investment measures.

The second Difu survey showed that resources are pooled in more than ninety percent of the program districts. However, the quality and intensity of this pooling cannot be fully ascertained from the poll. Traditionally, urban development promotion has always attempted to apply several support strategies to the districts and to activate as many investors as possible. In the past this approach concentrated on supporting measures involving investment. The second survey, however, suggests that a variety of "new pooling benefits" have been created in implementing Socially Integrative City, while the old form of pooling continues to function.

Resource pooling as practised in the Socially Integrative City program requires establishing innovative, efficient organizational structures in government. In many cities and towns new interagency and interdepartmental cooperation and management formats are being tested, and personnel is learning from these approaches. "Progress in interagency and interdepartmental cooperation" is cited by surveyed municipal government represen-

4 Stolpe (2003).

tatives in seventy percent of the districts as a benefit of the program.[5] However, references are made to problems and difficulties – primarily by respondents from the pilot districts. The hurdles cited include departmental self-centredness and rivalry, which are far from being passé. Another shortcoming mentioned was tardiness in building cooperative structures to match changed decision-making powers and procedures. The question of who is to be the coordinator has not been adequately answered in the numerous interdepartmental control and steering panels which have come into existence. It appears that joint coordination by socially oriented and spatially focused organs is an advantageous approach.

In the light of the new challenge of establishing an unprecedented resident-friendly onsite presence, we deem it to be a resounding program success that government feels it has developed greater rapport with the people in the street during the course of program implementation. The survey indicated that this phenomenon is seen as the second-most-common benefit of the program. It was mentioned in responses from 85 percent of districts.

The preamble to the 2002 administrative agreement states: "The federal government and the *Länder* coordinate and pool all available federal and *Land* resources and measures needed to develop urban districts to exploit synergy effects ..." Pooling resources for development projects in urban districts has proved to be the persistent Achilles heel impeding program implementation. By now remarkable pooling successes have been reported, however. Spokespersons for ninety percent of all districts confirm that resources have been pooled – and the majority of such incidences involve pooling with programs outside traditional urban development support. However, acquiring and coordinating these resources continues to demand substantial efforts, particularly from players acting at citywide, urban district and project levels.

---

[5] The second *Difu* survey asked municipal government contacts to assess the successes and failures in program implementation.

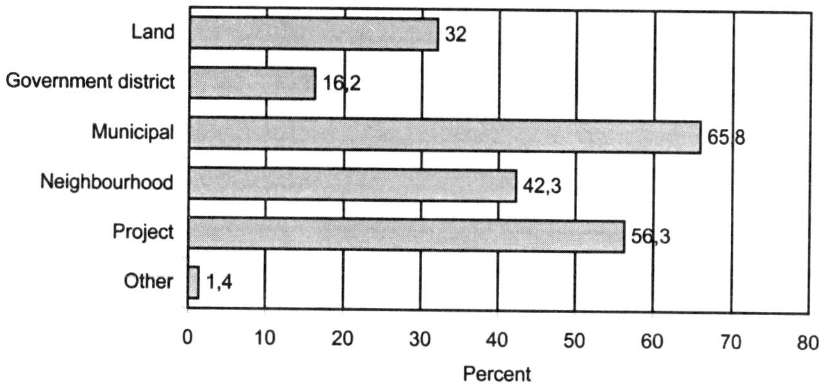

Figure 5: Levels of Resource Pooling
(n = 222, multiple responses; second survey – Difu 2002)

Uncertainties about subsidies and how to apply for them remain. Almost three quarters[6] of the answers to the open question[7] requesting suggestions on how to change the program, which were to be passed on to participating federal, *Land* and appropriations authorities, mention incompatible support schemes with varying timeframes and different territorial coverage or target groups, or complicated pooling procedures with a plethora of points of contact. This jives with the fact that the most frequently mentioned program implementation problem is "limitations and stipulations on application of resources." Over fifty percent of the districts reported encountering this hurdle. Forty percent were said to face Land-level shortcomings in coordinating resources and shackling strings attached to allocations.

Housing companies are the largest private Socially Integrative City district investors. The second Difu survey reveals that slightly more than half of the districts profit from housing company investment. Like the housing companies, private property owners, who play a greater role in older communities, are also torn between short-term gain and long-term maintenance of real estate value, and between stabilizing the existing population structure and improving the area, which leads to displacement of current residents.

6 Seventy percent of all 175 answers.

7 Multiple choices were not given.

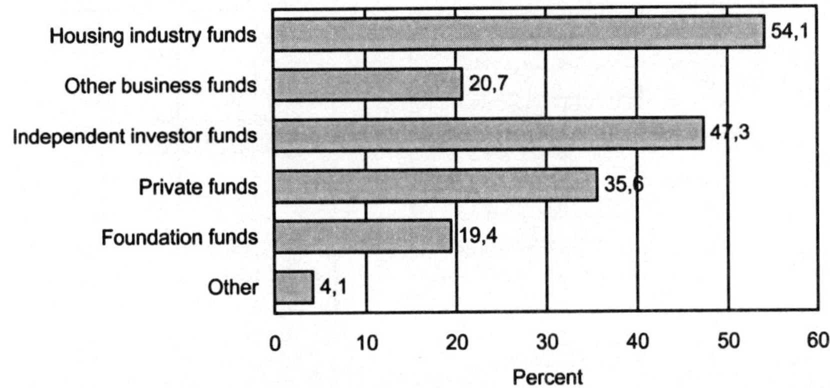

Figure 6: Application of non-governmental aid
(n = 222, multiple responses; second survey – Difu 2002.)

Neighborhood management

Neighborhood management is universally recognized as a key tool in performing the complex operations of integrative urban district development. However, organization, tasks and self-definitions vary. Process-oriented neighborhood management ensures horizontally and vertically networked cooperation and management structure at government and district levels, between these levels and with all other locally relevant players. In over eighty percent of the program districts, neighborhood management has consequently been instituted at all three control and operation levels: government, neighborhood and intermediate. Eighty percent of the municipal respondents assess neighborhood management as a “success.”

In Berlin, Hamburg, Hessen and Nordrhein-Westfalen neighborhood management is stressed more heavily than in the other *Länder*. This is reflected in particularly detailed recommendations and specifications on establishment of neighborhood management.

There is considerable room for improvement in the interaction of the three control and operation levels. Pilot area studies exhibit this shortcoming most clearly. A major, looming dilemma for local neighborhood management is the fact that time limits on many contracts jeopardize personnel continuity. In two thirds of the districts the contracts run for no more than three years. One half expire after only one year. Under these circumstances trust cannot be established.

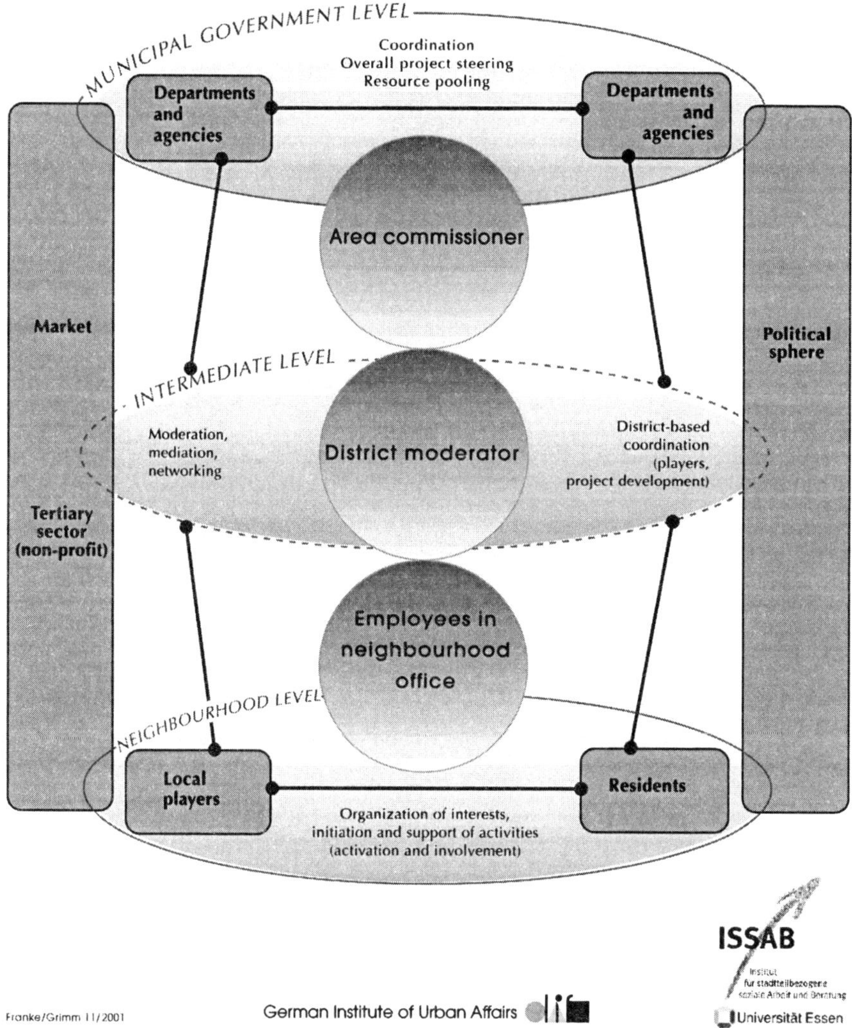

Figure 7: Neighbourhood management. Areas of responsibility and organization

That takes much longer. Frequently there is a lack of suitable equipment in the onsite offices, which have proved themselves as a sine qua non of neighborhood management. Considering the special qualifications, specifically communication and organization skills, that neighborhood management requires, it is encouraging that several institutions now offer further training and studies in neighborhood management.

Experience shows that serious commitment, profound personal dedication and perseverance in often very draining activity are fundamental prerequisites for the sound establishment of neighborhood management. Many additional ingredients for success are actually formal and organizational matters. Detailed *Land* program guidelines recommending implementation of neighborhood management at all control and operation levels impinging on integrative urban district development are therefore helpful. Tips on finance options and various applications of this new instrument can be supportive. Efficient municipal-level participation can be fostered by political involvement, good communications, sufficient decision-making power, adequate qualifications and ongoing training of (local) neighborhood managers and continuity.

Activation and participation

Establishing stable neighborhood social networks, organization of stakeholders on site, interlacing local initiatives, agencies and businesses, establishing neighborhood participation structures and expanding the individual problem-solving scope by operating in the sphere of "activation and participation" – all of these are fundamental preconditions for breakthroughs in integrative urban district development. The pilot districts present evidence that locations with efficient neighborhood management have the best chances of motivating people to get involved.

Administrators in three quarters of all program districts are encouraged by "activation of previously hard-to-activate population segments." In the pilot districts there was greater scepticism about the openness of neighborhood citizens. This finding indicates that efforts to energize residents must be redoubled and become more innovative. Some population segments have hardly been reached (in-migrants and their families, the long-term unemployed, senior citizens). These groups require special attention and personal contact on subjects tailored to their current predicaments. The "thresholds" for availing oneself of an opportunity, sometimes constituting real barriers, must be lowered, e.g. by offering services abounding in unpressurized communication, interaction and entertainment.

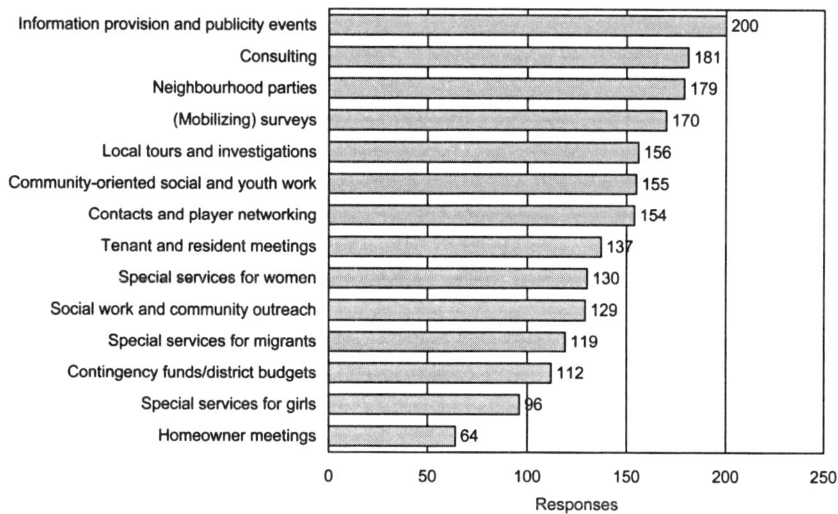

Figure 8: Employment of Activation Techniques
(n = 222,multiple answers, second survey – Difu 2002)

"Improved opportunities for residents to participate" was mentioned by government respondents from ninety percent of the districts as the most important benefit of the program. But in-depth investigations in the pilot districts cast doubt on the extent to which the task forces, urban district conferences and forums, planning and future workshops really achieve neighborhood involvement. Sometimes participatory events and strategies are only attractive to the middle class. Their formalized communication systems and routines deter and exclude population segments that act informally and spontaneously.

Willingness of civil servants and political leaders to delegate authority to citizens and local organizations has proved to be a key variable influencing activation and participation. Partial success has been achieved since more than half of all program districts have been endowed with contingency funds, creating the wherewithal for neighborhood players to accomplish small projects and measures swiftly and unbureaucratically. If no contingency fund is in place, it is difficult and laborious to mobilize small amounts – for example, to buy supplies and equipment or to impart knowledge and know-how to local activists. This issue is mirrored in records showing how often onsite operators claimed "logistical support"[8] dedicated to the program and how they applied the aid. Decentralized decision-

8 Cf. Chapter 2.2 Onsite program support

making powers and contingency funds or district budgets facilitate and stimulate neighborhood activism. The relatively generous neighborhood and "action" funds in Berlin have provided major impetus for civic activities. Public relations is also being employed as a means of activating people and getting them involved. Participation-oriented, two-way public relations is making strides in the program districts.

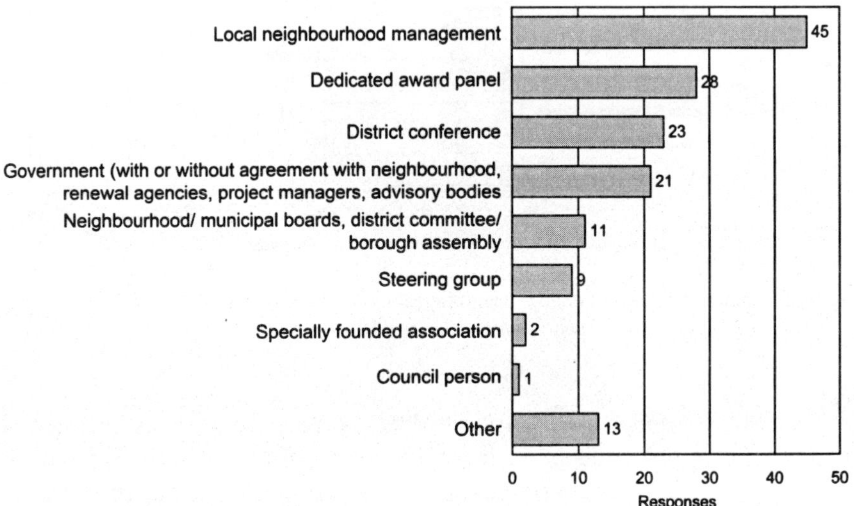

Figure 9: Contingency Fund Allocation Decision-Making Bodies (n = 222, multiple responses; second survey – Difu 2002)

Key topics for action

In rankings of specific measures and projects to improve situations and prospects in Socially Integrative City districts, the construction and space management activities and social policy areas are growing closer and closer. "Living environment and public space" is the most frequently mentioned area of activity in the second survey, given for 81 percent of the districts, but others such as "image improvement and public relations" (77%), "child and youth welfare", "sports and recreation" (70% each) and "social activities and social infrastructure" (68%) aren't far behind. The youth welfare offices responsible for Development and Opportunities for Young People in Social Hotspots (E & C) were included in a written survey that also dealt with Socially Integrative City districts. The juvenile offices give almost equal priority to youth, education, employment, housing and urban planning policies.

	Measure Action Theme			Salient Action Theme		
	abs,	%	Rank	abs,	%	Rank
Living environment and public space (security)	180	81,1	1	83	37,4	1
Image and public relations	171	77	2	72	32,4	3
Child and youth welfare	156	70,3	3	66	29,7	5
Sports and recreation	155	69,8	4	43	19,4	11
Social activities and social infra-structure	151	68	5	80	36	2
Urban district culture	142	64	6	49	22,1	10
Schools and education in the district	140	63,1	7	63	28,4	6
Integration of diverse social and ethnic groups	128	57,7	8	70	31,5	4
Qualifications and training	124	55,9	9	58	26,1	7
Employment	121	54,5	10	50	22,5	9
Local housing market and housing industry	119	53,6	11	51	23	8
Transport	118	53,2	12	22	9,9	12
Environment	94	42,3	13	12	5,4	14
Family services	91	41	14	9	4,1	15
Senior citizen services	74	33,3	15	8	3,6	16
Accumulation of neighborhood assets	64	38,8	16	15	6,8	13
Health	64	28,8	17	5	2,3	17
Other	2	0,9	18	2	0,9	18

Table 1: Action Topics of Measures and Projects
(n = 222, multiple responses; second survey – Difu 2002)

Key projects have acquired particular significance for urban district development. They provide powerful stimuli for neighborhood life and district profiles and send signals that affect the local atmosphere and mood. In the survey the existence of the issue of such projects was affirmed for almost ninety percent of program districts. The activity area termed "living environment improvement and public space" also takes first place in the salient project list. It is followed by "social activities and social infrastructure". "Local housing market" is a distant third.

It is becoming very clear that still more distinct priorities should be set among the Socially Integrative City topics. Such is the case with the preventive fields, "school and vocational education" and "health promotion." Schools are proving over and over again to be key institutions in the Socially Integrative City districts. They can be catalysts for overcoming the social isolation of young people in a demoralizing, impoverished milieu. Language support by schools and conflict management and dispersion of prejudice against foreign ideas and persons give students skills that create more favourable conditions for district integration. To do this, however, schools require additional support. Problem-ridden schools cause dislocation of those households which could contribute heavily to positive trends in urban districts.

"Health promotion," underemphasized thus far in integrative urban district development, is now receiving more attention, and rightly so. Particularly services for women – including some in schools – can initiate multiplier effects, since women are the ones who most often impart decisive knowledge of activities and everyday life to families and neighborhoods.

Boosting the local economy is the most frequently mentioned item – associated with 61 percent of all districts – but this ascribed importance is not yet reflected in specific measures and projects. "Asset accumulation in the district," which is a consequence of local economic strength, ranks a poor second. Only 29 percent of the districts have measures and projects to foster such growth. Also-rans include "improvement of employment and education" (named for 29% of the districts) and "commitment of private enterprise" (23%). Strengthening the local economy is apparently preached more than practised. Obviously channelling instruments have so far failed to route the economic promotion resources into local small business. Chambers of commerce and industry, chambers of handicrafts and job centres are still insufficiently integrated into the program. The same applies to the local business world. We must pay more attention to social, cultural and private components of work situations in the districts and neighborhoods.

"Motivation is a by-product of perception" was a frequently heard mantra at the Starter Conference for the Socially Integrative City program in March 2000. This is another reason why we should not underestimate the emotional consequences of the blight and physical neglect of disadvantaged districts. Carelessly designed spaces engender careless treatment. The spatial environment of a neighborhood constitutes a permanent element of a good or bad "address" and is a major enhanceable constituent of residents' self-confidence. Combating blight and neglect at an early stage checks the emergence of feelings of insecurity and inferiority. This is an indication of the great importance of public spaces in Socially Integrative City neighborhoods.

The extent to which images can affect perception is demonstrated by inhabitants' reports of massive feelings of insecurity in many districts, mainly mirroring subjective fears and reactions to the tarnished and distressing image and to a lesser degree reflecting exposure to alarming facts and statistics. Upgrading the current negative image of many program areas and nurturing a positive image requires tangible improvements in the neighborhood, accompanied by comprehensive application of aggressive public relations.

	Very negatively		Negatively changed		No change		Improved		Greatly Improved		No opinion	
	abs,	%	abs,	%	abs,	%	abs,	%	abs,	%	abs,	%
Outsider's image of district (n=205)	1	0,5	10	4,9	93	45,5	69	33,7	18	8,8	14	6,8
Insider's image of district (n=204)	-	-	4	2	45	22,1	121	59,3	22	10,8	12	5,9
Identification with district (n=203)	-	-	4	2	49	24,1	110	54,2	24	11,8	16	7,9
Press coverage (n=204)	-	-	7	3,4	35	17,2	113	55,4	38	18,6	11	5,4

Table 2: Assessment of Affects of Public Relations to Date (second survey – Difu 2002)

Apparently, the broad spectrum of measures designed to improve the neighborhood image is bearing fruit already. Observers of almost eighty percent of the program districts have noted an "improved atmosphere" in the neighborhoods, while almost seventy percent of the districts are credited with "image gains". The substantially positive estimates of public relations performance to date strongly suggest that improvement in insiders' image of and identification with the districts as well as in press coverage has been achieved for two thirds of the areas. However, respondents tended to doubt whether the image of their district held by outsiders had improved. Change for the better was attributed to only 42 percent of the territories.

Municipal support strategies

Implementation of the Socially Integrative City program requires municipal support in terms of complementary policies to provide legitimacy and medium-term guarantees to measures and projects. Here, strategies include organizing political backing, process evaluation for permanent quality control of management, citywide monitoring as a basis for well-founded selection of districts and as an early warning system for dangerous trends in other urban districts as well as coordination of neighborhood and municipal development models. Moreover, it is essential to establish structures and strategies to consolidate and sustain the gains in the districts.

Soliciting political support

Political backing for program implementation is a fundamental ingredient for the success of Socially Integrative City. This means, primarily, that district selection and integrated action plans as well as the new cooperation and management formats should be endorsed in resolutions – or at least in acknowledgements – by the city council or assembly, and that political platforms express commitment to Socially Integrative City strategies and concepts. Apart from this formal involvement of municipal government, participation of all local political parties elected to the city council and to borough committees in projects and measures is a vital means of increasing public awareness of risks and opportunities in the city districts and of the approaches adopted to solve their problems.

Municipal politicians face new decision-making structures alongside the traditional control functions mandated to elected officials. Reservations persist in some quarters about the shift of decision-making powers to the grassroots level. Many officials resort to blockades and revert to an authoritarian view of policymaking, for fear of loosing authority. This attitude can only be changed by creating win-win situations and clarifying decision-making responsibilities.

Government proximity to the front line is vital to build new partnerships and to ensure that citizens assume responsibility and commit themselves to the program. Having said this, we are delighted that municipal government respondents have claimed overall "success" in "bringing politics closer to (sixty percent of) the districts." It is widely stressed that recruitingmunicipal politicians as campaigners for urban district development and partners for all involved population groups should be promoted by more appealing, comprehensive information.

Process evaluation to assure quality

Researchers and others have repeatedly complained that the impact and acceptance of the program have not been systematically investigated. In fact, Socially Integrative City communities are not embracing implementation of evaluation despite this element of the integrated action plan being required by the *Länder*. Restraint and scepticism are related to uncertainty about evaluation methods and procedures and to inadequate explanation of the purpose and benefit. The strong emphasis on evaluating the results aggravates the reluctance of those who feel it is too soon to measure the impact of the recently launched program.

Municipal government players, however, anticipate positive effects of an evaluation in terms of practicality and initiation of learning processes. They tend to favour give-and-take process evaluation. Strategically oriented process evaluation enables investigators to qualify strategies, plans and projects, to redress misguidance and to dismantle obstacles to program implementation. Project and measure auditing, for instance by commissioning status reports, has an impact, but only if continuous feedback takes place.

Initial evaluation-related statistical appraisals on the basis of survey findings suggest positive impact of centrally initiated program implementation tools. More active process control – gauged by whether neighborhood management has taken root at all three activity and steering levels and an integrated action plan is in place – is evidenced in markedly positive estimates of program results, e.g. improved cooperation between agencies, higher resource pooling efficiency, healthy proportions of investment and non-investment measures, higher action plan viability. Process evaluation can also have a positive impact. Evidence for this effect can be found in responses to onsite program support and elsewhere. Evaluation and monitoring systems should be used more frequently than they have been so far. In fact, they should be established as program control routines.

One result of the nationwide survey is particularly conspicuous. Just under one quarter of the program districts (a total of 53) have no evaluation and have not planned any, which is in clear contradiction to the Socially Integrative City philosophy. However, this figure is affected by the year in which each district joined the scheme. In those districts that enterd the program in the second half of 2000 and in 2001, evaluation and monitoring have rarely become issues. Almost one quarter of all program districts (55 units) report that evaluation has been introduced. Almost half (98) of all districts state that an evaluation is still in the planning stage. Three quarters of the 153 program districts with implemented or planned evaluation say that investigation has been limited to the district. In one fourth the evaluation has also covered the area surrounding the district. In 56 percent of the cases, the municipality is the commissioner; in about twenty percent it is the *Land*; and joint initiation ensued in the rest.

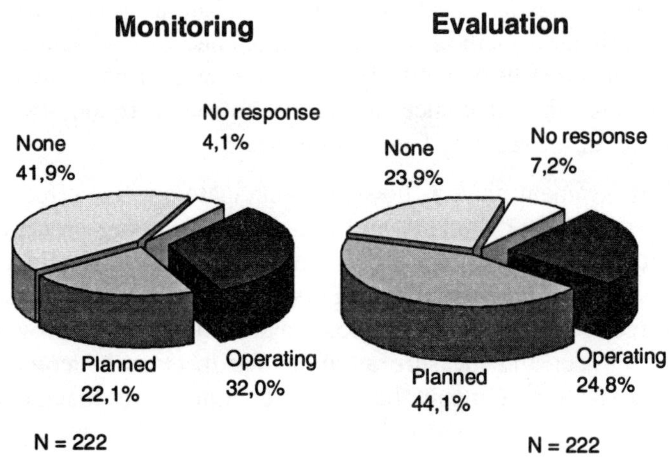

Figure 10: Evaluation and Monitoring in Socially Integrative City Program Districts (n = 222; second survey – Difu 2002)

Monitoring as a reasoned determinant of district selection

Indicator-based monitoring enhances the subjective evaluative approach. So far many cities lack microspatial datasets to differentiate social venues according to indicators of social situation, housing variables such as duration of residence, rate of removal and vacancies, health variables, local economics, etc. Well-founded screening of "urban districts with special development needs" requires detailed knowledge of conditions in the entire city. Since continual sociospatial reporting systems have only been introduced in a few cities, systematic indicator-based district selection has been a rare occurrence.

If monitoring systems were employed as permanent microspatial territorial observation, the choice of districts would be more scientific and the program approach would shift from reactive to preventive. Detecting adverse trends in restricted zones early enough for timely countermeasures to be installed is important. Permanent updating of data inventories could be harnessed eventually to factor analysis and territorial typologies on the basis of additional qualitative features and characteristic problem solutions and strategy patterns.

Integration of district policies in citywide planning

Localizing the Socially Integrative City in the spatial living environment with direct interfaces to ambient problems and potentials has proved to be both correct and indispensable. Criticism has been voiced where the districts boundaries have been delimited in too narrow fashion, excluding important infrastructure features or local economic sites.

However, successes in area based approaches are jeopardized when improvements in Socially Integrative City neighborhoods entail the socio-geographical shifting of problems to neighboring zones. Such displacement of underprivileged population segments, or citywide policies that threaten the standard achieved in the favoured district have counterproductive repercussions. These risks concentrate on school and education, labour market and employment, housing and infrastructure development policies. The bottom line is that district-oriented, area based policy must always consider the entire municipality.

Sadly, dovetailing programs that incorporate district-oriented measures, projects, procedures and strategies with citywide development planning has generally remained lip service. The important question of how to establish a relation to overall city efforts has hardly been addressed. Few proposals for organizing and practising such collaboration exist. To accomplish this goal, we need to develop additional organizational structures – e.g. advisory committees at the municipal level or city development concepts like those pursuant to City Renewal East – to coordinate processes in the district with those in the overall city in a reciprocal relationship. Only a few cities have established such structures.

Municipal strategies towards sustained effects

As in traditional urban development, follow-up is an issue. Safeguarding the improvements in the long-term is a pillar of the Socially Integrative City program. Nordrhein-Westfalen districts, where program support is expiring soon, have long been debating this aspect of phasing out or "exit." This fact suggests that the subject of follow-up should play a much larger role from the start of program implementation.

The main goal is sustaining major institutions and services that benefit the neighborhood, especially by reconstituting them as self-contained structures. This takes more time than we originally believed. An average of fifteen years were needed for the far less complex renewal focusing on buildings and architecture in past urban revitalization programs. In this context we often pose but rarely answer the question of terminating or perpetuating institutionalization of endeavours such as neighborhood management. It looks as though grassroots offices are indispensable as contact and coordination points for civic involvement and as the hub of player networking systems. They are the only means of guaranteeing endurance of district improvement and must be permanently and generously staffed and budgeted.

Considerations for refining the program

It is the responsibility of the federal government and the *Länder* to organize the discussion of results and transfer of knowledge between cities and towns participating in the program. As in the case of the sharing of experience by the *Länder*, the focus is on good practice and quality standards, particularly those related to instrumental-strategic fields of activity. Ultimately the performance of the program depends on how successfully the federal government and the *Länder* cooperate to give permanence to Socially Integrative City and to tear down barriers and eliminate weak links. Without additional reforms of public service systems, and particularly national economic and labour market policies, successes in implementing the program will be limited to territorial is*Land*s and isolated subject areas, reducing their long-term impact, because problem causes in the urban districts cannot be eradicated with an update of the urban development support program.

Sharing experience and player networking

Implementing a program as complex as Socially Integrative City, which also embodies a new policy approach, demands a large amount of experience in sharing information, knowledge transfer, cooperation and public relations. The German *Länder* support exchange among their cities and towns to a greater or lesser extent. Hessen, Nordrhein-Westfalen, Sachsen and Saar*Land* are particularly instrumental in organizing comprehensive sharing of findings among their program municipalities. These *Länder* commission expertises and accompanying research in support of this effort.

Besides targeted counselling and further training services, the *Land* measures that have proved to be especially useful in the day-to-day implementation process include numerous published operation and orientation guides. The works range from tips on how to draft integrated action plans and set up neighborhood management and how to obtain funds and pool resources to evaluation proposals and models. *Länder* recommendations on elaborating and updating integrated action plans are available in Bayern, Hamburg, Hessen, Nordrhein-Westfalen, Saar*Land* and Sachsen. Particularly detailed neighborhood management specifications have been issued in Berlin, Hamburg, Hessen and Nordrhein-Westfalen. Funding guidelines or comparable catalogues have been published by Bayern, Niedersachsen, Sachsen-Anhalt and Thüringen. Bayern, Bremen, Hamburg and Mecklenburg-Vorpommern are starting to think about evaluation. Saar*Land* and Sachsen-Anhalt's evaluation activities are decisively shaped by simultaneous implementation of EU Structural Fund programs which specify evaluation as a grant requirement. Berlin, Hessen and Nordrhein-Westfalen have the most advanced designs and have made the most progress on implementation.

Harmonization of funding programs is lagging. The federal government and, to a greater extent, the *Länder* are challenged to do much more in this area. Despite efforts to provide information and foster coordination via interministerial task forces, counselling on grant application procedures and resource pooling, the idea of efficient pooling has not yet come to fruition. The conventional vertical organization of government departments still appears to dominate administration behaviour. Nordrhein-Westfalen and Hessen are doing their own thing, establishing *Land* programs in each pertinent government department to directly address urban districts with special development needs.

One of the main goals of *Land* and nationwide experience sharing is elucidating the enforcement of regulations and gauging the scope for interpretation. Among other things, this concerns the eligibility of projects and measures in the non-investment sphere for financing within the framework of the Socially Integrative City program. The example of the hurdles created by Article 104, Paragraph 4 of the Basic Law for federal aid to the *Länder* demonstrates that the *Länder* enforce the rules in a variety of ways. A broad interpretation of the clause permits employment of Socially Integrative City resources not only for neighborhood management, but also even for contingency funds, public relations work and further training if they are needed to prepare, support and sustain investments and foster public acceptance.

Quality standards should also be discussed more extensively and plausibly than has been the case so far. They should be incorporated into grant approvals and be enforced, e.g. in the realms of integrated action plans, neighborhood management, resource pooling, evaluation and monitoring.

This would promote quality competition. Overall, the terms for applying for public funds seem to attach too little importance to quality standards. Awarding resources should encourage good ideas, innovations and creative concepts seems much more appropriate than to fan competition into demonstrating the direst needs.

Sustaining the program

The Socially Integrative City program is currently supported and managed by many professions and institutions, including on-site actors. But commitment and enthusiasm wane when uncertainties arise. Two basic prerequisites for successful implementation of the program are continuity and reliable frameworking. The procedures of traditional urban development promotion took fifteen years on average, despite widespread urging of "expedience," and led to the conviction that urban revitalization is a never-ending task. It would therefore be unrealistic to expect proof of sustainable improvement at this stage, only four years into such a complex and complicated program as Socially Integrative City.

The complex problem in many program districts have turned out to be even more complicated than originally believed. They require stronger financial support, particularly in the start-up phase – and the Socially Integrative City funds must be tapped to this end. Organs furnishing local neighborhood management support are frequently dramatically understaffed and unable to tackle the variety of claims on their resources or the jobs they are assigned. Moreover, the program cannot function with any degree of independence in some districts because it overlaps with better-financed schemes. Under these circumstances increasing resources appears to be sensible and desirable, particularly when the measures and projects are subject to auditing in the course of process evaluation.

However, the precarious municipal financial situation in some cities and towns erects barriers for raising local funds. Responding in this vein, respondents from ten percent of the program districts name the "lack of local municipal resources" or "empty coffers" as an obstacle. One fifth of all program districts use additional resources by way of cofinancing. The problem of raising matching funds has already knocked several cities out of the program and observers fear that others will follow. Therefore there are plans to reduce the required local share or allow communities to enlist aid of third parties who do not receive any federal aid.

The program districts assume functions which disencumber the municipalities as a whole, like providing a home for the homeless, and they serve as a test bed for sustainable development of entire cities. Already this alone legitimizes a greater injection of resources, which is also justified by the extreme problem density in the needy neighborhoods.

In the future, we should explore notions of how and when to move integrative urban district development from reactive emergency control and ad-hoc intervention toward permanent preventive action. In the Nether-*Lands* neighborhood action has been supplanted by integrated municipal development planning. New impulses can certainly be expected from the output of the City 2003 Idea Competition.[9] This asks contestants to develop citywide models of "future integration of a mutually supportive urban citizenship to combat tendencies toward inequality, exclusion and fragmentation" which can provide orientation for decisions on necessary processes and projects.

Legal underpins of the program approach

The Socially Integrative City program is a source of new light on urban regeneration, already beneficiating other forms of urban renewal. According to data provided by several *Länder*, the program is stimulating the expansion of revitalization objectives and reinforces resource pooling. Nevertheless, uncertainty, unconducive to sustained prosecution of Socially Integrative City missions, persists. The doubts concern not only the continuity of supporting funds, but also the viability of the program's participatory, cooperative and integrative approach. It therefore seems appropriate, to promote the stability and implementation of the program and to increase its impact, especially at the municipal level, to integrate its principles into the special building law of Articles 136 ff of the Building Code (BauGB) once incorporated in the new Article 171(BauGB).

While objectives and principles of renewal are incontestably compatible with the Socially Integrative City program, enactment of the following central program approaches into law appears to be indicated:

First, expansion of regulations on citizen participation, empowering as many population segments as possible to become involved and share responsibility in the districts, and creation of organizations such as neighborhood management bodies with adequate personnel to permit this interaction;

---

9 See http://www.stadt203.de/ergebnisse.

Second, clear enunciation of the necessity and fundworthiness of establishing and continuing integrated action plans, including non-investment measures to pave the way for renewal;

Third, since finance and subsidies only need to be reported informally, as prescribed by other legislation, it would facilitate integration to enact binding obligations for other sponsors to assist Socially Integrative City districts in a special way. This conscription of other aid agencies would have to be matched by the obligation of the municipality to endeavour to obtain financing to support renewal measures that do not require investment.

National government reforms

The program was not created with the aim of solving all problems in urban districts with special development needs which encumber and stigmatize lifestyles and outlooks on life. Nevertheless, the basic problem of socially integrating cities must be tackled much more aggressively. The new awareness of the needs of the districts and their inhabitants, the diversity of projects and palpable improvements in urban neighborhoods should not disguise the fact that problems such as unemployment, welfare dependence, gaps in provision of homes for low-income households, and education and training deficits were not caused locally. Many policy areas which impinge on solutions are beyond the jurisdiction of cities and towns. There is a general consensus that neighborhood initiatives and activities must be reinforced by overarching macrosocial policies, primarily in the areas of job and housing markets, economic development, education and migration.

It also appears crucial to obtain a full account of the threats which are compounding the arguments for application of the Socially Integrative City program. Continued liberalization of housing markets, sale of municipal housing authorities and abolition of tenancy stipulations will increase the geographical concentration of tight-pinched households and, unless infrastructural measures are taken to alleviate the anticipated problems for immigrant groups in Germany and integration efforts are intensified, the country will run the risk of aggravated conflicts, bitter rivalry and xenophobia.

Adopting good practice from European neighbors

Taking advantage of solutions from Germany's neighbors will evolve into a best practice. We are observing a growing requirement to tap experience gained in other countries and to share German findings with them.[10] The July 1999 event which kicked off the Socially Integrative City program included a presentation of Dutch and British experiences, which have subsequently produced more advanced findings and continue to stimulate German thinking. In the Netherlands the Stedelijk Beheer approach accentuates monitoring, district typology and elements of integration, coordination, decentralization and citizen participation. Britain's New Deal for Communities stresses new local partnerships between private, charitable and public institutions and tying awards of grants to certain types of competition, and thus to model quality.

International comparisons point to shortcomings in the ministerial underpinning in Germany. The apportionment of tasks and the requirements of Socially Integrative City demand special tailoring of responsibilities. "What we really need is a Ministry of Urban Affairs" or a "Ministry of Urban Integration Policy" is the message Socially Integrative City activists are sending. They argue for adequate federal and *Land* ministry powers and responsibilities to handle the conspicuously worsening social problems in cities and towns.

Outlook

The district-oriented, integrative and participatory approach to urban district development propagated by the Socially Integrative City program has won great across-the-board acclaim. It is proving a necessary and correct avenue to construction of viable, high-performance organizational structures, elaboration of integrated action plans and implementation of stimulating measures and projects for development in disadvantaged parts of towns.

The Socially Integrative City program has encouraged the commitment and operation of all players and vindicated everyone who had previously advocated or launched an integrative, cooperative urban district improvement approach. The program is having a stabilizing effect which many perceive to be a great boon. It gives players who are new to the idea

---

[10] Several EU and OECD projects and a number of enquiries from beyond Germany demonstrate the great interest in Socially Integrated City.

the support and kick they need to explore integrative procedures and to draft and implement new schemes and organizational structures to develop urban districts.

Successes in implementing the program have so far centred on the instrumental, strategic sector (advancing full speed on integrated action plans and neighborhood management but only tentatively on resource pooling). In territories where integrative urban district development has long been practised, notable improvements in neighborhood housing and living conditions have been accomplished by diverse infrastructure schemes, employment measures and training courses as well as through upgrading the spatial environment and polishing the image of the community. However, sustained improvement of situations and outlooks can hardly be achieved with a strictly macro-spatial approach.

The socially integrative city is an ideal. As such, it will assume more distinct contours and will constitute a beacon for future development and a model of viability if the new policy approach is pursued aggressively and on a wide front in cities and towns, if the federal and *Land* governments agree on quality standards and program option refinements on the basis of municipal experience, and above all, if onsite policymaking on the local and grassroot levlel is accompanied by the necessary coherent reforms in federal and *Länder* governance.

References

Beer, Ingeboor/Musch, Reinfried (2002), Stadtteile mit besonderem Entwicklungsbedarf: die soziale Stadt, Modellgebeit Kottbusser Tor, Berlin-Kreuzberg, Final report of onsite program support, May, Berlin.

Deutsches Institut für Urbanistik, ed. (2002), Kongress "Die soziale Stadt: Zusammenhalt, Sicherheit, Zukunft," Documentation, Berlin, Arbeitspapiere zum Program Soziale Stadt, Vol. 8.

http://www.stadt203.de/ergebnisse. Accessed March 2003.

Stolpe, Manfred (2003), Program 'Die soziale Stadt' auf gutem Weg (Socially Integrated City on the Right Track), press release of the German Ministry of Transport, Building and Housing, April 8, No. 112/3.

Contributors

Dr Reinhard Goethert is an internationally recognized for physical planning and upgrading of low income settlements, focusing on design, participatory technique, policy development and training. He is Principal Research Associate in the School of Architecture and Planning at MIT, and teaches courses on housing and development. He is director of the SIGUS Program, a service oriented program targeting the informal sector in developing countries. He holds a B.Arch, M.Arch from MIT, and a doctorate from RWTH, Aachen.

Dr Horst Matthaeus has been a working in various positions in the fields such as urban development, urban conservation, regional planning in Asia, Latin America and Africa since more than 30 years. His recent focus is on good governance and the interrelation between state and the civil society in the context of strengthening local governments. Currently he holds the position of a coordinator and program director for "Capacity Building in Governance" in Ethiopia for GTZ.

Dr Alicia Ziccardi received her Ph.D. in Economy at the UNAM (Universidad Nacional Autónoma de México), a B.A. and M.A. in Sociology and a postgraduate degree in urban and regional development from the Torcuato Di Tella Institute in Buenos Aires. She is a member of the Mexican National System of Researchers and works at the Institute for Social Research of UNAM. She teaches at the postgraduate departments of political and social science and of urbanism and coordinates a joint master program in regional studies of IISUNAM (Instituto de Investigaciones Sociales of the Universidad Nacional Autónomade México) and Instituto Mora.

Arturo Mier y Terán received an MA in architecture and a diploma in housing from the UNAM (Universidad Nacional Autónoma de México). After postgraduate studies in housing at the Architectural Association in London, he received a MPhil in regional planning and urban design from the University of Edinburgh. He was awarded the National Prize in Urban Design 1992 and a National Prize in Housing 2002. At present he is consultant to CEPAL (Comisión Económica para América Latina), and teaches in the postgraduate programme in urbanism of UNAM. He is also doing research on housing related issues as a member of CONACYT (Consejo Nacional de Ciencia y Tecnología).

Christoph Stump worked for the planning unit of the Bronx Borough President's Office in 2002 where he got a close insight into the problems and developments of the South Bronx the administration and not-for-profit developers to help facilitate community revitalization. He returned to the Bronx after completion of his thesis "Sustainable and Affordable Housing in the South Bronx" at the Berlin University of Technology in Germany, which he developed in close cooperation with the not-for-profit community group Nos Quedamos. He currently works as an architect in New York City.

Monika El Shorbagi was born in Germany and has been living in Egypt for most of the past 15 years. She has studied political science and Islamic studies in Berlin and Cairo with a focus on international politics, political Islam and gender studies. During the past ten years, she has worked with different development organizations, mainly in integrated development projects in poor urban areas. She has also conducted a range of socio-economic research and studies and has contributed to publications and radio features.

Dr Debra Roberts currently heads the Environmental Management Department of eThekwini Municipality (South Africa). Her responsibilities include overseeing the preparation and implementation of Durban's Local Agenda/Action 21 programme and ensuring that environmental considerations influence all aspects of planning and development in the city. Prior to joining the municipality, Dr. Roberts lectured on urban open space planning and design at the University of Natal in the departments of Biology and Geographical and Environmental Sciences.

Dr Neelima Risbud is professor of housing at the School of Planning and Architecture in New Delhi, India. She is an architect and town planner. Her doctoral work is on "Slum Improvement and Tenure Regularisation Policies in Indian context." Her areas of research include informal housing and *Land* markets. She has extensively published on housing and tenure issues since 1987 and contributed to the Global Report on Human Settlements 2003 for U.N. Habitat.

Dr Anne Power is professor of social policy and co-ordinator for housing at the London School of Economics, Great Britain. Her work so far has covered such wide ranging subjects as American, European & UK urban problems; crime; housing & housing renovation; management problems; social exclusion; social problems; energy use in buildings; migration; international development; anti-social behaviour; policing; neighbourhood management; social policy on housing, race relations; education; cities; planning; urban problems & community.

Dr Mary Corcoran White is senior lecturer in the Department of Sociology, National University of Ireland, Maynooth. Her research interests have included the study of urban transformation and change. She has completed a collaborative national study on quality of life in local authority housing estates and is the author of a report on housing estates in Dublin and has also been involved in BETWIXT, "Between Integration and Exclusion", an interdisciplinary, multi national study of seven European cities and in the ENTRUST-network.

Dr Heidede Becker is senior research fellow at the German Institute of Urban Affairs (Difu), in Berlin, Germany - a research institute founded by the Deutscher Städtetag (German Association of Towns and Cities). She works in the department of urban development and law. Her research and publications focus on Urban Planning and Design, Housing, Urban Regeneration and Architecture. Over the last years she has headed the research and organisational unit that supported the German Program "Die Soziale Stadt" (Socially Integrative City).

Dr Rolf-Peter Löhr has started his career in the former German Ministry for Building, Housing and Urban Planning and is deputy head of the German Institute of Urban Affairs (Difu), in Berlin, Germany and has published widely on a variety of topical issues, particularly on social policy, legal aspects of urban development and Socially Inclusive Cities such as Area Management. He is co-editor of a reference manual on planning law in Germany.

Editors

Dr Peter Herrle is professor of architecture and urban development and head of the Habitat Unit at Berlin University of Technology (TUB). Since 2002 he is advisory professor at Tongji University in Shanghai, China. He has a long record of research on urban social and development issues and has been working as a consultant to international development organizations and NGOs in many countries in Africa, Asia and Latin America. Major topics of his work and publications include informal settlements, informal economies, housing, local governance, participatory planning and urban conservation.

Dr Uwe-Jens Walther is professor of urban and regional sociology at the Institute for Sociology, Berlin University of Technology (TUB). He was research fellow and lecturer at the University of Oldenburg and senior research officer at the Federal Research Institute for Regional Geography and Planning in Bonn (BfLR/BBR). His research interests and publications include the Experimental Housing and Building Programme (ExWoSt), Urban Regeneration and implementation of community oriented revitalisation programmes as well as the informal economy, social planning and social groups in thc city.

HABITAT – INTERNATIONAL

Schriften der Habitat Unit, Fakultät VII, Architektur – Umwelt – Gesellschaft der Technischen Universität Berlin
hrsg. von Prof. Dr. Peter Herrle

Steffen Lehmann
Der Weg Brasiliens in die Moderne
Eine Bewertung und Einordnung der modernen Architektur Brasiliens vor Brasilia, 1930–1955
Bd. 1, 2004, 320 S., 29,90 €, br.,
ISBN 3-8258-6939-3

Paula Santos
Neue Instrumente der Stadtplanung in Brasilien
Das Ende der illegalen Stadt?
Habitat International ist die Publikationsreihe der *Habitat Unit*, einer Lehr- und Forschungseinheit an der Fakultät VII der Technischen Universität Berlin. Die Reihe widmet sich soziokulturellen und entwicklungspolitischen Aspekten zeitgenössischer Urbanisierung und Architektur. In lockerer Folge werden damit an der Habitat Unit entstandene Dissertationen und Forschungsergebnisse vorgestellt.
www.habitat-unit.de
Bd. 2, 2004, 296 S., 29,90 €, br.,
ISBN 3-8258-6972-5

Ethnologie

Makilam
Weibliche Magie und Einheit der Gesellschaft in der Kabylei
Riten, verborgene Lebensweise und Kultur der Berberfrauen Algeriens
Beharrlich hält sich die pauschale Meinung, daß sich die Rolle der kabylischen Frauen lediglich auf Fragen der Natur, der Gefühle und der Fortpflanzung reduziert, und dies in einem System der Unterdrückung durch die männliche Vorherrschaft. Um die Ohnmacht, die durch diese Ungleichheit entsteht, zu umgehen, sei ihr Dasein von Zurückhaltung und Magie, insbesondere die Liebe betreffend, beherrscht. In ihrem Werk widerlegt die Autorin diese Vorurteile und zeigt auf, wie sich die weibliche Magie auf alle Gebiete des täglichen Lebens erstreckt. Die Kabylin war ebenso eine Magierin der Erde, in ihrer Arbeit als Töpferin, sowie bei ihrem Wirken als stillende Mutter oder am Webstuhl. In Wirklichkeit beherrschte sie die traditionelle Gesellschaft, die ohne sie gar nicht bestehen konnte, indem sie sowohl deren materielle als auch spirituelle Einheit sicherte. Dieses Buch ist eine Huldigung an alle Mütter, die ihr Wissen und Können über Generationen an die Töchter weitergegeben haben; gleichzeitig erinnert es aber auch an längst vergessene Wurzeln, die einst zur magischen, verborgenen Natur aller Frauen dieser Welt gehörten. Makilam, Historikerin und Doktor der Philosophie, wuchs bis zum Alter von siebzehn Jahren in einem Dorf des Djurdjura auf. Seitdem lebt sie in Europa, ist aber intensiv an ihre Herkunft gebunden. Ihre von persönlichen Erlebnissen durchzogene Untersuchung bietet viele neue, bisher unveröffentlichte Erkenntnisse über Riten und Mythen einer im Aussterben befindlichen Gesellschaft.
Bd. 1, 2001, 336 S., 20,90 €, br.,
ISBN 3-8258-5384-5

Knut Knackstedt
"Geheimbund"?: Yi He Ch'üan
Ein ethnologischer Beitrag zur Neubewertung des interdisziplinär relevanten Geheimbundbegriffs am Beispiel der "Boxer" in China (1774–1900)
Eignet sich der all(zu)bekannte „Geheimbund"-Begriff, verstanden als westliche Konzeption eines sozialen Phänomens, als wissenschaftliche Kategorie? Um dies zu beantworten, prüft der Autor seine Arbeitsdefinition „Geheimbund" auf ihre Anwendbarkeit am Beispiel der chinesischen Yi He Ch'üan, der „Boxer". Im Bemühen um größtmögliche Nähe zu den historischen Ereignissen wird unter anderem chinesisches Quellenmaterial ausgewertet, das größtenteils bislang nicht von westlichen Gelehrten wahrgenommen worden ist. Das Resultat überrascht.
Bd. 2, 2002, 344 S., 30,90 €, br.,
ISBN 3-8258-5806-5

Ulrich Oberdiek
Gespräche mit einem Brahmanen in Indien
Diskursanalytische Transkription und annotierender ethnographischer Kommentar
Während einer Feldforschung (1995/96) entstanden Gespräche mit einem Brahmanen, von denen hier vier vollständig diskursanalytisch transkribiert und um deutlich abgesetzte ethnographische Kommentare ergänzt sind. So entsteht eine andere Art von „Ethnographie": eine direktere und transparentere Repräsentation. Dies ist ein methodischer Unterschied zur „klassischen" Ethnographie, aber auch gegenüber modifizierten, neueren Formen (Dialogizität, Polyphonie), die die Anderen nur in kurzen Ausschnitten zu Wort kommen ließen. Die Gesprächsinhalte haben ein „interkulturelles" Gepräge (hinduistische Kultur, eine „globalisierte" Diskussion). Eine weitere theoretische Orientierung betrifft ethische Fragen des Unterschiedes bzw. der Gleichheit der Beteiligten: Kommunikations- und Machtbeziehungen.
Bd. 3, 2002, 240 S., 20,90 €, br.,
ISBN 3-8258-5689-5

Brigitte Steger
(Keine) Zeit zum Schlafen?
Kulturhistorische und sozialanthropologische Erkundungen japanischer Schlafgewohnheiten
Warum schlafen so viele Japaner in Zügen und Sitzungen? Was tun sie nachts? Keine Zeit zum Schlafen? – Diese erste Monographie über sozial- und kulturwissenschaftliche Aspekte des Schlafens behandelt Themen wie Zeitverwendung, Arbeitsethik, Geschlechterverhältnisse, soziale Beziehungen, den Umgang mit Ängsten und das Verhalten in der Öffentlichkeit. Steger untersucht Schlafmethoden zum Gescheiterwerden, erstellt eine Typologie von Kulturen der Schlaforganisation sowie eine Theorie des öffentlichen Schlafens und prägt den Begriff der „sozialen Tarnkappe". Sie zeigt, daß soziales Leben ohne Möglichkeiten der Erholung unerträglich wäre. Brigitte Steger erhält 2005 den Spezialpreis für herausragende Publikationen des Landes Vorarlberg, 2002 wurde sie mit dem Bank Austria Preis zur Förderung innovativer Forschungsprojekte an der Universität Wien ausgezeichnet.
Bd. 4, 2., überarb. Aufl. 2004, 504 S., 34,90 €, br.,
ISBN 3-8258-6993-8

Heiner Goldinger
Rituale und Symbole der Börse
Eine Ethnographie
Bd. 10, 2002, 216 S., 20,90 €, br.,
ISBN 3-8258-5690-9

Mongameli Mabona
Diviners and Prophets among the Xhosa (1593 – 1856)
A study in Xhosa cultural history
The South African anthropologist, Dr M. Mabona, uses the main title of this book as a convenient platform to launch an investigation into the roots of Xhosa culture and history. Many of the findings break new ground in Southern African anthropology and history such as: the original stock of the Bantu peoples arose from a cradle-land between the Orange and Vaal rivers in South Africa; the word 'Guinea' is identical with the Xhosa 'ebu Nguni' (Nguniland); Xhosa as well as Bantu history stretches back 50'000 years ago into the Middle Stone Ages (MSA) and into the Acheulian Age - the age of hominisation; the basic paradigmatic structure of Bantu speech; Xhosa thought structures; the fundamental relationship between the Xhosa language and mythology.
Bd. 12, 2005, 464 S., 35,90 €, br.,
ISBN 3-8258-6700-5

Marie-France Chevron
Anpassung und Entwicklung in Evolution und Kulturwandel
Erkenntnisse aus der Wissenschaftsgeschichte für die Forschung der Gegenwart und eine Erinnerung an das Werk A. Bastians
Das Buch behandelt Fragen der kulturellen Veränderung als Ergebnis teils historischer und teils evolutionärer Gesetzmäßigkeiten. Teil Eins beschäftigt sich mit Ansätzen der

frühen deutschsprachigen Ethnologie, wobei Bastians Theorie der Elementar- und Völkergedanken im Mittelpunkt wissenschaftlicher Überlegungen steht. In Teil Zwei werden der Erklärungszusammenhang zwischen kulturellen Gemeinsamkeiten und Unterschieden, die universellen Grundlagen des Mensch-Seins und der kulturellen Entwicklung aus heutiger Sicht dargestellt.
Bd. 14, 2005, 480 S., 35,90 €, br.,
ISBN 3-8258-6817-6

Kerstin Gudermuth
Kultur der Liebe in Indien
Leidenschaft und Hingabe in Hindu-Mythologie und Gegenwart
Gefühle sind soziokulturelle Konstruktionen, so auch die Liebe. In der Hindu-Kultur wird die Liebe durch zwei Begriffe, *kāma* und *prema*, zum Ausdruck gebracht, die hier anhand populärer mythischer und religiöser Texte analysiert werden. Während *kāma* das Ideal für eheliche Liebe ist, ist *prema* Ideal für Gottesliebe. Beiden gemeinsam ist die Hingabe. Die Untersuchung der gegenwärtigen indischen Liebesvorstellungen zeigt das Fortleben der tradierten Liebessemantik. Sie zeigt aber auch, dass Menschen diese Werte verschieden interpretieren und gleichzeitig neue Ideen in ihre Handlungen integrieren.
Bd. 15, 2003, 160 S., 19,90 €, br.,
ISBN 3-8258-6969-5

Makilam
Zeichen und Magie der kabylischen Frauen
Sexualität in der Kunst der Berber-Frauen
Entgegen einer weit verbreiteten Auffassung über die Große Kabylei in Algerien sehen sich die Kabylinnen in ihrer Rolle als Frau keinerlei Beschränkungen unterworfen. Die Autorin Makilam zeigt auf, daß sich mit der Interpretation von magischen Praktiken, graphischen Symbolen und Übergangsriten andere Auffassungen über die kulturelle Identität kabylischer Frauen ergeben als jener Zustand zwischen Schweigen und Isolation, der ihnen von westlichen Beobachtern zugeschrieben wird. Nach einer Initiation in die esoterische Schrift der Frauen, die sich auf Töpferwaren, Webstücken, Tätowierungen und Wandmalereien mitteilen, vermittelt Makilam eine erneuerte Sicht der symbolischen Grammatik dieser „Dekorationen". Die Kabylinnen erzählen in den Motiven eine Geschichte der Erotik.
Bd. 16, 2003, 216 S., 24,90 €, br.,
ISBN 3-8258-6921-0

Peter Lutum
Die japanischen Volkskundler Minakata Kumagusu und Yanagita Kunio
Ihre kontroversen Ideen in der frühen Entstehungsphase der modernen japanischen Volkskunde
Yanagita Kunio, der als Initiator der modernen japanischen Volkskunde gilt, erhielt nicht nur wesentliche Anregungen von dem wissenschaftlichen Außenseiter seiner Zeit, Minakata Kumagusu, sondern ignorierte bewußt dessen Vorschläge zu einer interdisziplinären Volkskundeforschung und begründete eine nationale Volkskunde. In dieser Studie wird die Kontroverse zwischen Minakata Kumagusu und Yanagita Kunio über die Leitlinien der ersten volkskundlichen Zeitschrift in Japan, Kyôdokenkyû, untersucht, die weichenstellend für die spätere Entwicklung der modernen japanischen Volkskunde war und als ihre „pränatale" Phase interpretiert werden kann.
Bd. 17, 2003, 112 S., 9,90 €, br.,
ISBN 3-8258-6949-0

Andreas de Bruin
Jugendliche – ein fremder Stamm?
Jugendarbeitslosigkeit aus aktionsethnologischer Sicht. Zur kritischen Reflexion von Lehrkräften und Unterrichtskonzepten im deutschen Schul- und Ausbildungssystem
Ein ursprünglich für drei Tage geplanter Referenteneinsatz in einer beruflichen Fortbildungsinstitution entwickelt sich als Initialzündung für eine langjährige Zusammenarbeit mit über 1500 arbeitslosen Jugendlichen. Der Autor beschreibt den Weg zu einem Dialog auf „gleicher Augenhöhe" und zeigt auf, dass

nur eine interdisziplinäre Vorgehensweise das Problem der Jugendarbeitslosigkeit lösen kann. Im Mittelpunkt des Buches steht die Fachdisziplin Aktionsethnologie und insbesondere die Auseinandersetzung mit Machtstrukturen, die einer konstruktiven Entfaltung junger Menschen im Wege stehen.
Bd. 18, 2004, 264 S., 24,90 €, br.,
ISBN 3-8258-7555-5

Ethnologie: Forschung und Wissenschaft

Günther Schlee
Identities on the Move
Clanship and pastoralism in Northern Kenya (second edition 1994, first published in 1989). This is a title distributed by LIT Verlag. The book was first published by Manchester University Press in 1989. The distributed version is part of the second edition published by GIDEON S. WERE PRESS, Nairobi, Kenya in 1994.
Clans are normally thought of as contained within ethnic groups. In the Horn of Africa the pastoral Rendille, Gabbra, Sakuye and some Somalis of northern Kenya and southern Ethiopia have many clans in common. As a result the clans are not always smaller or less important than the ethnic groups. How such inter-ethnic relationships came about is the subject of this study many go back beyond ethnic divisions to over 400 years ago. The book also examines the uses to which they are put, for instance in managing herds. Oral history is combined with cultural comparison and the analysis of social structure. The many original texts are themselves of linguistic interest. Blending synchronic and diachronic perspectives, the book synthesises historical ethnology in the Continental tradition with social anthropology. Historically it overturns some established ideas about how the Horn was settled. Anthropologically it shows how relations may exceed the bounds of the ethnic group as the conventional unit of study. It will be of interest to anthropologists, sociologists and social geographers or planners concerned with pastoral development.
Bd. 2, 2000, 288 S., 24,90 €, br.,
ISBN 3-8258-4800-0

Wim van Binsbergen
Intercultural Encounters
African and anthropological lessons towards a philosophy of interculturality
This book brings together fifteen essays investigating aspects of interculturality. Like its author, it operates at the borderline between social anthropology and intercultural philosophy. It seeks to make a contribution to intercultural philosophy, by formulating with great precision and painful honesty the lessons deriving from extensive intercultural experiences as an anthropologist. Its culminating section presents an intercultural philosophy revolving on the tenet 'cultures do not exist'. The kaleidoscopic nature of intercultural experiences is reflected in the diversity of these texts. Many belong to a field that could be described as "meta-anthropology", others are more clearly philosophical; occasionally they spill over into belles lettres, ancient history, and comparative cultural and religious studies. The ethnographic specifics supporting the arguments are diverse, deriving from various African situations in which the author has conducted participatory field research (Tunisia, Zambia, Botswana, and South Africa).
Bd. 4, 2003, 616 S., 40,90 €, br.,
ISBN 3-8258-6783-8

Gerhard Kubik
Zum Verstehen afrikanischer Musik
Aufsätze
Gerhard Kubiks bahnbrechendes Werk "Zum Verstehen afrikanischer Musik" gibt eine Einführung in die Grundbegriffe der neueren afrikanischen Musikforschung. Wesentliche Fragen der Ikonologie in der afrikanischen Musikforschung werden behandelt und Querverbindungen der Musikforschung zur bildenden Kunst, zur Tanzwissenschaft und dem Jazz aufgezeigt. Der Autor macht so auf

transkulturative Prozesse zwischen Afrika und der Westlichen Welt aufmerksam. Ferner widmet sich der Band historischen Arbeiten zum Xylophonspiel in Buganda, der Harfenmusik bei den Azande in der Zentralafrikanischen Republik und den mit Liedern verbundenen *'al'ọ*-Yoruba-Märchen in Nigeria. Ein aktualisiertes Vorwort und eine Liste mit neuerer, weiterführender Literatur runden das Werk ab.

Bd. 7, 2., aktualis. u. erg. Aufl. 2004, 448 S., 19,90 €, br., ISBN 3-8258-7800-7

Ethnologische Studien

hrsg. von Ulrich Köhler (Universität Freiburg)

Eveline Dürr
Mitla zwischen Tradition und Moderne
Wandel einer zapotekischen Gesellschaft in Oaxaca, Mexiko

Bd. 27, 1997, 392 S., 24,90 €, gb., ISBN 3-8258-2648-1

Brigitte Hülsewiede
Die Mayordomías in Tequila
Das religiöse Ämtersystem heutiger Nahua in Mexiko

Die Heiligenverehrung in Tequila liegt im Autoritätsbereich der indianischen Bevölkerung. Ein Amtsträger (Mayordomo) ist ein Jahr lang für einen Santo zuständig. In dieser Zeit wird nicht nur das Santo-Fest gefeiert, sondern mehrere rituelle Handlungen begleiten die Amtszeit. Die Gesamtheit der Feste bildet einen Jahreszyklus, der durch das Patronatsfest und die aufwendig gefeierte Karwoche geprägt ist. Ausgehend von einer ausführlichen Beschreibung wird der einzelne Amtszyklus als Lebenszyklus des betroffenen Santo und der Jahreszyklus als ein übergeordneter Lebenszyklus interpretiert. Der Jahreszyklus hängt mit dem Patron Tequilas zusammen, dem eine überragende Bedeutung zukommt. Das Schicksal Tequilas hängt am Patron, der nicht allein, sondern mit einem Begleiter existiert. Die Karwoche – verstanden als eine von den Santos begangene Familienfeier – ermöglicht seine Ankunft zum groß gefeierten Patronatsfest. Die Arbeit zeigt, daß christliche Ausdrucksformen in Tequila eine neue Singgebung innerhalb eines indianischen Weltbildes erfahren haben.

Bd. 28, 1998, 560 S., 35,90 €, gb., ISBN 3-8258-2649-X

Christiane Bögemann-Hagedorn
Hinter Opuntienhecken
Kulturwandel und ethnische Identität in einem Otomí-Dorf des Valle del Mezquital, Mexiko

Grundlage dieser Fallstudie ist die im Rahmen einer einjährigen Feldforschung erarbeitete gesamte Ethnographie eines Otomí-Dorfes. Im Ergebnis werden der auch nach Geschlecht und Schichtenzugehörigkeit differenzierte Prozeß des Wandels analysiert und die Folgen für die Dorfstruktur und die ethnische Identität dargestellt. Deutlich werden einerseits destruktive Auswirkungen den Wandels, die beispielsweise traditionelle Instrumente des sozialen Ausgleichs scheitern lassen. Hervorgehoben werden jedoch andererseits Kreativität und Strategien der indianischen Bevölkerung, die die Effekte von Akkulturation und enormen ökonomischen Druck zu neutralisieren suchen, um ethnische Identität zu bewahren und die Subsistenz abzusichern.

Bd. 29, 1998, 304 S., 25,90 €, br., ISBN 3-8258-2650-3

Ulrich Köhler (Hg.)
Santa Catarina Pantelhó
Ein Dorf von Indianern und Ladinos in Chiapas, Mexiko. Ansätze zu einer Ethnographie

Pantelhó ist aufgrund seiner komplexen ethnischen Zusammensetzung und der Lokalgeschichte atypisch für das zentrale Hochland von Chiapas. Einerseits wohnen in diesem Dorf mit den Tzotzil und Tzeltal zwei verschiedene indianische Volksgruppen und außerdem Ladinos, spanisch sprechende Mexikaner. Andererseits kam die indianische Bevölkerungsmehrheit Pantelhós erst in den